IN DEFENCE OF WELFARE

IN DEFENCE
OF WELFARE

Edited by
PHILIP BEAN
JOHN FERRIS
DAVID WHYNES

Tavistock Publications
London and New York

First published in 1985 by
Tavistock Publications Ltd
11 New Fetter Lane, London EC4P 4EE

Published in the USA by
Tavistock Publications
in association with Methuen, Inc.
29 West 35th Street
New York, NY 10001

Printed in Great Britain by
Richard Clay (The Chaucer Press) Ltd,
Bungay, Suffolk
Typeset by Keyset Composition, Colchester, Essex

British Library Cataloguing in Publication Data

In defence of welfare. — (Social science paperback)
  1. Welfare state
  I. Bean, Philip II. Ferris, John III. Whynes, David   IV. Series
  361.6'5 HN17.5

  ISBN 0-422-79090-7

Library of Congress Cataloging in Publication Data

In defence of welfare.
  Bibliography: p.
  Includes indexes.
  1. Welfare state — Addresses, essays, lectures.
I. Bean, Philip. II. Ferris, John. III. Whynes, David
IV. Title: In defense of welfare.
JC341.I5 1985 361.6'5 85-9984
ISBN 0-422-79090-7 (pbk.)

Contents

Contributors

Philip Bean is Senior Lecturer in Social Administration and Social Work at the University of Nottingham. He has worked as a research officer with the Medical Research Council and as a probation officer in the Inner London Probation and Aftercare Service. He has held visiting academic appointments in the USA and Canada and has published widely in the fields of criminology, mental health, and social philosophy. His recent publications include *Adoption: Essays in Social Policy, Law and Sociology* (ed. 1984) and *Mental Disorder and Legal Control* (1985).

Jonathan Bradshaw is Professor of Social Policy and Director of the Social Policy Research Unit at the University of York. His books include *The Family Fund: An Initiative in Social Policy* (1980), *Issues in Social Policy* (with Jones and Brown 1983), and *Reserved for the Poor* (with Deacon 1983). He is a member of the DHSS Small Grants Committee, the Social Security Research Policy Committee and, until 1984, served on the national executive of the Child Poverty Action Group.

Tony Culyer is Professor of Economics at the University of York. He is the organizer of the UK Health Economists' Study Group and is co-editor of the *Journal of Health Economics*. He has acted as an advisor to governments and to international organizations on health matters, and has held visiting academic appointments at universities in Australia, Canada, and New Zealand. He has published extensively in the social policy field, his most recent book being *The Political Economy of Social Policy* (1980).

John Ferris lectures in social policy at the University of Nottingham. He is a graduate of the London School of Economics and previously worked as a civil servant and as a community worker with a special interest in urban planning. His publications include *Participation in Urban Planning* (1972) and a contribution to *Introducing Social Policy* (ed. Marsh 1979). He is currently interested in non-violence and social ecology and their implications for social policy.

Hilary Land is Reader in Social Administration at the University of Bristol. She earlier worked as a research officer at the London School of Economics and was involved with the National Poverty Survey (1978). Her publications include *Change, Choice and Conflict* (with Hall, Parker, and Webb 1975), *Who Still Cares for the Family?* (1978) and *Poverty and Gender* (1983). Her current interests include feminist analyses of social policy, links between family, state, and labour markets, and welfare in the armed forces.

Alan Maynard is Professor and Director of the Centre for Health Economics at the University of York. He has held visiting academic appointments in Italy, New Zealand, and Sweden and has acted as a consultant for international agencies such as the World Health Organization and OECD. He was an examiner for the Faculty of Community Medicine of the Royal College of Physicians and is a member of the York Health Authority. He has written extensively in books and journals on the organization and regulation of health care systems.

Michael O'Higgins is Reader in Social Policy at the Centre for the Analysis of Social Policy, University of Bath. Since 1980 he has been a specialist adviser to the Social Services Committee of the House of Commons. He recently co-edited *The Future of the Welfare State* and is the author of a number of articles on income distribution, public expenditure, social security policy, and the 'hidden' economy.

Robert Pinker is Professor of Social Work Studies at the London School of Economics. He earlier held the Chair of Social Studies at Chelsea College and was the Lewisham Professor of Social Administration at Goldsmiths' College, University of London. His publications include *Social Theory and Social Policy* (1971), *The Idea of Welfare* (1979), and articles on various aspects of social welfare. He is currently interested in social work and comparative social policy.

Raymond Plant has been Professor of Politics at the University of Southampton since 1979, having previously been a Senior Lecturer in Philosophy at the University of Manchester. He has been a Visiting Fellow at Nuffield College, Oxford, and was Stevenson Lecturer at the University of Glasgow. His most recent books are *Philosophy, Politics and Citizenship* (with Vincent 1984) and *Equality, Markets and the State* (1984).

Hilary Rose is Professor of Applied Social Studies at the University of Bradford. Her teaching and research interests lie in the fields of social policy, the sociology of science, and women's studies. She has published extensively in these areas.

David Whynes lectures in Economics at the University of Nottingham, having previously held a research post at the University of York. He is the author of a number of books, including *The Economic Theory of the State* (with Bowles 1981) and *Comparative Economic Development* (1983). Most recently he has edited *What Is Political Economy?* (1984). His interests centre on public economics, political economy, and economic thought.

Arthur Willcocks has been Professor of Social Administration at the University of Nottingham since 1972. His research interests are primarily in the field of the health service and include studies of recruitment in medical specialities, of professions supplementary to medicine, and of planning structures within the NHS. He has served as a member of a number of health authorities and is currently Dean of the Faculty of Law and Social Sciences at Nottingham.

Barbara Wootton has, since 1968, been the Deputy Speaker of the House of Lords. In a career spanning more than sixty years she has held a variety of academic posts, including Director of Studies in Economics at Girton College, Cambridge, and Professor of Social Studies, University of London. She has served on four royal commissions and on many government committees concerned with economic and social issues. She has written widely on social matters, her most recent book being *Crime and Penal Policy* (1978). She has been a London magistrate for over forty years and was made a Companion of Honour in 1977.

Introduction

The idea for this book arose from the circumstances created by the change of government in Britain in 1979. Within the space of a few years it had become evident that the new administration was committed to what some of its more extreme supporters termed 'rolling back the welfare state'. This anti-welfare stance was hardly made explicit during the election campaign and only became clear as specific measures were introduced (principally, budgetary measures aimed at reducing the level of public spending). Thus, it appeared to us, Government intentions were being revealed in a fragmented and piecemeal manner, by selective expenditure cuts coupled with equally selective expansions and subsequent ministerial justifications. However, and irrespective of any limitations or inadequacies within the prevailing public welfare system, it seemed that there existed both general and specific problems of welfare characteristic of advanced industrial societies which were, quite simply, being disregarded. More precisely, the waste and inefficiency aspects of public welfare provision were being emphasized at the expense of addressing the problems that the existing system was designed to resolve.

In spite of optimistic beginnings, it had become fashionable by the 1970s to lament the failure of the state welfare apparatus erected after the Second World War. As academic social scientists, we were well aware of the proliferating literature in which the Keynes/Beveridge conception of collective welfare provision was tested and found wanting. In an earlier period, attacks on state welfare had tended to come from those on the political left, who saw state systems as insufficiently redistributive and repressive. More recently, however, the most strident (certainly the most publicized) attacks have come from the 'new right'. Reading through this modern literature, the broad consensus of social values which has supported the welfare state since 1945 appears to have collapsed (we say 'appears' because that evidence which is available remains far from convincing). As editors, we were concerned about the consequences that would follow from an uncritical acceptance of this populist welfare critique. Such populism had, we felt, a doctrinaire character which consistently turned away from the actual analysis of those specific, often chronic and intractable, problems that the main social services attempt to resolve. Indeed, the new right does seem almost to have assumed the character of an evangelical sect in preaching the 'down home' truths of old-time religion. Certainly it possesses its fundamental texts, in the form of selected doctrines of classical political economy up-dated by latter-day prophets such as Friedrich von Hayek and Milton Friedman. The principal weakness of the approach in political terms has been, we believe, its invitation to accept uncritically simplistic formulae encapsulated in slogans of the likes of 'privatization' or 'free market' or 'self-help and enterprise', almost as if the mouthing of such phrases could magically produce the solution to complex welfare problems. Accordingly, it was essentially not a concern to defend a Keynes/Beveridge welfare *status quo* which prompted this book, but rather a concern to defend the value of pragmatism and open-minded enquiry in dealing with social and economic issues.

Not surprisingly, the doleful anti-welfare literature of recent years has begun to produce a counter-current. Those who have already sought to defend welfare from within the discipline of social administration have generally done so from that which might be termed a collectivist Fabian position. This tradition of empirical social science has much to commend it, not least its in-built respect for patient statistical investigation and the presentation of carefully marshalled evidence. Whilst we naturally welcome all such contributions to the welfare debate we felt that our own defence of welfare would need to be multi-faceted, because the notion of a line of battle drawn up between the supporters of the welfare state on the one hand and the anti-welfare lobby on the other is far too simplistic. Whilst such an antagonism is both obvious and real it does not exhaust the possibilities; welfare is under threat in other ways. In intellectual terms, for instance, welfare needs defending from its friends as much as from its enemies. A fair proportion of the formal political debate over the future of the welfare state appears to consist of the exchange of platitudes and dogmas between occupants of entrenched positions and this style of argument has no more been the province of the 'antis' than it has of the 'pros'. The defence of welfare ideals against untruths is not best accomplished by the fabrication of further untruths, no matter how well intentioned. Thus, the unquestioning belief that the welfare state as it is presently constituted represents the embodiment of all that is good can be as detrimental to the cause of welfare as can the opposite.

We believe also that the defence of welfare needs to be multi-disciplinary because the arguments involved have many layers – economic, political, social, legal, moral. Attempts to move the whole subject of welfare towards an interdisciplinary perspective can assist in diluting the domination of the limited set of conceptual models existing hitherto, thereby opening up new possibilities in approach. *A priori*, there would seem no reason to suppose that any one academic discipline could legitimately claim the monopoly of interpretation in this or, for that matter, in any other area. Such a consideration guided our selection of contributors who have been drawn from a variety of disciplinary backgrounds. Only in one sense was our selection specifically biased. As it is clear from whence the recent attacks on welfare have been coming we saw no need to include any defences of new right policies. These arguments have already been made and it is this book's function to evaluate them.

We have grouped the twelve essays of the collection into three sections, the first comprising 'Ethical and Moral Questions'. Here our canvas is perhaps at its broadest. Raymond Plant's opening contribution serves as an introduction to the section and, indeed, to the volume as a whole, by providing a context. He explains, first of all, how the contemporary criticisms of the welfare state have arisen, by reference, *inter alia*, to the constraints of the present economic environment, the growing ideological acceptance of the neo-liberal defence of capitalism, and the fear of the state's observed tendency to expand its influence. Raymond Plant then concentrates his attention upon the ideological aspects by an examination of the neo-liberal rejection of welfarist assumptions. Far from being coterminous with distributive justice, he argues, market distribution can actually militate against its realization; there remains a need for a theory of need. He concludes that the 'moral attack on welfare mounted by the neo-liberals on the grounds that justice and liberty are not served by welfare provision is seriously flawed'.

Raymond Plant's views are very much in harmony with those of Barbara Wootton. In her paper, Barbara Wootton touches on the problems of ethical assessment, beginning with the impossibility of deriving non-metaphysical propositions about the issue. She too explores the neo-liberal predilection for interpreting economic morality as being synonymous with the free play of market forces. In tracing the moral fabric of our present welfare system she is at pains to point out that major problems have indeed arisen; we have, she believes, 'landed ourselves with an enormously expensive bureaucratic monster'. Thus, the neo-liberals may be correct in diagnosing that problems exist, although their own solutions still leave much to be desired. In terms of reaching the appropriate solutions Barbara Wootton believes that 'we should be more radical, with simplification the primary aim'.

The first two papers are directed quite explicitly towards the type of neo-liberal thinking associated with the name of Hayek. In contrast, the following two are more concerned to expose some of the moral dilemmas inherent within the Keynes/Beveridge welfare ideology as it has evolved in the post-war world. In John Ferris's paper, citizenship is the central concept, citizenship

being about the definition of individuality and therefore a fundamental moral issue. The implication is the existence and
acceptance of certain social and political rights held by each
member of society. John Ferris argues that, whilst neo-liberalism
can certainly be regarded as one modern threat to citizenship
(despite its claim to be concerned for individual liberty), the
roots of the general threat lie far deeper. In certain respects the
Keynes/Beveridge welfare state must carry part of the burden of
blame owing to its creation of welfare dependency: 'personal
autonomy remains restricted by many subtle mechanisms for
those obliged to depend upon state welfare'. In reality, citizenship is governed more by structure and less by ideology. Our
evolving industrial and technological society has constrained the
individual's freedom in the economic sphere and has re-defined
his/her communal association in the public sphere. Individuals
have become smaller as the political and economic machinery
has become larger. John Ferris examines corporatist and Marxist
visions for coming to terms with this experience but rejects both
in favour of a decentralized social ecology approach.

The rhetoric of welfarism has almost always defined concern
for others as a moral imperative. Practical manifestations of this
judgement have produced insidious consequences, especially
vis-à-vis the role of women, as the paper by Hilary Land and
Hilary Rose makes clear. Using both literary and sociological
sources, they establish the existence of a stereotype of womanhood, dating back to Victorian times, which has perceived
women as altruistic in their familial roles of wives and mothers.
Such selflessness has been interpreted as being both natural and
inevitable although the character of the theory developing this
view has changed over time. Hilary Land and Hilary Rose argue
that the 'angel in the house' stereotype of women was grasped
firmly by the architects of the welfare state and, as Beveridge's
'divine vocation', became embedded in its principles. They
show, for example, that men's welfare rights have been defined
with respect to labour market conditions but those of women
have been defined with respect to marital status. They conclude
that, whilst the social and economic position of women appears
to have improved since the 1940s, as a result of the operations of
the welfare state, the stereotypical imagery remains and modern

society retains the notion of a division of altruistic responsibility
on sexual grounds.

The theme of the second group of papers, entitled 'Welfare and
the Market', is explicitly economic. As the title implies, the
concern here is to investigate the workings of market processes in
the context of welfare provision. In examining the philosophy of
the market, David Whynes's paper serves both as an introduction to the section and as a linkage with the preceding group
of essays. He opens with an elaboration of the 'market model'
used by neo-liberals in criticizing collective welfare provision and
explores why markets are held to be both ethically virtuous and
efficient. As economists have long realized, market theory is a
powerful tool and David Whynes proceeds to examine its implications in a number of welfare-related areas – the design of
government, the nature of redistribution and the selection of the
size of the economic 'safety net' which even non-collectivists
agree ought to exist within society. He also explores the relationship between market theory and the current political dogmas
that purport to be based upon it.

Over the past two decades a strong economic case has been
built up to support the extended usage of markets within welfare
services. Tony Culyer's paper opens with a review of such
arguments, those in favour of markets believing, for example,
that a more effective demand/supply equilibrium can result from
market provision. Additionally, there will exist incentives for
efficiency and a desirable absence of interference from the
welfare bureaucracy. In contrast, the socialized welfare system is
said to generate inefficiency, to lack incentives, and to lead to an
excess demand for services. Tony Culyer argues that, up to now,
the greater part of the market debate has been conducted in
purely abstract terms and he moves on to consider how
abstractions must confront reality in cases where real-world
markets appear to operate in an imperfect and sub-optimal
manner. As an example of the need to deal with realities rather
than dogmas, Tony Culyer considers altruism or caring (a
central postulate of welfarism) as a scientific hypothesis. He
suggests ways in which we might reach positive, as opposed to
idealized, conclusions about the significance of such behaviour.

Two of the most important issues in the market debate form the themes of the remaining papers in this section. First, Alan Maynard considers the influence of the means of financing welfare systems on a supply and demand response. His comparison of public tax and private insurance financing reveals that, irrespective of the rhetoric of the ideologues, *both* methods can give rise to inefficient resource allocations because both share common features. A discussion of the characteristics of efficient allocation prefaces an explanation of the modifications necessary to both public and private systems to further this end. Alan Maynard argues that, although public and private systems both confront similar efficiency problems, they are actually seeking different distributional goals (based upon need on the one hand and ability to pay on the other). Accordingly, it is on these grounds that either system might be judged desirable or otherwise.

Whereas Alan Maynard's paper touches on distributional matters within specific welfare services, Michael O'Higgins looks at the record of redistribution policy in general. He notes that many people have experienced disillusion about the possibility of creating a more egalitarian society and have come to doubt the efficacy of government management in securing such a goal. He argues that, to some extent, this pessimistic vision has been created by problems of interpretation, by subscription to counter-factual 'evidence', and by the 'utopian' expectations of earlier periods. Using recent UK data, Michael O'Higgins appraises government income redistribution and reaches the verdict that 'the distribution of resources through state welfare is markedly more equal than the distribution of market-generated income'. He concludes with an assessment of the possible redistributive consequences brought about by permitting areas of existing public welfare provision to be market provided.

The first section of this book concerns itself with moral principles, the second with the economic manifestation of such principles. The emphasis of the final section, 'Consumers and Victims', is the application of principles in the context of the UK experience. Robert Pinker opens the section with an overview of contemporary trends in social welfare policy and the current political debate. He considers the present Conservative Government's attitude towards social policy and economic management in the light of both the economic climate and traditional Conservative thinking. Robert Pinker detects an undermining of earlier welfare ideals, for instance, a drift from universalism to selectivity in benefit provision. He is also concerned about the divisive nature of contemporary policy in its practical application, whereby a social consensus is being broken down and certain groups appear to be better positioned than others to take advantage. He also detects a cause for concern on the intellectual front: 'the radical nature of Thatcherist policies could eventually provoke collectivists into turning conservative in defence of the established order of social welfare'.

Fundamental to the functioning of any state is the maintenance of law and order. Philip Bean examines Conservative policy on this issue, focusing upon its relationship to welfare. In terms of legislative content, he argues, the present Government appears to have done little to destroy the 'law and order consensus' which has existed throughout the post-war period. There have, however, been changes of emphasis, for example, Conservative enthusiasm for re-establishing the family as an instrument for social control. Philip Bean goes on to analyse two prominent themes in modern law enforcement: first, the implications of the changing social role, organizational structure, and economic status of the police force. This established force is central to the notion of the 'protection of the State', a notion dominating contemporary thinking. Second, he suggests that general protection arguments can be superficial in that they do not respond to claims of specific interest groups whose problems are all too often defined away.

The final two essays in the collection form specific defences of welfare in their own right. The structure, and the intention, of each essay is broadly similar and together they encompass two of the most important institutions within the UK welfare state – Jonathan Bradshaw appraises the present system of social security and Arthur Willcocks examines the National Health Service. Each paper sets out the accepted objectives of the institution concerned and identifies its achievements, both over time and with respect to equivalent institutions in other countries. The specific problems with which each institution has had to cope are highlighted. In the case of social security, for example, the demand for services has been rising constantly owing to demographic change, growing unemployment, and the increase in the scope and level of benefits. Health care has likewise been subject to demand and cost escalation. Both authors accept that the institutions leave much to be desired on efficiency grounds: Jonathan Bradshaw notes that our present social security system sometimes manages to ignore those in need whilst distributing to those not in need and Arthur Willcocks accepts the criticism of bureaucratization. Both essays conclude that, although the record of service provision in terms of, for instance, equity and egalitarianism has been encouraging, there remains scope for improvement. However, following the arguments of the previous sections, welfare problems do not necessarily entail market solutions.

There remains little doubt that the Keynes/Beveridge idea of the welfare state, and the varieties of collectivism that have evolved from it, contain contradictory elements. Such a realization, coupled with the evidence of the economic recession which has developed since the 1970s, poses a very real threat to our established ways of thinking about welfare. In our view, there can be no defence of welfare which seeks simply to reimpose the solutions of earlier decades; herein, perhaps, lies a central weakness of the orthodox Fabian defence. One of the strongest of the new right's arguments has been the insistence that wealth must be created to sustain a viable public sector and, whilst we might feel that economic policies since 1979 have done little to create such wealth, the basic point seems to have appealed to the electorate on two separate occasions. It could well be the case that the economic growth which the UK experienced during the 1950s and 1960s, growth which supported significant extensions in state welfare provision, will be unattainable in the foreseeable future. Arguably, a repetition of that particular form of growth might nowadays be considered undesirable on other grounds. This being the case, the stereotypes and clichés of both the left and the right, ideas which have dominated our thinking about welfare in recent years, will have to be abandoned. At the public level, this new welfare debate is only just beginning and it will require open-mindedness, flexibility and, above all, political creativity. Sadly, it is just these characteristics that have been absent from discussions about welfare up to now.

Philip Bean
John Ferris
David Whynes   March 1985

PART ONE
ETHICAL AND
MORAL QUESTIONS

1

The very idea of a welfare state

RAYMOND PLANT

The idea of the welfare state is currently treated with more
scepticism across the political spectrum than at any time during
its development. In so far as the institutions of the welfare state
were consolidated during the period of Butskellite consensus
which lasted until the mid-1960s, it is now seen both on the right
and the left to embody many of the failures implicit in that
consensus. In the more polarized political climate of today the
welfare state seems to be part of that consensus politics, the
assumptions of which now appear to be questionable. It was
assumed, so it is argued, that the fiscal dividends of growth could
be used to increase welfare in a relatively painless way by maintaining the absolute position of the better off while increasing
public expenditure on health, education, and welfare to improve
the relative standing of the worst-off members of society
(Crosland 1975). In this way it was thought that the social and
economic rights of citizenship could be extended within a market
economy without putting excessive strain on that economy.
Obviously there were sharp disagreements between the political
parties about how far these social and economic welfare rights

should go and how far the welfare state should be seen as a vehicle of redistribution, but nevertheless, the existence of such a state, which would go well beyond a residual welfare state attempting merely to prevent destitution, was not seriously questioned by either of the mainstream political parties or by intellectuals. Indeed the degree of consensus over these matters, part of what has been called 'the end of ideology', effectively marginalized the writings and warnings of critics. Many of the basic ideas of contemporary critics of the redistributive welfare state such as Hayek and Friedman were formulated and disseminated during this period (Hayek 1960; Friedman 1962), but they did not make a very wide impact at that time and they were often thought of as eccentrics who were attempting to stand in the face of the tide in history because many, particularly convergence theorists (Kerr 1962), saw the development of the welfare state and the entrenching of social and economic rights of citizenship as a necessary concomitant of the development of a complex urban industrial society. The development of the moral critique of such a state by right-wing economists, heavily indebted to the writings of the classical political economists and rejecting the post-war Keynesian consensus, was thought to be an anachronism, not a genuine threat to the range of values which supported such a state. Of course, there were those, as much on the left as on the right, who pointed out that the welfare state, committed to meeting *needs*, was in principle profoundly anti-capitalist. The welfare rights of the citizen gave him a standing and a status based upon need which was independent of his performance in the market (Thompson 1958), but even those who saw this point seem to have dismissed it on the ground that the apparently limitless potential for economic growth within the mixed economy, plus fine tuning by Keynesian demand management, could cope with this implicit contradiction.

What then has led to the disenchantment and to the growth in importance of the critique of the welfare state developed by writers such as Hayek, Friedman, and Nozick (Nozick 1974), as well as Marxist critics such as James O'Connor (1973) and Claus Offe (1984)?

The first is undoubtedly the more constrained economic environment within which both Labour and Conservative governments have had to operate, particularly since the 1970s. This has had the effect of throwing into relief the problem of providing the resources for the extension of welfare rights within, broadly speaking, a capitalist economy. Many defenders of the welfare state had previously argued that the welfare state was necessary to secure the legitimacy of capitalism because it dealt with the inevitable side-effects of unconstrained capitalism – poverty and an unacceptable extent of inequality, which, if allowed to continue unchecked, would produce degrees of envy and resentment which might well threaten the maintenance of such an economy. On this view, the welfare state, while it embodied uncapitalist or even anti-capitalist assumptions, was nevertheless a 'necessary evil' which could be financed out of fiscal dividends of growth. However, the difficulties in sustaining growth and the deep-seated difficulties in securing increased productivity in the British economy led many to see the welfare state as a brake on economic development and to confront what O'Connor from the Marxist left has called 'the fiscal crisis of the state'. The fiscal crisis lies in the fact that in a constrained economy with a welfare state the government has two contradictory imperatives. The first is welfare expenditure, seemingly necessary to secure legitimacy, and the second is to secure the conditions of capital accumulation necessary for capitalist development. High rates of incremental growth might allow both of these imperatives to be pursued at once, but a constrained economy, on the other hand, would make this balancing act difficult to sustain. Faced with contradictory pressures, the new right is prepared to cut back welfare provision in order to secure the possibility of capital accumulation. This strategy, if it were to be successful, would involve more than attacks on 'waste' and would involve substantial cuts in the range of public expenditure which was directed to securing welfare rights.

This argument does not necessarily imply a lack of concern with the plight of the worst-off members of society because, if it was combined with a vigorous defence of capitalism (as found for example in the writings of Hayek and Friedman), it could be argued that the poor would in fact get relatively richer by a trickle-down or echelon advance process whereby, in a relatively unconstrained market, what the rich consume today will trickle down to the poor who will be able to consume these things eventually. Greater inequality might well, on this view, make society as a whole richer, including the worst off. A very minimal residual welfare safety net might be needed to meet the needs of the few with special problems who might miss out on the echelon advance. This is how Hayek makes the point about the trickle-down mechanism:

> 'If today in the United States or Western Europe the relatively poor can have a car or refrigerator, or airplane trip or radio at the cost of a reasonable part of their income, this was made possible because in the past others with large incomes were able to spend on what was then a luxury. The path of advance is greatly eased by the fact that it has been trodden before. It is because scouts have found the goal that the road can be built for the less lucky and less energetic . . . many of the improvements would indeed never have become a possibility for all if they had not long before been available for some. If all had to wait for better things until they could be provided for all, that day would, in many instances, never come. Even the poorest today owe their relative well being to the result of past inequalities.'
>
> (Hayek 1960: 44)

So if, confronted with the fiscal crisis posed by the welfare state, we choose to cut back the welfare state this will not mean that the worst off will be left to their plight. On the contrary, in so far as the welfare state acts as a brake on economic development it may well be doing harm to those whose interests might best be served by benefiting from the trickle-down effects of a freer economic system.

Coupled with this view is the argument that, if not tightly constrained, the welfare state has an inbuilt tendency to grow. The argument here, that there is a definite range of needs for the welfare state to meet at a definite level, which could then mean that it could reach a plateau of funding, is regarded by critics as a false one. Needs are open-ended and if they are seen as the basis of welfare rights there is no intrinsic limit to the extent of such rights and the claims on the resources of the state which such rights embody. Take the case of medical need and the National

Health Service. There is no class of basic identifiable medical needs which the NHS could meet in a straightforward and determinate way so that its funding would be predictable and level. On the contrary, on this view, medical needs expand with the growth of medical technology. For example the development of new surgical procedures, advances in preventative medicine such as cervical and breast screening, and the invention of technologies such as dialysis machines, mean that needs grow in relation to these possibilities, and the satisfaction of these needs is turned into a social right – a claim on the resources of the state. Consequently, welfare demands on the state are not clearly limited and as Enoch Powell has argued, if these needs are supposed to be satisfied at no cost to the individual at the point of delivery, then the demand is infinite (Powell 1966).

The state is under enormous pressure to meet such needs, particularly in the sphere of health. But the state has no resources of its own; it derives its income from taxation. But increasing taxation is likely to have an effect on incentives and thus on economic performance, and borrowing is likely to increase inflation or push up interest rates which again have effects upon economic performance. On this view a good deal of thinking about welfare is a victim of what Samuel Brittan (1983) has called the 'Wenceslas myth' – that welfare provision is a matter of generosity or stinginess on the part of the state, whereas the reality is, of course, that welfare provision comes out of taxation and borrowing and we cannot detach this from economic growth, which if Hayek is right is in itself likely to benefit the worst-off more than planning and welfare.

This problem about the insatiability of need is linked to another feature of the welfare state which the new right regards as both central and baneful – the connection between the welfare state and pressure groups. The elastic idea of welfare needs encourages the formation of pressure groups which seek to secure government funding to meet the 'needs' which they have identified. This pressure group activity, including the producer groups of welfare services (doctors, nurses, teachers, social workers), is unregulated and leads to important and deleterious economic consequences for government in the sense that the political parties in a welfare society are subject to continual electoral pressure to promise to increase the provision of welfare resources. Thus in a society with a large welfare sector politics inevitably takes on the character of an auction in which one party cannot afford to be 'outbid' by another in its promises over the provision of resources to meet the 'needs' of its citizens, with the consequences this has for the economy which has to produce a sufficient surplus to meet these 'needs'.

This is, broadly speaking, the political and economic case developed by the new right against the welfare state as it has developed in Britain since the war. The difficulties in implementing any kind of plan to cut back the growth of welfare in the interests of the productivity of the private sector of the economy are clear enough in the current British political context. Despite the apparent support of the then chancellor for the Central Policy Review Staff's paper to the cabinet on reducing public expenditure on welfare services, including the NHS, the outcry was widespread enough across the political spectrum to mean that Mrs Thatcher was forced to say during the general election campaign in 1983 that the NHS was safe in Conservative hands. The cutbacks which have been made, which are very marginal in terms of the radical surgery which the neo-liberal, new right diagnosis would require, have been met by widespread opposition not just by the producer interest groups concerned but also in the country at large.

However there is, in addition, a moral case made by the new right which has to be taken account of in any serious attempt to develop a defence of the welfare state and this is particularly associated with the influential writings of Hayek. This attack is an attempt to confront some of the values on which the welfare state might be thought to be based.

Two values which are often brought into play when defending the welfare state are that left to its own devices the economic market will limit freedom and cause injustice. On this view an unconstrained market will produce large inequalities and those at the bottom of the resultant stratification will not have the resources to make their demand effective in the market and thus their *freedom* will be diminished. Similarly, those who are at the bottom and suffer poverty and relative deprivation are the victims of *injustice*. Thus the argument is that the welfare state which seeks some measure of redistribution is an attempt to increase the freedom of the worst off and to rectify the injustices in distribution which the market creates.

Hayek decisively rejects both of these welfarist assumptions. It is central to his argument that coercion and injustice can only occur as the result of *deliberate* action – for example when person A threatens person B or intentionally causes B to do something he would not otherwise do. However, in Hayek's view, the outcomes of economic transactions do not have this degree of intentionality. In the market innumerable individuals make small decisions to buy and sell in the light of their own necessarily restricted knowledge and in the light of their own view of their best interests. In a complex economy some will no doubt suffer as the result of the aggregate of the individual decisions which are made, but these outcomes were not intended by the individuals who took the decisions. Indeed the very complexity of the economic relations involved makes it impossible for them to act deliberately to cause harm in this way. The suffering which may well be an outcome of a particular set of market transactions is an unintended, remote, and unforeseen consequence of an aggregate of individual decisions which were taken for all sorts of different and limited reasons.

Granted this view, the market cannot be criticized because it is coercive towards those who do not wield large economic resources. While these people may in fact suffer, they are not coerced because coercion has to be an intentional act. The *freedom* of the worst off is not diminished by their lack of resources. Similarly they do not suffer from injustice. Injustices equally are only caused by intentional actions. Therefore there is no moral basis for a critique of the market in terms of its coerciveness and injustice. The suffering which may be caused by the operation of the market is not to be rectified by claims to rights, justice, and equality, but by charity and voluntary action. The provision of a welfare safety net, whether by voluntary or political action, is a gift to be bestowed not a right to be claimed. There might be good pragmatic grounds for the provision of a welfare safety net but this is not a response to a moral imperative and certainly the provision of welfare for redistributive purposes has no moral legitimacy.

Perhaps two analogies will make the argument more clear. The weather is a natural phenomenon outside human control. The weather does not do anything deliberately and although it may cause suffering, it would be absurd to rail against it because it is coercive or because the suffering it causes is an injustice. These are purely naturalistic outcomes of a non-deliberate process and the consequences a matter of luck as much as anything else. Similarly, if someone is born with a genetic handicap we would see this as a matter of luck and ill fortune rather than an injustice. In both cases the *rights* of those who suffer as a result of these non-deliberate actions have not been infringed. They suffer from misfortune and they may indeed make demands on the virtues of charity and generosity, but none of this is a matter for rights or for justice. So it is with the market.

While it is of course true that the market consists of human actions, and is thus not like the weather or a genetic lottery, nevertheless they are similar in that their outcomes are un-intended. Hayek makes this point as follows in the context of a discussion of justice:

> 'It has of course to be admitted that the manner in which benefits and burdens are allocated by the market mechanism would in many instances have to be regarded as very unjust if it were the result of a deliberate allocation to particular people. But this is not the case. These shares are the outcome of a process the effect of which on particular people was neither intended nor foreseen. To demand justice from such a process is clearly absurd, and to single out some people in such a society as entitled to a particular share evidently unjust.'
>
> (Hayek 1976: 64)

It is perhaps worth noting in passing that this argument would apply to any theory of distributive justice and not just those embodying criteria of need. If we operated with a meritocratic conception of justice favouring merit and desert the same considerations would apply. The market does not and cannot distribute according to any particular set of moral principles, and it is a deep illusion to think it can. So those conservatives and liberals who extol the market because they believe it rewards the energetic and deserving are in Hayek's view as mistaken as socialists. The outcomes of a genuinely free market are in principle unprincipled (Hirsch 1977).

This argument about justice is backed up by a claim that in a morally pluralistic society there are no agreed criteria of distributive justice which could guide the allocative decisions of the state and that for the state to pursue redistributive welfare policies in such circumstances is deeply illiberal. In a liberal society the state should not pursue some particular view of the good life, because people will disagree about what the good life consists of, but if, granted the range of moral disagreement, the state seeks to impose *one* view of distributive justice as opposed to another then it cannot treat its citizens as equals. This point has been made very forcefully by John Gray, a libertarian critic of the welfare state, who argues as follows:

'Criteria of desert and merit are not shared as a common moral inheritance, mutually available to the inner city Moslem population of Birmingham and the secularised professional classes of Hampstead but instead reflect radically different cultural traditions and styles of life. It defies experience to suppose that any consensus on relative merits can be reached in a society so culturally diverse (and for that reason so free) as ours. . . . The objectivity of basic needs is equally delusive. Needs can be given no plausible cross cultural content but instead are seen to vary across different moral traditions. . . . One of the chief functions of the contemporary ideology of social justice may be, as Hayek intimates, to generate an illusion of moral agreement, where in fact there are profound divergencies of values.'

(Gray 1983: 181–82)

A redistributive welfare state, founded upon the pursuit of social justice, will be incompatible with the moral divergence of a modern society and to try to implement one conception of justice as opposed to another is not to treat this divergence with the respect that it deserves. On this view, despite often cited claims to the contrary, a redistributive welfare state does not treat its citizens with equal respect.

There is also a further and less abstract way in which this

might be thought to be true – namely that many of the institutions of the welfare state are inherently paternalistic and put far too much discretionary power into the hands of the 'welfare professionals' – doctors, social workers, teachers, DHSS civil servants, etc. In so far as welfare benefits are given in kind, in terms of personal social services etc., then the individuals who receive such benefits will experience very little freedom in relation to them and this again is an argument frequently used by critics of the present welfare state. Thus David Marquand argues:

> 'if the state takes my money away from me to give it to someone else, my freedom is thereby diminished. If those to whom it is given receive it in the form of cash, which they spend as they like, and if there are a lot of them and only a few of us, there may well be a net gain in freedom. If they receive it in the form of services, in the direction of which they have no say and over the allocation of which they have no control, there will be no gain in freedom'
>
> (Marquand 1980)

If we are to defend the welfare state against Hayek's strictures on its relation to personal liberty we shall have to be sensitive to this kind of argument. It would be paradoxical (to say the least) to defend the welfare state as a means to freedom while at the same time endorsing institutions and forms of service delivery which allow individual claimants very little in the way of freedom of choice in relation to those services. Marquand's point about the allocation of services is also well taken. If the claimant has very little say in the way the service is allocated his freedom of action may well be diminished, but equally importantly the area of discretion given to individual administrators may well be too wide and the decisions made too arbitrary.

All of this adds up to a formidable diagnosis of the political, economic, and moral dilemmas of the welfare state and it must be taken seriously. There is no possibility that repeating old certainties will somehow remove the challenge posed by the neoliberal critique. The force of this critique is based not just upon its intellectual thrust which is formidable, but also the fact that in the real world, the economy does seem to pose problems for the extension of welfare rights in the present constrained circumstances. Consequently the critique has to be taken seriously and in my view any future defence of the welfare state will have to take into account some of the points raised by the new right and modify its conception of the welfare state in the light of them. In what remains of this chapter I shall try to sketch the main lines of what a defence of welfare against this background might look like.

In the space available to me I propose to try to combat the *moral* critique of the welfare state just because I regard it as the most important. If the welfare state does not have the function of increasing freedom, rectifying injustices, and responding to the moral claims based upon needs, it hardly seems worth defending. It is only in so far as redistributive welfare institutions actually tap deep-seated moral sentiments among citizens about justice, fairness, freedom, and the recognition that meeting needs is a basic requirement of citizenship, that any defence is likely to be successful.

Let us take Hayek's critique of social justice first. What I have to say here falls into two parts. First I shall attack Hayek's view that unconstrained markets do not cause injustice; and second I shall argue for the centrality of a theory of needs in arguments about justice, as of course need is at the heart of the conception of the welfare state and is what its critics find most objectionable about it.

Hayek argues that the outcomes of markets when they adversely affect the position of an individual do not result in injustice. Of course, he may be poorer, of course he may suffer – but he does not suffer an injustice. The difference is crucial, for only if the individual were to suffer an *injustice* would there be a genuine moral claim on the resources of the state to rectify that injustice. As we saw earlier injustice is seen to be irrelevant because the outcomes of the market are not deliberately willed by anyone and maldistribution can only occur where there is a distributor intentionally making a maldistribution. However, this degree of intentionality is lacking in markets and injustices cannot arise. This is how Hayek describes the situation in *Law, Legislation and Liberty*, vol. 2, *The Mirage of Social Justice*:

'We do cry out against the injustice when a succession of calamities afflict one family while another steadily prospers, when meritorious effort is frustrated by some unforeseeable accident and particularly if, on many people whose endeavours seem equally great, some succeed brilliantly while others utterly fail. . . . And we will protest against such a fate although we do not know anyone who is to blame for it or any ways in which such disappointments can be prevented. . . . It is no different with regard to the general feeling of injustice about the distribution of material goods in a society of freedom. Though we are in this case less ready to admit it, our complaints about the outcome of the market as unjust do not usually assert that somebody has been unjust. Society has simply become the new deity to which we complain and clamour for redress if it does not fulfil the expectations it has created.'

(Hayek 1976: 68)

However, it is not clear that injustice is *only* a matter of how a particular outcome came about or arose, but rather is as much a matter of our response to the outcome. Certainly someone who was born with a severe handicap does not suffer an injustice because of the genetic lottery, but where justice and injustice come in is in our response to his position. If we can, at no damaging cost to ourselves, compensate him to some extent for the damage he has suffered, but wholly fail to do so, this is where the injustice lies – in our own response or lack of it. In any event, while the deleterious outcomes for some individuals and groups in the market may not be intentional they may still be fairly predictable and foreseeable given the already obtaining distribution of income and property, and to take steps to compensate people for the harmful consequences which this existing distribution is likely to have on them could well be seen as a matter of justice.

Underpinning Hayek's argument here is his conception of the social order in general and the market in particular as a spontaneous order which, while of course the product of human action, is not the product of design. Because of this we can only understand it in an abstract way and we could never acquire the detailed practical knowledge, a good deal of which is in any case non-propositional, to enable us to control it in the interest of some moral purpose such as social justice.

However, it is far from clear to me that Hayek has a consistent argument on this point, because he has argued in studies in *Philosophy, Politics and Economics* that a catallaxy or market order can be made to serve preordained human ends. Indeed, his argument is positively Rawlsian:

> 'An optimal policy in a catallaxy may aim and ought to aim, at increasing the chances of any member of society taken at random of having a high income, or what amounts to the same thing, the chance that whatever his share of total income may be, the real equivalent of his share will be as large as we know how to make it.'

(Hayek 1967: 173)

This kind of attitude would seem to require a drastic revision of the view that a spontaneous order or catallaxy cannot be constrained by some overall values. If this is so, then there is clearly a place for asking moral questions about the outcomes of such spontaneous processes.

We have to remember in this context that it is also part of Hayek's thesis that because we cannot appeal to any conception of justice to constrain the market we cannot provide any moral basis for either grounding or criticizing the existing structure of property rights against the background of which market transactions take place. These facts have to be accepted as given. Granted this, it is highly likely that some groups, those with low incomes and no property, are going to suffer as a result of the impersonal forces of the market and, if it is in our power to do something about this by way of compensating mechanisms and we fail to do so, we are involved in injustice because this is not to treat these individuals with equal concern and respect. Some will be rendered poor and deprived by a process whose justification is that it makes the bulk of the population richer. They can of course be forced to accept the poverty but they can hardly accept it in a way consistent with a right to equal respect and concern on the part of the government. Failure to attend to the welfare of those individuals who, through no fault of their own and largely owing to bad luck (remember intentionality is lacking), find that they are unable to live the kind of life which the culture of society defines as the norm of human fulfilment is deeply unjust. Granted that given the existing structure of property rights in the economy (which cannot be grounded in any theory of justice) the outcomes of markets for the worst-off groups are likely to be severe and that this is foreseeable irrespective of whether anyone intended it, then it seems merely an exercise in persuasive definition to argue that social justice is irrelevant in these contexts.

Even if we accept the above account, it still leaves one part of Hayek's critique untouched – that is that we have no shared criterion of distributive justice to guide the redistributive politics of a welfare state. Because we have no agreed criterion the effects of the welfare state are going to seem arbitrary. It might be argued that this is particularly true of the case of 'need' as a criterion of distribution because it might be thought that some attempt to mobilize collective resources to meet needs is a central feature of the welfare state. It is, one might say, its internal goal. For example, Forder in his book *Concepts in Social Administration* argues that 'the definition of need presents a central problem to the social services since this defines the objectives of the services' (Forder 1974: 39). Similarly, in 'The Concept of Social Need' Jonathan Bradshaw argues that: 'The concept of social need is inherent in the idea of social service. The history of the social services is the history of the recognition of social needs and the organisation of society to meet them' (Bradshaw 1972: 640). If need is the central distributive goal towards which the welfare state aims, and if the moral basis of need is almost wholly indeterminate and its nature and limits are undefined, then this clearly would represent a fundamental weakness in the general coherence of what might loosely be called the welfare state ideology, and this is precisely the conclusion which critics from the right have drawn. So for example, Alan Williams argues: 'The word "need" ought to be banished from discussion of public policy, partly because of its ambiguity but also because the word is frequently used in "arbitrary" senses' (Williams 1974: 6). This is echoed by many on the right. In their view it is not just a conceptual nicety which is at stake here. Because we have become accustomed to the idea that the welfare state should take responsibility for meeting needs, and because the notion of need is so elastic and arbitrary, there is no limit to the extent to which needs and the resources required to meet them can be put on the political agenda, and thus no inherent limit on the growth of the welfare state.

So here is a central and, I believe, genuinely important problem which an adequate defence of the welfare state has to face directly. Perhaps the argument could be divided into two: is there a defensible moral basis for claims to need? And if there is, are there any theoretical constraints which could be put upon the expansion of needs?

In dealing with the first part of the argument I shall draw upon some points made more fully in *Political Philosophy and Social Welfare* (Plant, Lesser, and Taylor-Gooby 1981). We have to see 'need' as an instrumental notion; needs are means to ends. If I need something it is always for something. Thus my claim to need certain resources is justified only if the ends for which I need the resources are justified. Because of the connection between needs and goals it is often argued by critics that needs must be intrinsically subjective and arbitrary in the sense that in our society goals and purposes are so diverse, and because there is disagreement about the range of valuable goals to be pursued then the needs which are defined in relation to these goals are going to be arbitrary and will depend upon the subjective moral evaluation of others in assessing the legitimacy of their claims to need. This is the burden of John Gray's criticism cited earlier.

However, the real situation is much less hopeless and relativistic than this. The mistake which critics of need make in the sphere of welfare is that they concentrate upon the diversity of needs in relation to specific goals. Obviously, the specific goals and purposes of individuals differ and thus their needs differ in relation to them, but if we turn our attention to the idea of goal-directed behaviour more generally and ask ourselves what people need in order to pursue goals and purposes of any kind at all, or what they need in order to act effectively in forming any purpose and pursuing it, then we are in a position to begin to define a class of basic needs – those needs which would have to be satisfied for an agent to be able to act effectively in the pursuit of any conception of the good, whatever it might turn out to be.

These needs might be regarded generally as physical well-being and autonomy; an individual would have to be able to function efficiently as a physical entity and have freedom to deliberate and choose between alternatives if he is to pursue any conception of the good. Clearly, while an individual who is brain-damaged may survive on a respirator, this is not sufficient for human agency, so it is some level of physical well-being (rather than just physical survival) which defines the basic material need here, understood as that class of goods necessary to pursue goals and implement them. Similarly, in the case of autonomy one might argue that my conception of the good or my plan of life is going to depend crucially upon my sense of what is possible, of what can be achieved, and this in turn will depend upon my beliefs about the world. These things have to be learnt and acquired; we are not born with them. In this sense, therefore, agency requires education and other goods of the same sort.

From all of this it follows that I cannot rationally respect persons and value their capacity as rational agents while at the same time being indifferent to whether they have the general resources to make agency effective. In this sense, therefore, basic needs, or the necessary conditions of action, are the primary goods – goods which have to be obtained whatever else I might want – and as such constitute a basic class of welfare needs which all citizens have in common (Rawls 1972).

However, while this argument is effective as far as it goes it needs to be supplemented by two subsidiary points, one about distribution, the other about the range of needs in question here. While the class of basic needs may define a class of basic welfare goods, it does not give any guidance about the sort of distribution required for such goods. Without such a principle, despite the fact that we might have been able to identify basic needs, the ambiguity of the nature of their distribution would still concede a great deal to the neo-liberal critic of welfare. However, as we saw earlier, it is part of the neo-liberal case that the state should be neutral over conceptions of the good and we might draw upon this ideal to provide us with some help over the distributional issue. Given that basic needs as I have described them are the means to any set of goals, then it could be argued that the basis of distribution of the resources to meet these needs should be strictly egalitarian in the sense that an *unequal* distribution of the resources required to meet such needs could only be justified if the state took the view that the goals and purposes of some persons were of so much less value than those of others that they should have a lesser share in the resources, or more extremely that some persons are so clearly of intrinsically less worth than others that they deserve a lesser share. Both of these principles would be incompatible with the basic morality of a liberal society, and thus an equal distribution of the resources to meet basic needs would seem to be the arrangement most consistent with liberal morality.

This might be regarded by some as too insensitive to the differences between persons in the sense that an equal distribution of basic need-related resources would in fact disadvantage those with the least capacity to transform these resources into effective conditions for agency (Sen 1980). Some may be so handicapped or crippled by circumstances, on this view, that to give them the same resources as others who are not so handicapped would be deeply unjust. This raises very deep philosophical problems about how degrees of incapacity can be compared and how differing forms of capacity might command different social resources. Intuitively the idea that we should move from equal provision of resources to that provision of resources which will, so far as possible, secure the greatest equalization of the capacities of individuals to pursue their good is an attractive one. No doubt very rough judgements can be made here about the level of provision which would for example go as far as possible to equalize the capacity of someone who is physically handicapped to pursue his conception of the good with that of an able-bodied person. But until there is some theory which would ground these rather intuitive judgements in something more theoretically secure, those who favour this view will have to admit the arbitrary and discretionary elements about it.

I defined the needs which the welfare state should seek to satisfy as being, broadly, physical well-being and autonomy, and in the last paragraph a just distribution of these welfare goods was seen as one which would do most to equalize the capacities of individuals to pursue whatever they find worth pursuing.

However, the class of welfare goods is rather indeterminate and might not the critic still argue that it does not really place any kind of theoretical limit on what could fall under the class of welfare goods, and thus on the demands made upon the state to satisfy them? Health care, education, and nutrition, all of which are basic welfare goods as I have defined them, do seem indeterminate and open-ended. Perhaps the first point to insist upon here is that there is no purely conceptual answer to this question, it has to depend upon contingencies, on the resources of society, and the political judgements of its citizens, and that this is unavoidable. If we accept a welfare state at all, however residual, and only very extreme libertarians such as Nozick (1974) do not, then the interpretation of what basic needs require for their satisfaction is always going to be a political issue. Hayek himself cannot avoid this issue by appealing as he does to a standard of absolute need – that absence of the resources which leads to destitution. The notion of absolute need is just as contentious as a relative conception and just as much a political and politicized matter.

There will clearly come a point, which cannot be specified in advance, at which the possibility of sustaining an incremental attempt to meet needs may be threatened by the resources consumed by welfare institutions. In the same way as there is often thought to be a trade-off between liberty and equality, so on this view the constraint on the expansion of needs will be the resources available to meet them. The limit will not lie in the nature of needs themselves, but in the circumstances and political judgements about them. The attempt to depoliticize this issue is impossible.

In the foregoing arguments I have stressed the moral basis of the claim that physical well-being and autonomy are basic needs and that society should organize itself on a collective basis to meet these needs as a basic moral demand on the political resources of the society. However, the emphasis upon autonomy leads fairly naturally to the other aspect of the neo-liberal critique of welfare, namely that the welfare state should not be seen as a means of extending freedom and indeed may well itself involve severe restrictions on the freedom of citizens, not least among those whom it purports to help. The argument here is that to be free is to be free from intentional coercion, and that since this is in any event missing from the outcomes of market trans-actions, economic markets are not coercive to the worst off; therefore an attempt by the state to increase their welfare cannot be defended in terms of an attempt to make them more free. The issues here are very complex and can only be touched on in a chapter of this sort. However, I shall try to suggest some answer to the argument.

The critic's argument trades upon a central and important point: we would not want to say that all impediments upon action are limits on liberty. For example, the blowing of the wind, which makes it impossible for me to ride my bicycle, does not infringe my freedom. I am still free to ride it, I am just unable to do so. The physical impossibility of my jumping to New York from Southampton is similarly not a limit on my freedom. Freedom, properly understood, is freedom from the intentional coercion of others. So if someone intentionally prevents me from riding my bicycle, my freedom is restricted. This view of freedom stands in contrast to a more extreme view in which freedom is identified with ability. But there must be a distinction between freedom and ability, otherwise all those things which I am unable to do would become infringements on liberty, and that would be absurd. I am unable to run the four-minute mile, but it would be absurd to say in the light of this that my freedom is diminished. These two points are crucial to the relation between freedom, capitalism, and the welfare state in the following way. If market transactions are impersonal, as Hayek argues, then their outcomes cannot be coercive because they were not intended; if someone lacks resources, capacities, or abilities, his freedom is not diminished because there is a logical gap between being free to and being able to; the first is to be free from intentional coercion, the second is quite a different claim. So no defence of a redistributive welfare state on the grounds that it increases liberty can be sustained.

It is possible to weaken the power of these arguments in the context of discussions about the provision of welfare and freedom without necessarily denying some of the basic insights involved in the critique. The first point would be to take issue with the view that freedom is infringed only when there are intentional impediments put on my activity. While this is true enough, it may not be sufficient to capture the complexity of our concept of freedom. In an argument which parallels the point about justice made earlier, we might well say that the actions of responsible agents which cause impediments to others to pursue their own actions can be regarded as infringements of liberty if these consequences were foreseeable, even if they were not intended by the agent in question. For example my flower bed may adjoin your lawn. I use a very powerful weedkiller which also kills grass and I use it in a liberal quantity. My intention is to rid my flower bed of grass but the foreseeable, although not the intended, consequence is that parts of your lawn are ruined by the weed-killer and your freedom to play croquet on a near-perfect lawn is diminished. Similarly it could well be argued that given the existing distribution of property rights in the economy free exchanges between individuals will have the foreseeable, although not the intended, effect of worsening the position of those with least, and that these foreseeable inequalities could in fact be construed as an infringement of freedom. Correspondingly efforts to mitigate these effects by measures of re-distribution could be seen as increasing the freedom of such groups.

In addition, it could be argued that there are dangers in insisting upon too sharp a gap between being free to and being able to, in the sense that even on a liberal definition of unfreedom as intentional coercion, the removal of such forms of coercion actually means corresponding increases in someone's abilities (Gewirth 1982). For example, if X intentionally prevents Y from leaving a room, Y's freedom is diminished. If X is prevented from exercising this power over Y, then Y is *enabled* to leave the room if he wants to. An increase in liberty in these circumstances implies a corresponding increase in the range of ability. Granted that arguments about welfare and freedom have often been about increasing abilities, then it would follow on this view that there could be specific circumstances in which such strategies could be seen as enhancing liberty. We value actions which remove impediments on freedom because they enhance the possibility that an individual will be able to live a life shaped by his own values and purposes, but in order to lead a purposive life shaped by my *own* values and not those of others I need both opportunities and resources. The limitations on freedom are not just those imposed deliberately by others but also those limitations which are subject to human alteration and which arise out of differences of birth and differing opportunities in education and welfare. To achieve this we need to organize economic and social resources more effectively to enable individuals to have the basic capacities to live the life they regard as good for them.

I conclude, therefore, that the moral critique of welfare mounted by the neo-liberals on the grounds that justice and liberty are not served by welfare provision is seriously flawed. However, this is not to say that we should not learn from the arguments at stake here. I believe that those who defend the welfare state as a means to freedom do have to be careful that the institutional arrangements which they endorse do actually secure the maximal range of choice and the maximal amount of responsibility for such choices by citizens. If the welfare state exists to promote and extend the freedom of citizens it would be paradoxical if this occurred in ways which made choices more difficult to exercise. As David Marquand pointed out in the quotation cited earlier, this might well argue in favour of more provision in cash to allow claimants to define their goods and their needs in their own way. Where provision is made in kind it should include as much participation as possible by claimants in the allocation and nature of the service. If the freedom of individuals in the welfare state is not to be seen as lip-service, this must be reflected in the institutional structures of such a state. There is no reason for example why state schools could not adopt different styles and traditions so long as their differences were not bought at the expense of others.

Finally, if the welfare state is to provide a fairer value for liberty, that is to say a fairer distribution of the necessary conditions for an individual to pursue his conception of the good whatever it might be, then it is arguable that the welfare state needs to be much more redistributive than it has been in the past (Le Grand 1982), and in fact greater redistribution may allow some of the more constraining features of the welfare state to be avoided. A good many of the bureaucratic and constraining features of the welfare state are a consequence of attempting to tackle the *symptoms* of a maldistribution of income and basic resources. Intervention, subsidy, compensation, and the network of rules which these require could be offset by a more egalitarian and redistributive approach to the taxation of income, wealth, and inheritance. This would require less bureaucracy and less direct interference in the lives of individuals (Plant 1984).

The final aspect of the moral criticism of the welfare state which I want to discuss is the vexed question of the nature of welfare rights. The point of criticism which I have in mind here is this: the welfare state cannot be seen as a necessary institutional embodiment of a set of basic human rights. There are no rights to welfare and the claims on which such rights are made are spurious. This kind of argument has been developed by critics such as Nozick (1974) and Cranston (1973) who think of political philosophy from a rights-based standpoint but who are not prepared to allow that there is a genuine right to welfare and the specific resources which such a right would entail. The issues here are abstract and conceptual but they do have a significant political edge. For example, drawing upon some of this critical material, Richard Rose argues as follows in his recently published *Understanding Big Government*:

'The benefits of the welfare state are far more numerous and claim far more money than civil or political rights, but they are discretionary, not constitutional programmes. Citizens are entitled to particular welfare state benefits by an ordinary Act of Parliament; they do not enjoy them as an entrenched constitutional right. The rhetoric of everyday party politics tends to blur the distinction between rights guaranteed citizens in a constitution, and entitlements under ordinary statute law. Constitutional rights cannot be revoked or repealed without threatening consent. Statutory entitlements can be changed by the decision of an elected government, just as they were adopted by an elected government.

Whereas the language of rights is the language of obligation, the language of benefits is the language of bargaining. . . . To confuse rights with entitlements, to assume that every demand must become an entitlement by statute and that every entitlement is an entrenched constitutional right necessary for popular consent, is to make the loyalty of citizens a by product of benefits (or bribes) from government.'

(Rose 1984: 235)

What are the grounds for this sharp distinction between civil and political rights to which correspond strict duties, and welfare 'rights' which are to be understood as demands to be met by bargaining and discretionary responses?

The first and in some respects the most fundamental argument is that whereas welfare 'rights' are always rights *to* something such as medicine, education, social services, and material resources of various sorts, civil and political rights are not. Characteristically civil and political rights require corresponding duties of *forbearance*, of abstaining from action rather than provision. As such, so it is argued, civil and political rights can always be respected because the grounds are negative and coreless – abstaining from killing, interfering, torturing, seizing property, etc. Given that I can only have duties which I am *capable* of performing and given that this condition also applies to government, then the negative content of the duties corresponding to civil and political rights is a feature of very great moral importance. Because such duties entail abstinence rather than provision, they are always practicable for both individuals and governments. Social and welfare rights, however, because they embody claims *to* resources, may not always be practicable and therefore the duties corresponding to such rights are not absolute and must embody elements of discretion and bargaining. Therefore welfare rights cannot be genuine rights if we understand by a right a categorical moral entity whose violation is always wrong. In *Right and Wrong* Charles Fried has put the points made above very elegantly:

'A positive right is a claim to something – a share in a material good, or some particular good with the attentions of a lawyer or a doctor, or perhaps a claim to a result like health or enlightenment – while a negative right is a right that something not be done to one, that some particular imposition be withheld. Positive rights are inevitably assigned to scarce goods and consequently scarcity implies a limit. Negative rights however, the rights not to be interfered with in forbidden ways do not appear to have such material, such inevitable limitations. If I am left alone, the commodity I obtain does not seem to be a scarce or limited one. How can we run out of people not harming each other, not lying to each other, leaving each other alone?'

(Fried 1978: 110)

This is a very clear statement of the standard criticism and it is repeated in Cranston and is implicit in Rose. On the face of it the question posed at the end of the quotation does have a good deal of force, but equally it does point us in the direction of the major weakness in the argument that a sharp distinction between positive and negative rights must be maintained; namely that while forbearance is not subject to a theoretical limit (as resources and services are), nevertheless in the world as we know it the requisite degree of forbearance necessary to ensure negative rights will not always be present. Consequently it is necessary for such forms of forbearance to be enforced by the police, the courts, the penal system, etc. Negative rights and the corresponding duties of forbearance, in order to be implemented and protected, require positive provision by the state in the form of institutions such as police, courts, etc. The degree to which these institutions should exist and the amount of public expenditure they command is going to be as much a matter of political debate and bargaining as welfare provision, so at this point it would seem that the distinction between negative and positive rights, based on the notion that only the latter require the commitment of resources, looks insecure.

However, the critic of the possibility of welfare rights still has a further argument open to him. He could argue that while in the real world the distinction does not hold in practice, nevertheless there is still a valid conceptual or logical distinction. *If* we were a community of saints and had an unlimited degree of forbearance, institutions for ensuring respect for negative rights would not be required and would thus not involve claims to resources; whereas welfare rights in such a world would still require absolute claims to scarce resources. However, if the critic of welfare rights can be allowed such a counterfactual in order to preserve the conceptual distinction, then the defender of welfare rights could equally claim that the distinction has no substance by invoking his own counterfactual – namely a world without scarcity. *If* there were no scarcity of material goods, the rights to such goods would not then be susceptible to the critics' strictures. There is nothing in this counterfactual that is more incoherent or far-fetched than the earlier one. Both arguments are basically about scarcity: in the case of negative rights a real-world scarcity of the human motivation towards forbearance, and in the welfare case a scarcity of material resources. A sharp distinction between these different sorts of rights cannot be maintained on this basis.

However, there are other grounds on the basis of which the distinction has been developed. Cranston for example has argued that rights must be universal if they are truly human rights. That is to say they must pertain to human beings as such rather than to humans under a particular description, whether that be of a social role, a race, or a gender. This point, which seems to be central to any theory of rights, is then used by Cranston to argue that while civil and political rights pass this test welfare rights do not. Welfare rights are held by individuals under particular descriptions and are thus not genuine rights. He takes for example the economic right to holidays with pay and he argues that this right is applicable only to those in paid employment and thus cannot be a genuine right. However, it is difficult to see what force this argument has. For example a right to a fair trial, as David Watson (1977) has noted, applies only to those who have been accused of a crime, and the same could be said of other civil rights – the right to vote for example applies only to those who have reached the age at which they are deemed to have reached political maturity. Of course, Cranston could always avoid this criticism by saying that all human beings have the *potential* for being accused of a crime or reaching political maturity and thus that these rights are universal, but similarly any human being has the potential for being in a particular socio-economic position so that rights to welfare or employment can equally be seen as universal rights.

However, Cranston's argument does bring out an important point about theories of rights, namely that there has to be some feature or characteristic in terms of which the assignment of rights is to be justified. These features have to be universal and not culturally specific otherwise they would not be *human* rights. The possibility, advanced on the basis of the earlier argument of this chapter, is that such features are to be found not in rationality as such (one of the usual candidates) or emotional affectivity (the other one), but rather in the basic needs for well-being and autonomy which I have argued are necessary conditions for the pursuit of any distinctive human purposes. Rights based upon such needs would be both constitutional and welfare rights. My well-being and autonomy clearly require certain kinds of forbearance on the part of others, but they also, as I have argued, require opportunities and resources. Where then does this argument leave Rose's distinction between civil and political rights which are crucial for legitimacy, and welfare 'rights' which are discretionary and have no bearing on legitimacy? Similarly, where does it leave the distinction between genuine strict obligations on governments and bargaining? We have already seen that the distinction between the different sorts of rights is overdrawn and there is no clear logical distinction between the two, but so too is the distinction between obligation and bargaining. Given the point that in the real world civil and political rights have to be protected, the organization and scope of this protection is also going to be politicized and subject to bargaining – thus producing the usual array of pressure groups (including producer interest groups) whose activities in the welfare sphere are so suspect in the eyes of the neo-liberal right. Of course we can still say that there is an obligation on government to provide these institutions but their nature, scope, and funding cannot be deduced from the nature of the obligation independent of normal political processes. However, all of this makes the position analogous to the case of welfare rights. I have argued that the provision of resources to meet basic needs has to be seen as a duty on government in the same way as the protection of civil rights is a duty, but here again what in detail will meet this obligation will be a matter of politics and bargaining. I do not see why neo-liberal critics of welfare rights should see it as a fatal objection to such rights that their implementation is politicized when exactly the same seems to be true of the forms of provision necessary to protect civil and political rights.

There are clearly definite limits to what can be settled by philosophical argument – and in the case of both civil and welfare rights this limit is reached once we have established that the state has a duty to protect both sorts of rights. These are benchmarks on the basis of which we are to judge the nature of the state's obligation. All the rest is for politics.

References

Bradshaw, J. (1972) The Concept of Social Need. *New Society* 19 (30 March): 640–43.

Brittan, S. (1983) *The Role and Limits of Government: Essays in Political Economy.* London: Temple Smith.

Cranston, M. (1973) *What Are Human Rights?* London: Bodley Head.

Crosland, C. A. R. (1975) *Social Democracy in Europe.* London: Fabian Society.

Forder, J. (1974) *Concepts in Social Administration.* London: Routledge & Kegan Paul.

Fried, C. (1978) *Right and Wrong.* London: Harvard University Press.

Friedman, M. (1962) *Capitalism and Freedom.* Chicago: Chicago University Press.

Gewirth, A. (1982) *Human Rights.* Chicago: Chicago University Press.

Gray, J. (1983) Classical Liberalism, Positional Goods and the Politicization of Poverty. In A. Ellis and K. Kumar (eds) *Dilemmas of Liberal Democracies.* London: Tavistock.

Hayek, F. A. (1960) *The Constitution of Liberty.* London: Routledge & Kegan Paul.

—— (1967) *Studies in Philosophy, Politics and Economics.* London: Routledge & Kegan Paul.

—— (1976) *Law, Legislation and Liberty,* vol. 2. London: Routledge & Kegan Paul.

Hirsch, F. (1977) *The Social Limits to Growth.* London: Routledge & Kegan Paul.

Kerr, C. C. (ed.) (1962) *Industrialism and Industrial Man.* London: Heinemann.

Le Grand, J. (1982) *The Strategy of Equality.* London: Allen & Unwin.

Marquand, D. (1980) Taming Leviathan. In *Socialist Commentary.*

Nozick, R. (1974) *Anarchy State and Utopia.* Oxford: Basil Blackwell.

O'Connor, J. (1973) *The Fiscal Crisis of the State.* New York: St Martins Press.

Offe, C. (1984) *Contradictions of the Welfare State.* London: Hutchinson.

Plant, R. (1984) *Equality, Markets and the State.* London: Fabian Society.

Plant, R., Lesser, H., and Taylor-Gooby, P. (1981) *Political Philosophy and Social Welfare.* London: Routledge & Kegan Paul.

Powell, J. E. (1966) *A New Look at Medicine and Politics.* London: Pitman.

Rawls, J. (1972) *A Theory of Justice.* Oxford: Clarendon Press.

Rose, R. (1984) *Understanding Big Government.* London: Sage.

Sen, A. K. (1980) Equality of What? In *Tanner Lectures on Human Values.* Cambridge: Cambridge University Press.

Thompson, D. (1958) The Welfare State. *New Reasoner* 1 (4).
Watson, D. (1977) Welfare Rights and Human Rights. *Journal of Social Policy* 6:
    31–46.
Williams, A. (1974) Need as a Demand Concept. In A. Culyer (ed.) *Economic
    Policies and Social Goals*. Oxford: Martin Robertson.

2

The moral basis of the welfare state

BARBARA WOOTTON

In capitalist societies such as have developed in western countries during the nineteenth and twentieth centuries, it is generally assumed that individuals will somehow or other manage to provide themselves and their dependants with an income. This is, for the great majority, achieved by getting some company, institution, or individual to employ them, while a lucky minority may inherit part or all of their income from their forebears. Another minority may themselves establish new business enterprises, the profits of which produce their incomes. Taken together, all these individual activities create an overall pattern of income distribution throughout the whole community, which, to borrow a phrase (alas! I forget from whom), is the 'result of human action, but not of human design'. Consequently there is no group or individual who can be held morally responsible for the pattern as a whole.

It is, however, a fact of experience that at least in relatively developed countries this undesigned pattern regularly turns out to be one of grossly unequal distribution. Thus in the UK in the income-tax year 1979–80 the richest 1 per cent of income recipients shared a total of £6410 million while the 10 per cent with the lowest incomes had only £3580 million to go round their much larger numbers (Central Statistical Office 1983). Although governments are not responsible for these initial patterns, they can and do modify them by the way in which they apportion between different income groups the tax liability necessary to pay for essential public services, such as defence or the civil service. Current taxation in this country does not, however, reduce the gap between rich and poor very dramatically. After tax deduction the top 1 per cent still share a total of £4140 million, while the bottom 10 per cent have to make do with only £3430 million between the lot of them.

In recent years many governments have gone so far as actually to pay out money to individual citizens in order to make sure that everyone has an adequate supply of basic necessities such as housing, education, fuel, food, drink, and medical care, in spite of the hazards of unemployment, widowhood, sickness, or disablement. Collectively such policies have become widely known as the hallmark of a 'welfare state', a title for which I know no recognized definition, nor is there any agreement as to the dates of its origin in different countries, except that it is in general a twentieth-century phenomenon. In Britain it has been variously supposed to date from the introduction of old-age pensions in 1908, from the Beveridge Report of 1942, or even from the immediate post-war government of Clement Attlee. In any case one might suppose the term 'welfare state' to be superfluous, since, at least in democracies, the objective of any government must surely be promotion of the welfare of the governed.

In the absence of any more precise definition we can, I think, follow customary usage in classifying as welfare states those in which the government takes positive steps to establish minimum living standards. That is the policy, the morality of which we have to assess; but before that assessment can be made, there are three obstacles to be overcome, one which is inherent in all moral judgements, one which applies to every form of government expenditure, and one which affects only judgements about welfare states. The first and most fundamental of these difficulties is derived from the fact that no moral judgement can be logically or experimentally verified as can such propositions as that two and two make four. Put two objects on the table, add two more, count them, and that settles the matter of the total; whereas moral questions can only be logically decided by reference to some fundamental principle which cannot itself be empirically tested. For Christians and believers in many other religions this 'act of faith' is a conviction that our standards of morality are interpretations of the will of God. If God wishes us to love our neighbours as ourselves (or to behave as if we did), that will give the welfare state a moral basis. The moral judgements of the agnostic must likewise be derived from some ultimate assumption acceptable to him personally, and is just as much an 'act of faith' when it is founded not on religious belief, but on some such formula as that happiness is better than misery, and that moral actions are therefore those which seek to maximize the happiness, or diminish the misery, of as many people as possible.

In practice, of course, most of us do not thrash out a personal moral code for ourselves. I myself, in the course of a long life with many opportunities to observe human life-styles in different parts of the world, have come to only two possibly relevant conclusions: first, that the normal human being (though there may occasionally be abnormal exceptions) has an innate need for some kind of moral code by which to guide his life; and second, that the content of that code is in the main culturally, not innately, determined, with the result that it varies greatly as between one country or one social class and another. Accordingly, I accept, with certain personal reservations, the current code of the community in which I live, respecting honesty, kindness, and generosity as morally admirable, while deprecating violence or indifference to the needs of others; and this will be the criterion governing any moral judgements that appear in this chapter.

The second and more limited obstacle in the way of assessing the morality of a welfare state is the hypothesis (apparently not unattractive to Professor Hayek (1976) and his disciples) that it is inherently immoral for the state to take money away from one person in order to give it to somebody else. American philosopher Professor Nozick (1973) has carried this one stage further by postulating that our property rights in our bodily organs are analogous to our rights in our material possessions, and that obligatory transfers of money from the haves to the have-nots are therefore comparable in principle (though not presumably in their degree of iniquity) to compulsory transfers of healthy kidneys from their owners to patients suffering from renal failure. That proposition many will surely dismiss as merely academic raving, impossible to be taken seriously. Moreover, since practically every form of public expenditure raises objections of principle amongst some of those who are obliged to provide the money for it, any general endorsement of the rule that it is morally wrong to make anyone pay for what he disapproves of is impracticable, even without its extension to our bodies as well as our incomes, since it would eventually make all government impossible for lack of money. What then, we may well ask, is the peculiar iniquity of compelling the prosperous to contribute to the welfare of their less fortunate fellow-citizens? Why should this be more immoral than compelling pacifists to share the cost of the armed forces? Can it be the fact that the transfers of money involved in welfare expenditure are more conspicuously personal than their equivalents in public expenditure generally which explains this peculiar sensitivity?

The third attack on the morality of the welfare state as such, and that which is today most popular in top Tory circles, is specifically directed against that institution alone. It is based on the doctrine that in a modern economy the distribution of income should in general be left to market forces. If, however, this results in the payment of really miserable wages to some groups of workers, it is proposed that the deficiency should be made good not by government but by private charity.

This I find utterly contemptible. For one thing, its advocates must be aware that, although there are many laudable charities active in many countries, these have never anywhere near produced minimum living standards for the whole population, such as should be the hallmark of a modern civilized society, and there is no reason to suppose that they ever will. Moreover, this proposal is an insult both to the recipients of such charity and to the donors, inasmuch as it relies on the sufferings of the former to provide a stimulus to the supposedly virtuous actions of the latter.

In spite of Professor Hayek's diatribes against what he sees as the 'mirage of social justice', the rapid proliferation of welfare states is sufficient evidence that root-and-branch objections to state expenditure on citizen welfare have not been effective. Moreover, even amongst those to whom the very idea of a morally based welfare state is anathema, I suspect that few would dispute that the motives of those pioneers who have been mainly responsible for the birth and growth of today's welfare states were and are in general morally laudable, even if ill-judged and even if they may have been reinforced by less altruistic considerations, such as the fear that failure to give help to a deprived minority might provoke reactions dangerous to social stability.

Good intentions, however, are not enough; we all know the destination to which they pave the road. A morally based welfare state might be acceptable in principle, but it would still have to make decisions about the practical application of that principle, and to grapple with any moral problems encountered in so doing. For example, how is the money for welfare expenditure to be raised, how are the intended beneficiaries to be identified, and how far can we be confident that in fact they do get the help that is meant for them?

In contemporary Britain no single consistent policy determines the answers to these questions. One rather unusual plan is the policy of a universal free distribution of benefits in kind financed by taxation – as exemplified in the original formula for the National Health Service. This purported to cover without charge every citizen's every need for medical help throughout his life. Much of this service is, however, no longer free, owing to the imposition of charges for prescriptions and other items, although exemptions for the elderly and for persons requiring regular treatment for chronic illness are doubtless motivated by morally admirable considerations. Nevertheless distribution in kind inevitably restricts the beneficiaries' freedom of choice, for which reason it seems desirable that this form of welfare provision should be confined to goods and services about which the consumer needs some specialist knowledge, if he is to make the best choices for himself. Accordingly, such free distribution of benefits in kind, not based on any specific contribution from the beneficiaries, is quite exceptional. Probably the example most nearly

comparable with the original NHS formula is the current entitlement of children of compulsory school age to free education. But
for the most part, the British welfare state has decided to compensate its citizens in hard cash for such hazards as unemployment, sickness, or widowhood.

For this purpose, as we all know, the instrument most commonly employed is the social security insurance scheme financed
by (mainly obligatory) contributions from employers, employees, and self-employed persons, and supplemented by a
regular grant from the Treasury. This system, which first
appeared on our statute book in 1911, was modelled on one
sometimes associated with the name of Bismarck in late nineteenth-century Germany. I doubt whether, if we were starting
now, we should have chosen this particular model. Although
presented as an insurance scheme, today it would hardly satisfy
any rigorous actuarial test, but that is a semantic matter of no
great importance. What does matter is the steady growth of the
scheme, both in regard to the contingencies against which it
makes provision, and in the range of the population which it
covers, until it now includes practically everybody who does any
kind of paid work. Although there are now five classes of contributors, to wit employers, employees, and three categories of
self-employed, the basic trio of employer, employed, and self-
employed is still the foundation upon which the whole structure
ultimately rests. But it is questionable how far this is appropriate
in the modern world. Contributions are not directly related to the
contributor's personal income: each of the five groups of contributors spans a range of incomes between a lower and an upper
limit. Individuals are then assigned to the group within whose
limits their personal income falls, and all the members of each
group are charged at the same rate.

All this adds up to an excessively complicated way of imposing
an inaccurate means test, while retaining the trio of employer,
employee, and self-employed, which is itself open to criticism,
especially as concerns the employer's place in the picture. It may
well be thought morally commendable that the workers should
take a modest share in the cost of their own protection against the
financial perils of the future; and they themselves often express
satisfaction that this contribution gives them a moral and legal

title to benefits. Being able to say that 'we pay for what we get' wipes off any possible stain of the ignominy and uncertainty of charity. By contrast, the employer's position seems somewhat anomalous. He alone contributes to other people's benefits, and not to his own. It can, of course, be argued that, since it is his decisions which are the immediate cause of unemployment, it is right that he should pay for that, and that 'we pay for what we do' is for him the equivalent of the workers' 'we pay for what we get'. On the other hand an employer can plead that he is not a free agent since his action is only the final link in a long chain of economic pressures which make redundancies inevitable.

Probably the truth of the matter is that the tripartite structure of our social security system reflects the conditions and concepts of a bygone age, in which industrial enterprises had not generally reached the scale of today's major undertakings, and in which the relations of employer and employee were more personal and more paternalistic than is commonly the situation today. Moreover, even if employers may be held to carry special responsibility for creating unemployment, the same can hardly be said about all the other contingencies against which the social security system now makes provision. The upshot is that we have landed ourselves with an enormously expensive bureaucratic monster which, under the innocent-sounding name of insurance, requires that millions of claims to benefits must be checked against each claimant's contribution record, and in which the cost of protection against common hazards is spread in a way that is only roughly related to ability to pay. Is there not also something reminiscent of an outdated class system in the practice of defining a citizen's welfare rights by his position in the industrial hierarchy? In a democracy are we not citizens first, with only a secondary role in what the economic textbooks like to describe as 'one of the factors of production'?

Surely the first step in the path towards common sense and fairness is to transfer to the taxpayer the whole cost of whatever benefits the welfare state may provide. For all its imperfections the distribution of tax burdens in our society is much better adjusted to the individual's ability to bear them than is the complex muddle of the social security tripartite contribution system.

Having decided where to look for the money, we have next to consider how best to use it, so as to guarantee to every citizen a standard appropriate to contemporary concepts of civilized living. In the days of the researches of Charles Booth and Seebohm Rowntree in the late nineteenth and early twentieth century, and indeed right down to the Beveridge Report of 1942, acceptable minimum standards were mainly calculated on a biological base, that is to say as estimates of the quantities of food and such other consumables as are generally held to be necessary for normal healthy living. Today more attention is paid to public expectations, including 'conventional' as well as biological necessities. Thus a MORI poll (summarized in the *Sunday Times* of 21 August, 1983) compiled a list of thirty-three items selected by a sample of the public as goods or services which in their view are essential to civilized living in contemporary society. From this the pollsters calculated that 51 per cent of the British population regard a TV set as an essential; two-thirds of that population also cite as essentials (amongst other items) adequate domestic heating, an indoor lavatory, a damp-free home, a bath not shared with any other household, and even a washing machine, while a more restricted poll representing over half, but less than two-thirds, of the population, would add to the above list 'new, not second-hand, clothes and a week's holiday away from home once a year'.

The pollsters then proceeded to pick out, from the totals thus collected, twenty-two items which seemed to be regarded as particularly urgent, and asked the respondents to say whether they themselves were unable to afford any of them. From the replies it was calculated that more than three million people in Britain were unable to afford adequate heating for their homes, while more than seven million had to go without some essential article of clothing such as a warm coat or a spare pair of all-weather shoes.

The validity of these conclusions must of course depend, as does the validity of any similar poll, on the assumptions that the sample questioned gave truthful answers, and that they fairly represented the population as a whole. MORI is, however, a reputable polling organization, and their findings can, I think, be accepted at least as indicators that we have a long way to go before our welfare state can guarantee that all its citizens really fare well; which perhaps imposes a moral obligation on the state to try to do better.

In practice, however, quantifying welfare benefits is a tricky business, quite apart from the obvious limitation set by the total that the nation can afford, which is itself not easily calculable. For one thing, doubts have been raised, notably by Julian le Grand (1982), as to whether our present machinery really does ensure that the money allocated reaches its intended target. Not only do the authorities have to be satisfied that every claimant is entitled to what he claims; there is also the problem of take-up. Some potential claimants are unaware of their entitlements – and not always much wiser after reading the relevant forms of application. Moreover, expense may be involved, particularly in the NHS, in reaping a benefit in full. Visits to the doctor cost time and money for transport, and it is just the poorer claimants to whom this may be an effective deterrent. The poor are also more likely than those in better-paid jobs to lose their wages for the time away from work involved in a visit to the doctor. Last but not least, in spite of some gallant but unsuccessful attempts to amalgamate NHS and private waiting lists, the difference in the waiting period for some quite serious operations, as between the NHS and the private patient, is notorious. And it is significant that the risk of chronic sickness or death increases for both men and women from top to bottom of the social hierarchy.

Apart from the NHS, most outrageous of all misdirections of welfare policy is perhaps the topsy-turvy effect of the remission of income tax on mortgage interest paid by house-owners. Obviously, the more expensive the home, the greater will the value of this concession be. Julian le Grand (1982) calculates that this results in some wealthy landowners enjoying 'negative income tax', the owners being paid to live in their own houses, which is hardly what any 'welfarist' intended. He finds that in general the chief beneficiaries of the welfare state are not the poor but the middle classes.

Generosity in welfare payments beyond a certain point also creates the 'poverty trap', in which an unemployed worker stands to lose money if he returns to work because his social security benefit exceeds his prospective wage. It seems to be widely believed that a considerable number of unemployed persons find themselves in this theoretically possible position, and that they therefore deliberately eschew employment. However, Alan Walker (1982) produced some useful statistics showing how matters work out in practice. His conclusion is that 'what our tax-benefit system has achieved for couples with three children, whose earnings fall into the bottom quarter of the income distribution, is that it does not matter what they earn . . . their living standards will be the same as anyone else's'. Higher up the scale, however, the situation is different. A similarly constituted family would have to be earning more than about £130 a week before a £10 rise in wages would give them a £5 clear increase in net disposable resources. Walker further observes that there is 'little or no evidence of the effect of the poverty trap on the behaviour of those caught in it'. His readers will certainly get the impression that for someone in the trap to calculate whether any given employment would or would not improve his position would require encyclopaedic knowledge, comparable to Walker's own, about the complex tangle of relevant regulations.

To sum up: probably the best we can do with the present social security scheme in the short run will be to abolish its contributory basis, take the existing benefit scales and wage rates as benchmarks, make such modifications of these as appear necessary to keep them in line with contemporary life-styles and reasonable public expectations, *and then send the bill to the taxman.*

In the long run, our policy should, I think, be much more radical, with simplification the primary aim. In 1942 Lord Beveridge reckoned that modern society had to wrestle with five giants: want, disease, ignorance, squalor, and idleness. His report only tackled the first of these, but he might indeed have listed a sixth, namely 'complexity'.

The obvious opposite of complexity is simplicity, and the simplest method of establishing a universal standard of civilized living would be to make a regular welfare payment from the tax revenues to every citizen without regard to his wealth or income, his health, his employment or unemployment, or indeed any other personal circumstances. It is of course Utopian to suggest that such a welfare payment, on a scale adequate for every recipient to maintain a civilized way of life on that allowance alone, can be more than a dream until at best a remote future. But when I observe how the Utopian dreams of my youth have developed into the commonplaces of today, I am prepared unashamedly to uphold such a universal 'social wage' (as it is often called) as the ultimate goal towards which welfare states should direct their policies. After all, in this country the principle has somewhat surprisingly been already conceded in one example – that of so-called child benefit. The parent or guardian of every child born alive in Britain, be he rich or poor, is entitled to a weekly non-taxable payment from the Inland Revenue (£6.50 at the end of 1983) until that child reaches the age of sixteen, or nineteen if he continues his education up to that age at a 'recognized educational establishment'. Even in this apparently straightforward case there are a few minor complications, such as higher pay for the child of a single parent, or what happens if the child gets married while still eligible for the benefit, but these are hardly sufficient to undermine the children's claim to be the first class of persons in this island towards whose maintenance the state makes a virtually *unconditional* payment, without any specific contribution having been made by or on behalf of the beneficiary.

Cries of horror will doubtless greet the 'monstrous extravagance' of any proposal to extend this type of welfare payment to all adults, including millionaires. The cost of such a 'social wage' is however affected by many variables, operating in opposite directions. It would be inflated by the inclusion of all those potential claimants who, as things are, fail to take up the benefits to which they are entitled. On the other hand, handsome economies would result in the administration of a scheme in which it was no longer necessary to consider either a claimant's contribution record or the particular circumstances (e.g. unemployment, sickness, widowhood) on which his entitlement was based. Nor would a beneficiary's activities have to be restricted while he was in receipt of benefit, in the way that anyone now drawing unemployment benefit is banned from earning anything 'on the side by moonlighting' and so forth. Finally, it would be the end of the 'poverty trap'.

Admittedly, the net effect of these variables cannot be calculated in advance, and the image of a living wage sufficient to satisfy modern ideas of a civilized life-style being payable to everybody in all circumstances, merely because they are alive and presumably wish to remain so, is somewhat startling in the contemporary world. But even so, I wonder if it would be considered more revolutionary than, in some quarters, was the introduction in 1908 of our first old age pension Act, giving non-contributory pensions at – in the money of the day – five shillings a week to persons with incomes not above £21 a year. My childhood memory is that my mother thought this was the beginning of the total corruption of the working classes. 'They would never hereafter save a penny for themselves' – not a very impressive warning to an eleven-year-old child. The comparable comment today on the proposed social wage would be: 'they would never do a day's work again'.

In the interim, while we still have a scheme for payment of benefits to meet only certain specified misfortunes, though this is hereafter to be wholly tax-financed, we shall have to work the social wage in conjunction with that scheme. The unemployed worker must be in receipt of both unemployment benefit and the social wage in the same way as he now retains the non-contributory child benefit payable for his children regardless of whether he is in or out of work. When all welfare payments are directly tax-financed, it will be a relatively simple matter gradually to substitute the new system for the old, and we should therefore look forward to a process by which the social wage takes over by degrees the responsibilities carried by the present insurance scheme. Or, to put the matter in another way, child benefit should gradually grow into an adult social wage paid and financed exactly as its predecessor is for children.

Although many of its supporters are enthusiastic equalitarians, the typical welfare state is concerned, I think, more with absolutes than with relativities. A universalized social wage would protect the vulnerable, without grudging the more fortunate their success as it would if linked to a means test; and it would be a practical expression of that concern for others which, as already observed, is the foundation of both the religious and the secular morality upon which the welfare state of today is built.

Up to this point I have ignored the promise (or threat?) that the economic and social structure of our society may soon be disturbed by the vastly increased productive power inherent in the 'new technology'. If this expectation is realized, much will depend upon the scale and the speed of the change. In the short run any development of new industrial techniques, especially, of course, those that are 'labour-saving', is likely to give rise to social and economic problems at least for a time. But if these are wisely handled, history shows that rewards are eventually reaped. After two centuries of improvement in productive techniques in this and other countries, the size of our work-force, and of those of some of our neighbours, has steadily increased, with only intermittent phases of serious underemployment, and this has brought a significant rise in living standards especially in the present century. At all times the first task imposed by a considerable rise in industrial productivity is to ensure that the way is clear for the additional products to find their way from those who produce them to those who want to make use of them. That is mainly a technical monetary problem. Money itself, being mostly made of paper, has no appreciable value, but it serves as an ingenious device for keeping open the necessary channels from producer to consumer. In my previous statement about the generosity of the welfare state being limited by what it can afford, the reference should be understood as relating not to money, but to the actual quantities of food, fuel, textiles, and all sorts of more frivolous articles which are available and ready to serve the purposes for which they were intended. In this context their monetary value is merely a convenient form of notation which makes it possible to add together a collection of miscellaneous items.

However, this is no place for a discourse on the technicalities of monetary policy in our economic system. Suffice it to say that it is for government and the financial institutions of the City to provide the mechanism for directing any new resources towards their destinations. What those destinations should be is another matter, and one for parliament and people to decide. Here, I think, we should be wary. What in my view is a dangerous and immoral myth seems to be gaining popularity in forecasts that any large expansion of our national production will inaugurate the 'leisure society', and that the pattern of regular daily work for most of one's life will become the exception rather than the rule. The immorality of this lies in the blatantly false assumption that at least in this country everybody has enough of everything that he legitimately requires; and that further production is therefore a waste of energy. As a rule this assumption is implicit, rather than spelled out, but there are occasional exceptions when it is dragged into the limelight by authors who see no shame in it. Notorious amongst these is E. J. Mishan (1967) who envisages this country as some sort of 'power-house in which every grown man or woman is a potential unit of input to be harnessed to a generating system from which flows this vital stuff called industrial output'. Thus he suggests that we are endlessly driven to expand steel output so that every family in Britain should have a motor car. (Whether the author himself had a car, when he fulminated in these terms from within the walls of the London School of Economics, is not disclosed, but his thesis necessarily implies either that all families who want cars are already able to get them, or that it is socially desirable that some should go without.) In this context the attitudes of working men and women are significant. Overtime is still a generally coveted privilege, not a detestable deprivation of enjoyable leisure, as witness the recent protests of miners' wives against strike action or overtime bans in the production of coal, even though this is one of the best-paid employments in the country.[1]

Strictly speaking, 'welfare' is indefinable and immeasurable. Nevertheless it does seem a misnomer to label as a 'welfare state' a government which uses the distribution of newly acquired resources to increase the leisure of the prosperous, rather than to supply the needs of the needy. What can be the moral justification of such a policy? In the end, as I emphasized at the outset of this chapter, all moral judgements can be traced back to social or personal choices. The values which have inspired the concept of a welfare state are deeply rooted in our own, and in many other, cultures in Europe and elsewhere, and they extend far beyond the boundaries of self-interest. But up till now progress in universalizing welfare has been slow. In 1942 William Beveridge believed that his plan would conquer poverty: yet forty years later Peter Townsend could publish a volume of over 1,200 pages on *Poverty in the United Kingdom* (1984). Nevertheless the moral values to which we owe the creation of today's welfare states give ground for hope that, by a wise use of our resources, we still have the opportunity to build a future in which we can be proud that the abolition of poverty, which is inherently evil, has taken precedence over the abolition of work, which is not.

Note

1 Throughout this chapter I have concentrated attention on the welfare state as exemplified by Britain. This is the only example that I know with sufficient intimacy to have any confidence in my own comments and criticisms. Nevertheless, there are important lessons to be learned from wider research and I should like to call the attention of those who are prepared to cast their nets more widely to the volume *Responses to Poverty: Lessons from Europe*, by a team of distinguished British authors, published recently by Heinemann Educational Books (Walker, R. *et al*. 1984).

References

Central Statistical Office (1983) *Social Trends* 13. London: HMSO.

Hayek, F. A. (1976) *The Mirage of Social Justice*. London: Routledge & Kegan Paul.

Le Grand, J. (1982) *The Strategy of Equality*. London: Allen & Unwin.

Mishan, E. J. (1967) *The Costs of Economic Growth*. London: Staples Press.

Nozick, R. (1973) *Anarchy, State and Utopia*. Oxford: Basil Blackwell.

Townsend, P. B. (1984) *Poverty in the United Kingdom*. Harmondsworth: Penguin.

Walker, A. (1982) *The Poverty of Taxation*. London: Child Poverty Action Group.

Walker, R., Lawson, R. and Townsend, P. B. (1984) *Responses to Poverty: Lessons from Europe*. London: Heinemann.

3
Citizenship and the crisis of the welfare state

JOHN FERRIS

The new authoritarians

The social policies of the new right[1] are founded on two public
arguments and an eerie silence. The public arguments have been
about economics and are trivial. They have received considerable publicity and have been cleverly packaged by advertising
men for public consumption. In their populist ad-man versions –
as mouthed ceaselessly by politicians and the media – they could
be said to have a plain 'good housekeeping' ring about them.
First, it was held that public expenditure had to be restrained in
order to promote new private investment. This, it was believed,
would ultimately provide the wealth to pay for essential services
(the difference between essential and inessential remains
obscure). Second, it was argued that public services could be
made to operate more efficiently by introducing commercial
practices and market discipline. Three main methods were
advocated:

1. Social services could be 'privatized' by contracting them out to private firms or simply by leaving them to the market to provide.
2. Cash limits could be imposed by central government on social welfare spending bodies like the NHS and local government.
3. The demand for social services could be shifted by means of charges for services used by the public.

Overall, the new right is seeking to shift the balance of social service provision from the public sector towards the market sector. This, it is claimed, would extend personal freedom, increase individual responsibility, and enhance consumer choice. Public debate has focused on paying for welfare and methods for achieving greater efficiency and reducing waste. The new right has given scant attention to the substance of social service provision. In this sense it has not been concerned with social policy. We are not concerned with their economic policies here except in so far as they do touch on substantive social policy matters, or contain, as we think they do, a hidden agenda. This hidden agenda is now showing itself in policy decisions as the creation of a highly centralized and authoritarian state. This in itself is a substantial social policy concern. If the market is so transparently beneficent, why is it so difficult without a big stick to persuade people to adopt it ? Of course, the answer normally given is that market rules here are to be imposed by government. But how big and strong does government have to be? New right intellectuals like Friedman and Hayek are fond of talking about a minimal state. The state in Britain and the USA has never been more intrusive and its representatives so noisily present in our daily lives. It is this growing state authoritarianism which is surrounded by an eerie silence by those who claim to love freedom, and it has received insufficient attention from those who are seriously concerned with social policy.

Indeed it is still the case that many journalists and academics who should know better accept the claims of the new right that their policies will reduce state interference and promote liberty. Since 1978 the surveillance of private citizens has been increasing steadily, and civil liberties formerly taken as established are now under attack. The substance of new right social policy is not the provision of welfare for those in need, but rather what is called 'law and order', or what I prefer to call state repression of dissent. Under the slogan 'law and order' the rights of citizenship, painfully achieved over the years, are being systematically restricted by both executive acts and legislation. Citizenship as an idea is central to how we think of welfare; it defines how we give and receive in society. Within the public sphere[2] citizenship acknowledges and reflects our inherent interdependency and need for community (Sennett 1977).

The concept of citizenship was related to social policy in T. H. Marshall's justly celebrated essay 'Citizenship and Social Class' (Marshall 1963). According to Marshall, citizenship consists of civil, political, and social rights; he was unable to accept fully the notion of industrial citizenship, although he came close to doing so. We are not concerned with the validity of Marshall's argument, although we do believe that the great merit of the essay is that it provided significance to a key concept for thinking about social policy and shifted attention away from welfare as something for the 'poor' to an area where we are all affected. This essay still provokes fundamental questions about the society we live in. Sadly, Marshall and the idea of citizenship have been too easily dismissed by many on the left whose intellectual and political virility are proclaimed by their rejection of 'idealism' and espousal of 'materialism'. Good materialists know that 'citizenship' refers to mere bourgeois freedom and is an idealist concept (Taylor-Gooby and Dale 1981).[3] With the example of 'actually existing socialism' before us we are hardly in the position to dismiss as trivial the rights and freedoms that have been achieved (Bahro 1978).[4] Certainly we can agree with those critics of Marshall who argue that he displays an overly optimistic evolutionary complacency in regard to the security and rootedness of citizenship in capitalist society. Against his somewhat sanguine portrayal of bourgeois benevolence in the extension of civic rights we would do well to remember E. P. Thompson's salutary remarks on the subject: 'these liberties, which were divested from authority and not granted by it, were greatly disliked by governments and created intense difficulties for them' (Thompson 1980). Citizenship within capitalist societies is vulnerable and fragile. The freedoms that exist depend for their continued existence on populations who take them very seriously indeed in the conduct of their public life. Citizenship as it was fought for by men and women in the past is now under attack from the state directly and is also in danger of being eroded by developments within industrial society.

The threats to citizenship that we discuss cannot simply be attributed to the new right, although in their desperate measures designed to solve 'accumulation problems' they are responsible for recent state attacks. Nevertheless the threats to citizenship have deeper roots in advanced capitalist society. The economic recession has raised them in a more striking and obvious way. Latent tendencies have now become manifest and the state has adopted a more overtly coercive posture in recent years. All the same we do argue that there are certain structural features characteristic of modern industrial societies that conflict with the realization of democratic citizenship and that it will not do to focus solely on the new right. It is after all salutary to recall that whenever civil liberty issues emerge in the House of Commons, Conservative ministers are invariably able to cite valid precedents from the record of previous Labour governments. For this reason we consider not only immediate threats posed by the new right; we also have to keep in mind the wider context. It is necessary to consider the major alternatives to the social policies of the new right. In this British context these are the Labour Party and the Liberal/SDP Alliance. We argue that there is a responsibility placed upon us to pass on to future generations a democratic heritage that includes a wide conception of the public sphere and the role of citizens within it.

Although there are important differences in the policies advocated by the Alliance and the Labour Party we consider that the differences are basically on how to reconstitute the Keynesian welfare state (for convenience we will refer to this as the KWS). This was of course the context of Marshall's essay. It is tempting now to look back and contrast the more expansive social policies of the 1960s with those now being implemented, and this, basically, is what I think both Labour and the Alliance are doing. A reconstituted KWS does not any longer offer a viable solution to the kinds of problem that exist in the 1980s. The conditions and possibilities of the 1980s and 1990s differ from those that existed between 1950 and the early 1970s.

While it is not feasible or desirable to offer a blueprint it is becoming evident that neither the new right nor their major political opponents in parliament can offer adequate solutions, and fresh approaches need to be developed. While practical solutions to today's problems are necessary I want to stress here that an important part of being practical in social policy is ethical acceptability. The failure of the KWS, which can be precisely dated from the oil crisis of 1973, was not just economic; the failure also involved a failure of moral vision. The war socialism which provided the basis of the post-war reforms did contain powerful moral elements, but these soon disappeared. Over the following decades political utilitarianism replaced the ethics of citizenship as the basis of the KWS. Thus the emergence of the KWS implied the devaluation of the moral components of citizenship as they were reflected in war socialism and in the solidarity of working-class struggles for basic rights and freedoms in the preceding centuries.

The moral failure of the KWS

In 1946 Lord Robbins argued that social policies adopted by the 1945 Labour government were self-contradictory and self-defeating: 'The belief that in normal times it is particularly sensible to try and mix the principles and run an egalitarian real income system side by side with an inegalitarian money income system seems to me simplistic' (Marshall 1963). T. H. Marshall later provided the appropriate sociological response to this exercise in economic logic:

> 'The policy in fact may not be simplistic at all, but subtle, a new fangled application of the old maxim "divide et impera" – play off one against the other to keep the peace. . . . I believe on the contrary that this conflict of principle springs from the roots of our social order in the present development of citizenship. Apparent inconsistencies are in fact a source of stability achieved through a compromise which is not dictated by logic.'

(Marshall 1963)

Marshall's insight into the structural foundations of the KWS, even if it was not entirely shared by Keynes himself, was certainly implicit in his work. Moreover, Marshall's insight has generally been acknowledged by other sociologists and political scientists of both liberal and Marxist persuasion. Following Marshall, the post-war settlement has been seen as a truce in the class war based on a trade-off between the rights of citizenship and an acceptable level of inequality.[5] Since 1974 there has been a gradual disintegration of this 'truce' and of general acceptance of the ground rules on which it was founded. Nevertheless the memories linger on and an unstable and disintegrating truce seems more attractive than the chaos of all-out conflict with its uncertain outcome. There are still many on the left who try to represent the post-war reforms as an unequivocal victory for democratic socialism. Marxists have been more ambiguous about them; they have generally felt free to criticize what they call the 'limits of welfare' and to focus attention on the more repressive aspects of state welfare.[6] Despite past negations of welfare state provision, Marxists since 1979 have in substance been prepared to opt for what amounts to the lesser evil of a reconstituted KWS, even though they dress their arguments in radical garb. Provision previously attacked as 'repressive' is now defended as the 'fruit of working class struggle'. This about-face manifested itself most embarrassingly in the campaigns to oppose new right measures like the sale of council houses, education cuts, and hospital closures. While we should recognize and acknowledge a very real degree of ambiguity in social service provision it has come to seem that there is even more ambiguity in Marxist approaches to social policy. Despite a resurgence in Marxist writing in this area and the emergence of what is some-times called the 'new' social administration, it turns out that the 'materialists' have not been able to free the subject from its 'idealist' Fabian origins. They can offer no alternatives to the forms of welfare developed in the years of the KWS. The Marxist critics are as élitist and statist as their Fabian opponents.[7]

Retrospectively it is nevertheless evident that both Fabians and Marxists from their differing angles of vision were able to demonstrate that the welfare institutions of the truce had not significantly reduced inequality and moreover had generated new forms of dependency and inequality. It turned out that citizenship in the moral climate of political utilitarianism of the KWS was altogether more fragile than Marshall had assumed – all in all neither a victory for democratic socialism nor a resounding defeat for capital. Inequality was masked and, as Marshall pointed out, provided with a new legitimacy.

The real, and open, secret of the KWS and its relative success in maintaining 'the institutions of the truce', to use John Rex's phrase, was not citizenship but the capacity of capitalism to sustain economic growth over a period of nearly thirty years. Economic growth enabled political élites to buy consent. Thus all social strata and social groups did benefit in varying degrees, but not in equal measure. Costs and benefits arising from growth were distributed unevenly and almost certainly exacerbated feelings of relative deprivation. Capitalist growth in this context created the 'me too society' (Walzer 1980). Talk of consensus in this context is misleading if we understand consensus in Talcot Parsons's sense of sharing in the normative values of a 'societal community'. The consensus that did prevail was not normative in the sense of resting on the shared values of citizenship or an acknowledgement of mutual interdependency.

There was a consensus among state officials and political élites, namely that social welfare and income were counters that could be used to gain party support in electoral competition. The institutions of the truce therefore were as precarious and conflictful as the processes and mechanisms of economic growth on which they were founded. When growth failed these institutions failed. Economic growth itself created many new conflicts and problems while it was able to postpone the satisfactory resolution of old problems. Growth in the service of capitalism becomes a mass education programme in the benefits of high consumption, and this spirit affected the welfare sector just as powerfully as it did the market sector. All this contrasts markedly with the hopes of Richard Titmuss who saw state welfare as popular moral education in the 'art of giving' (Fromm 1967).[8] Titmuss understood what the moral climate of the KWS really was and never ceased from attacking its political utilitarianism. Unfortunately, he also accepted industrial society as inevitable and was an unashamed élitist; in this he was classically Fabian (Titmuss 1967).

The social rights that Marshall identified turned out to be not so much the 'universal rights to real income' but provisional and highly circumscribed obligations accepted by the political managers as necessary to secure consent and to meet certain forms of manifest need created by high intensity market society. The circumscribed and provisional nature of these 'rights' is very clear when we consider the wilful legal and administrative complexity of social security provision. What do we mean by 'rights' when the basic necessities for existence are so wrapped around with administrative rules and legal procedure that all too frequently they can only be claimed with assistance from quasi-professional technicians? Furthermore many of these 'benefits' that are loosely called rights are discretionary and subject to stigmatizing means tests. A society that was seriously concerned with human welfare would not use words like 'claimant', 'client', 'benefit', 'right', to describe the acts of sharing in the face of the collective need that arises from our interdependency (Bookchin 1982). We are stuck with this language because it reflects the sad reality we are embedded in, but we should at least use it with a decent embarrassment and shame. While the KWS was no doubt more generous (it could afford to be) than anything that preceded it, the break with the poor law and market conceptions of welfare was never as sharp as has been made out.

Welfare dependency was shifted from charity to the state over a long period but it remains dependency. Personal autonomy remains restricted by many subtle mechanisms for those obliged to depend upon state welfare. To assert the values of individual and cultural autonomy is not necessarily to subscribe to the economic and philosophical individualism advocated by authors like Hayek and Friedman. They are not the advocates for freedom they claim to be because they have nothing worthwhile to say about the nature and forms of economic coercion, though they seem happy to accept the necessity of state coercion, even state violence, in order to impose 'market rules' or to create circumstances where they can be applied. Citizenship is important because it implies a public ethic that can transcend the contradictions between individual and society. It has always sought to reconcile our inherent interdependency with an equally inherent human need for personal autonomy and ethical self-determination. The political significance of citizenship is that it points to a public sphere prior to 'market' and 'plan', both of which are simply more or less expedient means for realizing collective ends depending on circumstances and what needs to be done.

Both 'market' and 'plan' have been fetishized in liberal theory, but the central failure of the KWS was not in this area of economic means but in the moral dimension. Liberalism, Keynesian and otherwise, cannot recognize limits to growth or the need for economic restraint, although it is strong on the need for political restraint by groups seeking social justice and equality. This blind pursuit of growth cannot but foster amoral cynicism and the unconstrained pursuit of sectional and individual interest. This was the moral failure of the KWS which virtually made growth and consumption into a new religion. No amount of compensatory welfare could alleviate the social and natural consequences of industrial growth as we have known it since the Second World War.

This 'fiscal crisis of the state' identified by James O'Connor (1973), where all social strata and groups want more from the state in the form of income, welfare benefits, subsidies, grants, etc., but at the same time resist paying the taxes which permit such payments, may simply indicate the human propensity for taking rather than giving, as conservatives would argue. Whatever the limits of human altruism, it is more relevant surely to consider the institutional arrangements which provide the immediate determinants of social behaviour. The KWS sanctified forms of competitive inter-group rivalry and replaced customary cultural restraints by technical manipulation of need. The competitive trade unionism of the 1970s, where groups were struggling for rank in the wages pecking order, had little to do with socialism as it has been traditionally conceived. During the 1970s the amoral logic of political utilitarianism degenerated into a Hobbesian pursuit of sectional interest. Without growth it was no longer possible to buy civic or industrial peace. Citizenship was revealed for what it had been all along in this context – purely instrumental. This essentially moral crisis created the political opportunity for the new right.

The limits of citizenship in the KWS

Although Marshall's elaboration of the major components of contemporary citizenship has probably been the most influential among academic social scientists, certainly in Britain, it seems to me that authors like Parsons, Bendix, and Lipset have more accurately conveyed how the concept has been understood by mainstream political opinion in the liberal élites. There is a tentativeness about Marshall's essay, a readiness to make qualifications, that is absent in American sociology. For all his evolutionary optimism, Marshall lacked the bland self-assurance and political complacency that characterized American social science during the 1950s and 1960s. It is worth noting two of Marshall's qualifications because they have been glossed over by other writers.

First, he noted that citizenship arose from structural conflicts in the social order and that this paradoxically provided a source of social stability, although he did not suppose that this stability would last indefinitely: 'It may be that some of the conflicts within our social system are becoming too sharp for the compromise to achieve its purpose much longer' (Marshall 1963).

Second, although collective wage bargaining and trade unionism were discussed as having some of the characteristics of what might be called industrial citizenship, Marshall was careful to distinguish this from political citizenship: 'Trade unionism has therefore created a secondary system of industrial citizenship parallel with and supplementary to the system of political citizenship' (Marshall 1963). It is precisely at the boundary, elusive as it is in reality, between the economic and the political that the new right stop in their talk of individual freedom. For them trade unions are essentially illegitimate, an unacceptable form of monopolistic power. Anthony Giddens has rightly argued that one of the major distinguishing features of capitalist society is the unrelenting effort given to maintaining formal and institutional separation of the 'political' and the 'economic', a distinction that the labour movement and trade unions frequently have to contest, although they will comply with it in the everyday transactions of industrial relations. Marshall accepted the separation, at least implicitly; indeed it appears to be the most important source of his qualifications and the hesitations in what was in other respects an optimistic essay. Giddens has in our view stated the issue very clearly:

'Rather than being permanent and stable the insulation of the polity and economy is fragile, incorporating as it does a strong ideological element – for notwithstanding the real political progress that is inherent in the transition from liberal to liberal democratic state, one element of Marx's critique of the capitalist state still applies. The capitalist labour contract, the sale of labour power and alienated labour, remain the other face of the liberal democratic state. Democratic organisation does not extend to the work place, in which the power of those in subordinate positions remains largely negative.'

(Giddens 1981)

Liberal-democratic formulations of citizenship are confined to having relevance in the sphere of the polity and are seen as having no application to the economy, where different 'rules' regulating the relations between labour and capital are held to apply. Trade unions and processes of collective bargaining are recognized in legal and institutional terms, but they do not have that aura of legitimacy that is inherent in the idea of citizenship with its reciprocal rights and duties. Within the framework of the KWS and liberal democratic theory, 'industrial citizenship', despite the high profile of economic problems, remains shadowy. This was the most important limitation of citizenship in the KWS. Moreover the 'fragile insulation' that Giddens notes continues to be a major source of conflict. Defending this particular line during the past decade has given rise to most of the justifications of state encroachments on civil liberties. Unfreedom at work presents a constant threat to liberties that have been won elsewhere. The counterpart of freedom in the political sphere is domination in the economic sphere. Industrial democracy should therefore be the next step in the extension of citizenship, for its own sake and to safeguard existing liberties.

The second major limitation of citizenship has to do with the kind of political community/culture in which citizenship rights and obligations are rooted. Marshall could take it for granted that citizenship had meaning within the framework of the nation state and that this would provide the major focus of loyalty and political obligation. We can no longer take the nation state as simply given. The problems are highlighted by Parsons in a discussion of the position of the black minority in American society (Parsons 1965). This essay by Parsons has the merit of being one of the most lucid liberal-democratic expositions of citizenship. It is also interesting because Parsons seeks to avoid the cruder forms of political utilitarianism that pervaded the KWS.

Parsons, unlike many liberals, does not seek to deny that black Americans are excluded from the rights of citizenship; according to him they are treated as second-class citizens. He offers a plausible, but not convincing, explanation of why this is the case, and unfortunately ends up 'blaming the victims'. His definition of citizenship is of interest in this context:

'The concept of citizenship, as used here refers to full membership in what I shall call the societal community. This term refers to that aspect of the total society as a system, which forms a *Gemeinschaft*; which is the focus of solidarity or mutual loyalty of its members and which constitutes the consensual base underlying its political integration.'

(Parsons 1965)

It is this notion of 'societal community' which seems rather forced to us. Modern 'total societies' are precisely societies where the word *Gemeinschaft* is not applicable, and if we are to use this term to denote political obligation in the modern nation state it is even more inappropriate. The nation state is also the welfare state, at least in the advanced industrial societies, and distinctive welfare measures are arguably the real basis of mass loyalty. Any politician who claims that citizens should give more to the state than the state gives to them is a demagogic charlatan. Patriotic *Gemeinschaft* is fraudulent; it is a spectacle in which a passive audience can watch the rise and fall of political gladiators and the parading of culture heroes on the national stage of the mass media. Commitments and purposes are invoked which belong to no one, they are not yours, mine, or ours. Participation offered by this kind of patriotic loyalty is always vicarious and illusory (Walzer 1980).

The nation state may be virtually inevitable, as Gellner has argued very persuasively, simply because few credible alternatives exist in the modern world (Gellner 1983). At the present time it may be equally inevitable that citizenship can only be defined by national identity in its legal aspects. All this may be so, but to use terms like *Gemeinschaft*, community, or mutual loyalty in the context of the modern nation state is simply ideological and mystifying. For Gellner the nation state is the natural home of industrial society. Where Parsons links loyalty to moral sentiments, shared values, and feelings of belonging, Gellner sees rather basic material interests.

> '[Industrial society] . . . was the first society to want the ideal of progress, continuous improvement. Its favoured mode of societal control is universal Danegeld buying off social aggression with material enhancement, its greatest weakness is its inability to survive any temporary reduction of the social bribery fund, and to weather the loss of legitimacy which befalls it if the cornucopia becomes temporarily jammed and the flow falters.'
>
> (Gellner 1983)

If Gellner is correct in this observation then the absence of the moral sentiments that are crucial for Parsons does, with the absence of economic growth, raise serious problems of legitimation. If the state cannot provide social harmony and material improvement what else can it provide other than a patriotic spectacle? The moral sentiments that Parsons invokes as the focus of solidarity to the 'societal community' have in the past been linked with what Gellner calls the 'given intimate structures of traditional society'. These kinds of attachments and sentiments cannot be simply transferred to the modern nation state in the way that Parsons suggests, certainly not without being transformed into something else. Human needs and feelings are not as easily divided and packaged as Parsons appears to think, one bit (the largest?) for the societal community, another for the family, another for co-religionists/ethnic fellows, etc. The point that Gellner drives home is that it is the nature of industrial society to transform these communal loyalties and ultimately to offer a different kind of identity, which, however 'folksy', 'national', or 'cultural' it might appear on the surface, actually requires substantial material underpinning to become compelling. We may still ask whether this is an adequate identity in human terms and whether the material benefits that flow from the nation state are sufficient to compensate for deeper moral attachments. Human nature is such that community is among the basic needs – however elusive it might be. The KSW in any event eroded those associations that we customarily think of in the context of community. This is a highly paradoxical feature of modern industrial societies.

The functional organizations of modern societies – trade unions, professional organizations, and so on – are the crucial representative organizations. Their strength and inclusiveness provide the best guarantee that the state will act benevolently, so that in the modern nation state unorganized citizens are unprotected citizens (Walzer 1980). The KWS requires functional groups that command loyalty and even provide a form of community for individual citizens. Such organizations are successful to the extent that they can intermesh with the state system, at which point they become agents of distributive justice and social control. Once integrated they tend to lose the characteristics of community and cannot be expected to function as arenas of democratic citizenship. They acquire the bureaucratic hierarchical form of the state itself. The attributes required for participation in such a system are those of the functionary, not the citizen. This is so in all units, for example schools, cities, universities, churches, factories, offices, etc. These are of course the places where citizens' views are relevant and likely to be well informed. In the perfected welfare state these arenas will have been broken up by bureaucratic organizations and popular resources will be withdrawn or flow elsewhere. The individual members turn out to confront a powerful state – the source of all benefits. Isolated from viable communal and cultural groups, individuals become materially and emotionally dependent upon centralized authorities. Of course it is to such 'liberated' individuals that inflated patriotic rhetoric is addressed. This is why citizenship requires a 'public sphere' and this in turn suggests decentralization and participatory self-government. The KWS and liberal-democratic theory are premised on centralization and management in all areas of life by political and functional élites.

A third alternative?

The fundamental dilemma that the KWS failed to resolve, and the new right is not even trying to resolve, was the contradiction between the imperatives of legitimation and capital accumulation. Legitimation here refers simply to popular support and consent. Another name for accumulation is growth. What was unique about the KWS was that it was able for a long period to secure legitimacy by means of growth and from this to operate what Gellner so aptly called the 'social bribery fund'. It could only be a temporary solution; it generates its own demise by undermining the basis of capitalist growth – the exploitation of labour power. By increasing the power of trade unions in collective bargaining and by having to increase taxation to fund social programmes the KWS reveals its limits. Economic growth did make it possible to conceal the contradiction and to postpone the consequences. It was possible to export the cruder and more primitive forms of exploitation to the Third World (and also import them along with migrant workers). Third World workers whether in their 'homelands' or in the metropolitan centres were excluded from citizenship rights that had been won by indigenous workers in the capitalist heartlands (or at least partially admitted). The truce between capital and labour was purely domestic; it did not exist in the Third World.

The anomic politics of the KWS did not end poverty and inequality; it modernized them perhaps and most certainly extended them globally. The particular role of welfare in the capitalist heartlands was to secure the integration of those groups of workers who were seen as functionally indispensable. Other groups lacking the power that comes from essential functions and/or organizational means remained invisible and unheard and therefore *de facto* second-class citizens. To this extent the KWS was more successful than even Marshall anticipated but at the very high cost of marginalizing many social groups and by imposing ecological damage on a global scale.

Industrial society now presents a very real and tangible threat to the organic basis of life itself on this planet (nuclear weapons are the logical outcome of this system). It would be rash to offer predictions about the probability of comparable growth rates being attained in the future; given the possibilities of technological and economic substitution they may be. However, we are no longer innocent and we now know that the social and ecological costs would be very high indeed. The prospect of overcoming scarcity defined in purely quantitative terms can never again be as attractive as it has been in the past.

For this reason variants of the KWS solution to the present crisis are not adequate. If the ecological critique is taken seriously it should surely lead to major reassessment of our attitudes towards 'actually existing' capitalism and socialism. Such knowledge would have a major influence in the consideration of alternative policies. Above all traditional definitions of scarcity and ways of overcoming it would no longer be relevant. These need to be revised from the standpoint of social ecology (Bookchin 1982). The new right of course has totally ignored the ecological evidence and puts forward its regressive programme as if we could simply go back to the early nineteenth century. It cannot be seriously considered as offering any kind of solution to the real problems of the modern world.

Ian Gough in a useful analysis of the crisis of the welfare state from a Marxist standpoint has proposed that we need a third alternative to the KWS (centre-right version) and social democratic reformism. Gough sees the new right as a problem rather than solution, and calls for a 'third alternative' (Gough 1983). Where I differ from Gough is that he does not question the need for further industrial growth, nor does he refer to the ecological critique of industrial growth. His Marxian alternative still seems rather orthodox. The political consequences of wider ecological awareness would be demands for radical decentralization, redistribution of power to the base (e.g. factories, offices, colleges, neighbourhoods, etc.). This calls into question Gough's implicit centralism.

Gough invokes the new social movements (feminism, ethnic groups, urban movements, the peace movement, etc.) as having prefigurative potential. I share these hopes, but unfortunately he fails to mention ecology or the fact that what defines these movements as new (at least the most numerous groups) is, first, their rejection of the Marxist truisms and orthodoxy that Gough still adheres to, and second, non-violence and ecological thought has informed the theory and practice of many of these groups. The implicit vanguardism of Gough's position is revealed when he suggests that the 'new movements' should relate to 'sections of the labour movement' (possibly the Labour Party although Gough steps back from this). He does not specify which sections; are Women for Peace to be offered the leadership of Arthur Scargill? Given the break-up of the industrial working class it is problematical even to talk of the working class in the traditional sense (Gorz 1981). What M. Bookchin called 'workeritis' in the 1960s is still around (Bookchin 1971).

What Marxists like Gough, who is not unaware of the issues, somehow resist seeing is that in the midst of the present crisis of the welfare state something new is being born. The kinds of problem we now face will demand new political responses; yesterday's Utopia becomes today's necessity. The terms of the debate and the categories that have been around since 1945 are becoming irrelevant. Gough knows this in a way but does not confront the problem directly, and the major political parties and political commentators for the most part do not even see the problem. Since 1980 new collective actors have emerged and with them new values and modes of action. They simply do not fit the old liberal/Marxist boxes and should not be analysed automatically from those assumptions.

Despite the claim that industrial societies are achievement societies, particularly capitalist societies – this has been virtually a sociological truism for over twenty years – they still depend for their functioning on very high degrees of ascriptive inequality, especially in the economic sub-system. One of the features that characterizes the political scene of the 1980s is the number of political groups which simply cannot be classified in the categories of class and therefore as aligned with either capital or labour. Many of these groups are challenging the ascriptive definitions that continue to influence the division of labour and the distributive mechanisms of the welfare state, for instance youth, women, ethnics, homosexuals, the elderly, and the disabled. For this reason the demands they raise nearly always have a moral dimension – moral because they are demands for inclusion (in Parsons's sense), but also because they imply qualitative transformation of society. Inclusion could not occur without radical changes in attitudes and values. The distributive mechanisms of welfare tend to follow rather than lead such change. If the demands were purely distributional in character then the KWS solution might be appropriate; but they are not. The new right simply seeks to repress all such demands and use the state to support the particular interests who gain from ascriptive role definitions. This is one reason why the line between the economic and political spheres needs to be obliterated. Citizenship, because of these factors, is therefore central to debates about a third alternative. A broader view of citizenship is necessary to secure the rights and freedoms of those groups who are to varying degrees excluded from full participation in social and political life (both *de jure* and *de facto*).

A wider concept of citizenship is also necessary for the protection of such non-capitalist 'spaces' as do exist within the existing social order, and of course for their extension. Such 'spaces' might be thought of as bases from which a qualitative transformation might be initiated. This presumably is what Ian Gough means when he uses the term 'prefigurative potential'. However bleak the prospect of this might seem now such spaces are a necessary defence against the destructive forces unleashed by industrial society with its instrumental rationality. Enough damage has already been done in the service of modernization and economic growth. I agree then with Ian Gough in his call for a debate about a third alternative but I also say that there are particular threats to democratic citizenship that will have to be met if this alternative is to be created.

Three threats to citizenship

First, industrial society, capitalist and socialist, is gradually destroying the idea of a public sphere where democratic politics are both ends and means. The ideas of citizenship and democracy share an ethical core that has gradually been shaped in a long historical development. These ideas, and the social practices from which they are derived, are in danger of being reduced to triviality and banality by economistic conceptions of citizens as passive consumers of private and public goods. While satisfaction of basic material needs is an important objective of welfare, it is not the only objective or even the most important.

Welfare state socialism has been primarily concerned with the aim of meeting material needs, assuming implicitly that aesthetic and cultural needs would automatically follow. It has not addressed itself practically to qualitative and cultural transformation. Socialist 'morality' is built in with words like 'fraternity', 'solidarity', 'co-operative'. This morality does not mix easily with the instrumental rationality of the modern bureaucratic party and state. More than fifty years of 'socialist realism' now induce feelings of embarrassment when we hear this language used. It has been debased by political cynicism. Despite the genuine moral concerns of democratic socialists like Tawney and Titmuss, welfare state socialism has converged with liberalism in its understanding that satisfaction of material needs would leave individuals free to pursue private happiness. Because of this, the public sphere in the KWS became an arena for the instrumental politics of distribution. Its wider expressive and ethical dimensions were allowed to wither. For any particular group, once its collective distributional claims are met, public life (politics) simply becomes an irksome burden to be left to salaried functionaries. Individuals are released from this 'burden' to meet their desires in the market – the citizen becomes consumer. Bahro and others indicate that behind the monolithic bureaucratic façade of 'actually existing socialism', similar, if not identical, processes are operating in eastern Europe. Bahro uses the term 'compensatory consumption' to describe the distributive incentives offered in the east. He also observes that 'compensatory consumption' is encouraged to suppress the emergence of emancipatory interests in personal growth and self-realization. With the emergence of the KWS, capitalism met the socialist challenge and showed itself as being more effective in providing 'compensatory consumption' and correspondingly just as effective in suppressing emancipatory needs.

These issues were acutely prefigured in the political writings of

William Morris back in the 1880s and 1890s, in particular in his arguments with the Fabians, like G. B. Shaw and the Webbs (Williams 1961). Morris consistently stressed that material satisfaction was a qualitative as well as quantitative objective, and moreover that it was a necessary but by no means sufficient condition for socialism. Morris recognized very clearly our interdependency and the need for participatory citizenship. Both Marxism-Leninism and social democracy in the twentieth century have departed from this socialist morality and implicitly, if not explicitly, encouraged consumerist conceptions of citizenship. This then is the first threat to citizenship.

The second threat to citizenship arises from technological developments in industrial society and poses the danger of eroding our capacity to be active and responsible agents. It is necessary to stress that this is not an assertion of technological determinism. What is involved is the disappearance of the political frameworks of decision-making in which citizenship is meaningful and in which ethical choice can be relevant and effective. The dilemma we are now confronted with has been lucidly outlined by Hans Jonas and has profound implications for the way in which we think about citizenship and social policy.

> 'The human condition, determined by the nature of man and the nature of things, was given once and for all, that the human good on that basis was readily determinable, and that the range of human action and therefore responsibility was narrowly circumscribed.'
>
> (Jonas 1972)

These conditions no longer hold; neither human nature nor the natural environment can any longer be taken as given. We now actively create both, with the emergence of modern technologies. Jonas argues that traditional ethics, religious, Kantian, or utilitarian, no longer correspond to scientific, social, and political reality. While they may still guide private conduct they are not effective guides to action in the public sphere.

To what extent can ordinary citizens have valid knowledge of nuclear energy and radiation risks such as to make their contributions to public decisions relevant? Conversely, are we content to leave such decisions in the hands of scientists who for the most part are on the payrolls of powerful public or private corporations? Politicians also represent particular interests. These dilemmas now pervade social policy – genetic engineering, the use of drugs in prisons and psychiatric hospitals to control social behaviour, high-technology medical intervention, electronic surveillance of citizens by the state. Modern science and technology have no inherent limits, and ethical concerns are external to the activity of producing such knowledge and techniques. Limits are no longer inscribed in the nature of things. We are obliged to choose although we now lack the political institutions in which to do this adequately. The sacred is no longer binding although we need to establish limits. Where else than from the public sphere could such limits come? Citizenship then is the means whereby we approximate as nearly as possible the universal interests, those interests that are inherent in issues that transcend sectional and individual gains and losses. Social ecology, in its critique of industrial society, raises a new categorical imperative. 'Act so that the effect of your action is compatible with the permanence of genuine human life' (Illich 1977).

Neither representative liberal democracy nor socialist 'party and state' democracy are constituted so as to be able effectively to represent the rights of non-human nature or those of future generations; quite the opposite. Ecological thinking has not yet had much influence on mainstream political philosophy. In so far as ecological arguments are acknowledged they tend still to be viewed as having relevance within existing intellectual frameworks and bureaucratic/organizational structures – scientific disciplines like botany, biology, and zoology, or organizations like environmental ministries and single-issue pressure groups. It does appear to us that the implications of the argument developed by Jonas is that social ecology – as philosophy, theory, and practice – is pre-eminently a matter for social policy and has relevance to the organization of welfare in society. Ivan Illich perhaps more than anyone has understood this in his writing over the past decade. Unfortunately Illich's extreme anti-professionalism has made it too easy for him to be dismissed as a wild polemicist. Illich nevertheless has taken Hans Jonas's argument seriously and attempted to outline directions which social policy may follow. In this, his critique of industrialism converges with that of William Morris and while it cannot (and should not) specify detailed content, it clearly suggests an extended concept of citizenship and participatory democracy.

A third threat to citizenship that has emerged is the growth of what a number of political scientists call corporatism (Cawson 1982). This, it is becoming clear from the literature, has relevance to understanding recent developments in social policy and the provision of state welfare, although the primary concern for many researchers has been industrial relations. Within the literature there is still controversy about an adequate definition of corporatism. For our purposes it is sufficient to say that corporatism can be understood as a state-supervised bargaining process that occurs between representatives of key interest groups. Much of the literature is concerned with what might appropriately be called extra-democratic horse-trading between 'capital and labour', the interest of the state being to alleviate chronic fiscal and planning problems and to secure discipline and constraint. These processes also extend to social policy. Caught as they are between government and professional interests, local and regional authorities, and the unions, all the major social services are affected to varying degrees, e.g. health care, housing, education, and personal social services. Corporatist strategies have been adopted in order to develop and maintain consensus among power élites and to adjust social policy-making with the requirements of the economy. It is important to stress that these political arrangements tend to remain inaccessible to the public. They are power élite negotiations and involve, quite frequently, the suppression of open debate. They also require extensive surveillance in order to provide information to state officials involved in the bargaining. The public are told as much as is considered desirable to secure support for agreements, usually via 'off the record' press briefings and 'leaks'.

The new right came to power in Britain with the declared aim of ending these corporatist arrangements by means of the extension of markets and privatization. However, I do not think that advanced capitalist societies can be simply transformed into pure market societies, even with all the 'resolute government' in the world. Modern societies are unthinkable without collectively provided social services like housing, education, health care, and social security. The question is not public *v.* private, but big *v.* small, or local *v.* centralized provision. If extensive re-commodification fails, as seems likely, then corporatism offers another complementary response to resolving conflicts over the production and distribution of public goods. What cannot be achieved via the coercion of the market may perhaps be achieved by political coercion in these essentially unequal bargaining arrangements (some producers may have some power, but never as much as the state). For example universities, threatened with financial cuts, will comply with pressures to shift resources between areas of research and teaching, irrespective of student demand or intellectual and scientific considerations. Secondary and further education experience similar pressures. The professions involved cannot be simply assumed to represent the interests of potential students, parents, and the public; their priorities, of necessity in this context, will be to save jobs, status, and pay. Likewise, unions will oppose hospital closures. Obviously educators, doctors, and social workers will claim to represent universal interests. However, because the public as users of services are excluded from decision-making, such claims will be treated with scepticism. Moreover, in the wider context of corporatist bargaining, power still resides with the representatives of capital, to invest or not to invest. Unfortunately, these interests will have the power to define the agenda and to place limits on what can and cannot be negotiated.

Some social policy analysts, although regretting the decline of pluralist liberal-democratic arrangements in policy-making, have welcomed corporatism as a means of saving the welfare state from the attacks of the new right. The basic assumption is that the functional interests of social service professionals will serve to represent user interests as well (Mishra 1984; Pinker 1979). A not dissimilar line of defence can be found in recent Marxist writing about the welfare state (Gough 1979; Corrigan and Leonard 1978). This kind of defence of welfare is problematical; even if we discount Illich's extreme anti-professionalism we know that producer groups in the social services will seek to maintain their position in the system irrespective of user benefit, and in fact often do act repressively and exploitatively. This is why I would argue against a corporatist version of the KWS as proposed by Pinker and Mishra. Corporatist arrangements are inherently inequitable. Morever, by definition they exclude representation of many interests. Their most common outcome is to shift the costs of decisions on to those who do not have a place at the table. Corporatism ignores the requirements of citizenship. However in some formulations it comes close to syndicalism. This suggests that it may be possible to envisage forms of functional democracy coexisting and overlapping with territorial forms. Given equal bargaining power this might work. But such measures, to be meaningful, require extensive decentralization, participation, and the enhancement of citizenship. C. B. MacPherson has proposed a model of how this might operate (MacPherson 1977).

Conclusion

Our concern in this chapter has been with citizenship and its links with more general frameworks for explaining and ordering welfare in society. Whatever the pragmatic merits and ethical acceptability of the particular components of citizenship, if they are not supported by coherent and widely accepted political values along with a positive view of a public sphere then citizenship will be effectively devalued and become vulnerable to economic fortune and the kinds of political hucksterism that have become prevalent in recent years. This was the fate of citizenship in the KWS, and it prepared the ground for the new right. What social gains had been achieved in the post-war years came to be considered as structurally irreversible by many social scientists, even though it was also held that popular attitudes were instrumental ('What's in it for me?') rather than based on normative commitment to values of co-operation and equality. These illusions have been brutally dispelled by the new right in power. The most fatal illusion fostered in the KWS was that the situation of the 'have-nots' could be improved painlessly without redistribution or taking anything away from the 'haves', a neat positive-sum game that assumed the possibility of virtually infinite economic growth.

The economic and social problems that confronted western capitalist societies after the oil crisis of 1973 had their roots in the structural nature of the KWS, which, in turn, was related to the western nations' increasing dependence upon the exploitation of Third World economies (a process which has been aptly called uneven and unequal development). In one sense the new right argument that there had to be a radical break with this 'Keynesian' past was more realistic than that offered by supporters of the KWS who sought to buy time and hoped that the problems would go away with a new upturn in the world economy. This was as far as realism went. New right policies are self-contradictory because capitalism is both endangered and made possible by extensive state welfare provision of the kind we have become familiar with. Collective welfare provision is necessary in an economic system which makes all of us dependent, that concentrates us in cities and urban areas, that ceaselessly disorganizes social life through its investment priorities. On the other hand, welfare, to the extent that it makes the conditions of workers secure, creates disincentives to work in the kind of way and at the level of intensity required by capital. Given new technology and the possibilities of resource substitution, it is possible that there will be a new cycle of growth. However, this possibility fails to attract in the way it might once have done; for every social problem temporarily relieved it would create deeper ecological problems. While growth might create the possibility of 'buying' legitimacy, as suggested by Gellner, it also means continued exploitation of the Third World and ecological disaster. Without either normative or 'instrumental' legitimacy the future we face will be increasing state repression and the erosion of civil liberties. The first victim of the recession has been citizenship; we have witnessed growing state authoritarianism with concerted and sustained attacks on local and industrial democracy. Expenditure on the police and defence has steadily increased over the past five years.

One alternative to these trends is that outlined by Murray Bookchin, which he calls *social ecology* (Bookchin 1982). As it has developed over the past decade the ecological critique has for the most part been the property of single-issue pressure groups and technical experts. The power élite have been able to keep it insulated. The rise of the West German Green Party as a political force encourages hope that it cannot be so confined much longer. Ecological concerns are now becoming social policy concerns. We do need urgently to develop these ideas in practical ways in social policy that will give rise to qualitative growth. In Bahro's terms we need to start addressing 'emancipatory needs' (Bahro 1978).

I believe that social ecology contains the values that would sustain citizenship as we conceive it. It is not, as many Marxists and liberals argue, backward looking or romantic. Claus Offe has pointed out, rightly in my view, that it is a response to a possible future that is distinctly threatening; it offers an alternative to industrial modernization that relies exclusively on instrumental reason and strategic rationality (a future predicted by Max Weber very chillingly many years ago). The new social movements are reacting to this impending disaster; the peace movement, feminists, and the environmental groups have all to varying degrees now absorbed the ecological critique of industrial society (Offe 1984).

In terms of social organization, it means creating alternative social bases of local power against the centralism of the state and the multinational companies that dominate the world economy. This requires local and decentralized participatory initiatives along the lines envisaged by C. B. MacPherson. The prospects seem bleak and the odds overwhelming but the protest has begun and will no doubt continue. The new social movements in this do reflect the practices and values of citizenship as it has developed historically and it is certain that the story is not over yet.

Notes

1 By 'new right' I mean the policies advocated by authors like Milton Friedman and F. A. Hayek and to varying degrees adopted by the Thatcher and Reagan administrations in the UK and USA since 1979.
2 In using the term 'public sphere' I am following Richard Sennett who discusses the 'fall of public man' in liberal capitalist societies. Sennett draws a distinction between 'public life' and 'private life' and sees them as governed by different rules. Liberalism, in Sennett's argument, has tended to devalue 'public life' and correspondingly overvalued personal happiness and 'private life' (Sennett 1977).

3 Peter Taylor-Gooby can be taken as representative of the position adopted by many Marxists who became interested in the substance of social policy during the 1970s.
4 Rudolph Bahro uses the phrase 'actually existing socialism' to describe the state socialist system that prevails in eastern Europe as opposed to the 'dreams and aspirations' that have existed since the Communist Manifesto of 1848.
5 The term 'truce', which seems to me to capture very neatly what Marshall was trying to convey, has been used by John Rex in his writing about the position of ethnic minorities in Britain (Rex 1970).
6 For a summary of the debates about welfare see Ian Gough's book *The Political Economy of Welfare* (Gough 1979) and especially the various reports that emanated from the Home Office CDP projects during the 1970s.
7 There is an implicit admission of this failure in Norman Ginsberg's book *Class, State and Social Policy* (Ginsberg 1979) where, despite the parading of Marxian theoretical categories, the analysis remains rooted in orthodox Fabian service approaches. Gough is more explicit and acknowledges the debt to Fabianism (Gough 1979).
8 In his essay 'Social Welfare and the Art of Giving' (1967) Titmuss alludes to the idea of social welfare as moral education for the masses. State welfare is how we can give to strangers.

References

Bahro, R. (1978) *The Alternative in Eastern Europe*. London: Verso.
Bookchin, M. (1971) Listen Marxist. In *Post-Scarcity Anarchism*. Berkeley, Calif.: Ramparts Press.
—— (1982) *The Ecology of Freedom*. Palo Alto, Calif.: Cheshire Books.
Cawson, A. (1982) *Corporatism and Welfare*. London: Heinemann.
Corrigan, P. and Leonard, P. (1978) *Social Work Practice under Capitalism: A Marxist Approach*. An International Symposium. London: Macmillan.
Fromm, E. (ed.) (1967) *Socialist Humanism*. London: Allen Lane.
Gellner, E. (1983) *Nations and Nationalism*. Oxford: Basil Blackwell.
Giddens, A. (1981) *A Contemporary Critique of Historical Materialism*. London: Macmillan.
Ginsberg, N. (1979) *Class, State and Social Policy*. London: Macmillan.
Gorz, A. (1981) *Farewell to the Working Class*. London: Pluto Press.
Gough, I. (1979) *The Political Economy of Welfare*. London: Macmillan.
—— (1983) The Crisis of the British Welfare State. *International Journal of Health Services* 13 (3).
Illich, I. (1977) *Limits to Medicine: Medical Nemesis*. Harmondsworth: Penguin.
Jonas, H. (1972) Technology and Responsibility: Reflections on the New Task of Ethics. *Social Research* 40: 31–54.
MacPherson, C. B. (1977) *The Life and Times of Liberal Democracy*. Oxford: Oxford University Press.
Marshall, T. H. (1963) *Sociology at the Crossroads*, ch. 4. London: Heinemann.
Mishra, R. (1984) *The Welfare State in Crisis*. Brighton: Wheatsheaf Books.

O'Connor, J. R. (1973) *The Fiscal Crisis of the State*. New York: St Martin's Press.

Offe, C. (1984) *Contradictions of the Welfare State*. London: Hutchinson.

Parsons, T. (1965) Full Citizenship for the Negro American. *Daedalus* 94 (4) (November): 1009–054.

Pinker, R. (1979) *The Idea of Welfare*. London: Heinemann.

Rex, J. (1970) *Race Relations in Sociological Theory*. London: Weidenfeld and Nicolson.

Sennett, R. (1977) *The Fall of Public Man*. Cambridge: Cambridge University Press.

Taylor-Gooby, P. and Dale, J. (1981) *Social Theory and Social Welfare*. London: Edward Arnold.

Thompson, E. P. (1980) *Writing by Candlelight*. London: Merlin.

Titmuss, R. (1967) Social Welfare and the Art of Giving. In Fromm (1967).

Townsend, P. B. (1979) *Poverty in the United Kingdom*. Harmondsworth: Penguin.

Walzer, M. (1980) *Radical Principles*. New York: Basic Books.

Williams, R. (1961) *Culture and Society 1780–1850*. Harmondsworth: Penguin.

4

Compulsory altruism for some or an altruistic society for all?

HILARY LAND AND HILARY ROSE

'Self-development is a higher duty than self-sacrifice.'
(Elizabeth Cady Stanton, Seneca Falls 1848)

'The whole joy of William's Scheme is its unconscious fairness to women.'

(Janet Beveridge 1954)

The angel in the house

Women and women writers have understood altruism very well, for selflessness to the point of self-effacement was the cardinal quality of Victorian bourgeois womanhood (Murray 1982). George Eliot's great novels, *Middlemarch* and *The Mill on the Floss*, have at their centre women struggling in the miniature world of domestic life to achieve that ideal of perfect selflessness. In *Middlemarch*, Dorothea marries Casaubon in order to become the helpmate of someone she regards as having a higher purpose. 'It seemed to me', says Dorothea, 'that the use I should like to make of my life would be to help someone who did great works, that his burden might be lighter.' Dorothea constantly seeks the one path where duty and tenderness go hand in hand. In her marriage to Casaubon her project is foiled, not because she is unwilling to sacrifice herself, but because Casaubon's scholarship is inadequate to bear the weight of her hopes. After Casaubon's death, Dorothea marries Will, his cousin, and sharing in his reforming activities finds a richer outlet for her ideals. Towards the close of the book Eliot permits herself to comment:

> 'Many who knew her, thought it a pity that so substantive a creature should have been so absorbed in the life of another, and be only known in a certain circle as a wife and mother. But no one stated exactly what else there was in her power she ought rather to have done.'

> (Eliot 1965: 894)

Not for nothing have women who have wanted something more than loving self-effacement seen the 'angel in the house' as someone to be placated or contested. Elizabeth Gaskell, comforting an aspirant woman writer, urged placating the angel and preserving one's strength so that, after the worst strains of child-rearing were over, one could then write (Gaskell 1982: 90). Jane Austen followed a different course. Her heroines may have found contentment with their Mr Darcy and Mr Knightley, but she herself elected not to marry and was indeed wittily ominous to her cousin Fanny on the hazards of marriage (Chapman 1979: 478). Thus women writers portrayed the perfect selfless woman, but lived their lives rather differently.

Maggie Tolliver will not and cannot choose happiness with Stephen Guest because she is unwilling to hurt Lucy, her dearest friend, to whom Stephen is engaged. Refusing him, Maggie says, 'Many things are difficult and dark to me – but I see one thing clearly – that I must not, cannot seek my own happiness by sacrificing others' (Eliot 1979: 571). But while Maggie is the unquestioned heroine of *The Mill on the Floss*, whose loving self-sacrifice stands as the heart of the book and indeed of Victorian womanly values, Eliot herself was to hazard the social opprobrium of an adulterous relationship with George Lewes. Where

Maggie accepted the constraints imposed on her personal life by her adored brother, Eliot in real life did not, choosing rather to use her pain to write her book.

Even women with an ambivalent, possibly hostile, relationship to feminism, but who acted outside the domestic sphere, understood the problem. Florence Nightingale, writing in *Cassandra*, observed that 'women have accustomed themselves to consider intellectual occupations as merely selfish amusement, which it is their *duty* to give up for every trifler more selfish than themselves'. Echoing many contemporary feminists she writes, 'Women never have an half-hour in all their lives (except before and after everybody is up in the house) that they can call their own, without fear of offending or hurting somebody' (Nightingale 1982: 91).

Virginia Woolf described the 'phantom woman' or 'angel in the house' with whom she had to do battle before she was able to write:

> 'She was intellectually sympathetic. She was immensely charming. She was utterly unselfish. She excelled in the difficult arts of family life. She sacrificed herself daily. If there was chicken, she took the leg; if there was a draught she sat in it – in short she was so constituted that she never had a mind or will of her own, but preferred to sympathise always with the minds and wishes of others.'
>
> (Barrett 1979: 59)

It is impossible to write and do something else at the same time so Virginia Woolf had to kill the angel in the house (by throwing an inkpot at her). She also had the resources to free herself of some of the more arduous and repetitive household tasks that filled so much of the time of her working-class sisters. They had a hard struggle and had to find ways of combining self-fulfilment or political activity with their household responsibilities. Hannah Mitchell, a suffragist active over seventy years ago, propped up poetry books while she did the washing up, for example. In her autobiography she recalls that her first feminist feelings were aroused when, as a girl, she used to sit mending socks while her brothers read books or played games. One of the founder members of the Co-operative Women's Guild commented:

'It was unheard of, when I was a child, for a woman's hands to
be idle. . . . At the early meetings of the Guild, the women
used to bring their sewing with them, unable to rid their minds
of the notion that there was something wrong in sitting with
their hands in their laps, while they listened to speeches or took
part in discussion. It has taken us 50 years, you might say, to
get over the idea that a woman is idling and wasting her time
when she is using her brain without her hands, and doubly so if
she is a married woman.'

(Gaffin and Thomas 1983: 14)

Women today may not take their sewing to meetings but still
they have to negotiate or arrange to be away from home. Bea
Campbell reported on the difficulties facing politically active
working women in her recent book *Wigan Pier Revisited*. One
woman who had been active in the women's section of the
Labour Party for years said:

'If I go to meetings and get back in time to make a supper and
look after all his comforts as far as possible, I don't know if it's
ruthless or selfish, but they go in for sulks, men. I just ignore it
and get on with it. Going to conferences I've sometimes walked
out of the door with sullen silences behind me.'

(Campbell 1984: 193)

Another, commenting on what happened when she was active in
a strike, said, 'Nobody in my home went without dinner. I saw to
everything.' A third woman contrasted their position with that of
men: 'Unlike the men, none of us ever come home and think only
about ourselves. That's what drives me batty about Trade Union
men, they don't even *know* they're exploiting their wives'
(Campbell 1984: 194).

Women as outside moral reasoning

We have begun with Dorothea and Maggie, not simply because
so many of us have read them and loved them as women finer
than ourselves, as heroines who stood as altruistic exemplars, but
because within scientific culture, as against the world of the

novel, women have been portrayed as *outside* moral reasoning. Women are characterized as nurturant, emotional, intuitive, conforming to rules, and the origins of these qualities are located in either, or both, their biology and their socialization. As Carol Gilligan (1982) has demonstrated, the patriarchal philosophies of Kant and Hegel which set women outside conscious moral action have by no means passed away, but are alive and kicking within human life-cycle theory. At times the social sciences have claimed too much for socialization theories, which seek to reduce women – and men – to nothing more than their upbringing. Nonetheless, the present flourishing discourse which actively sets women outside moral reasoning lies in the present renaissance of biological determinism – sociobiology.[1] But while sociobiology actively seeks to reduce women to their biological nature, social science, not least social policy, has silently colluded in the 'naturalness' of women's altruism.

By contrast, our discussion here, like that of the Victorian novelists, is written within a conception of women and men as not being reducible to their biological matter, even though personal biology inevitably acts as a constraint on what people can and cannot do. Thus there is little or nothing in common between our use of the concept 'altruism' which relates to conscious action, and the misuse of the concept within sociobiology, where it is reduced so as to point solely to actions which ensure the survival of oneself or one's genes. This rampant biological determinism is not merely scientifically inadequate, it coarsens moral and cultural life. Finding its populist expression in such crudities as 'There's no such thing as a free lunch' in which even the possibility of disinterested gift-giving is precluded, the new 'realism' fostered by sociobiology seeks to move towards Hobbes's 'War of all against all' in which order can only be maintained by force. While we have not the space to take issue in any detailed way with the attack on moral reasoning and actions proposed by sociobiology it would be wrong not to acknowledge the virulence and negative implications, not least for women, of its growth.

Gilligan gives new weight to Woolf's insight that 'It is obvious that the values of women differ very often from the values which have been made by the other sex. Yet it is the masculine values which prevail' (Woolf 1929: 18). We are left with the paradox that 'the very traits that have defined the "goodness" of women, their care for and their sensitivity to the needs of others are those that make them deficient in moral development' (Gilligan 1982: 18). It is not simply that Piaget's theory of the moral development of the child is based solely on the study of boys' games and their rule-making behaviour (girls' games did not show appropriate rule-making behaviour and they were silently erased so that boys might become the ungendered 'child'), but that the price of this erasure meant that the development of girls and women was to be measured against a scale specific to boys and men. It also meant that the values of women were not recognized as values, implicitly casting woman's morality into the realm of nature.

Presently we are in a Heraclitan flux of values. Sociobiology and new right politicians seek to restore Victorian values (that is, *male* Victorian values, for it is clearly not the loving self-sacrifice of Dorothea and Maggie Tolliver they have in mind, or at least not as a universal value). At the same time there is evidence of men – particularly men in mid-life – becoming aware of caring and intimacy as positive values. Even management journals speak, in the USA if not in the UK, of the merits of softer, feminine styles of management. While men celebrate these, for them, new values, women have long known altruism as a basis for social interaction. Distinctive patterns of interaction associated with women have been seen as 'instinctual' or 'intuitive' – a function of anatomy coupled with destiny – and thus have facilitated a situation in which psychology has long neglected to describe the development of women's values (Gilligan 1982).

Of course, it is not only psychology which has interpreted women's values as natural and, therefore, unnecessary to acknowledge as an, at times, personally costly moral act. Social policy, because of the significance of altruism in maintaining social solidarity, has a long history of lovingly detailing the self-sacrifice of women, above all poor women, and yet it sees neither the engendered character of the act nor does it feel it necessary to determine its social origins. Indeed, the discussion of personal altruism has not been marked by significant theoretical development until the last fifteen years. In 1970, Richard

Titmuss published *The Gift Relationship* and the subsequent years have witnessed a profusion of feminist enquiry into altruism as the moral basis of women's interaction with others. It is common ground to both that social science has tended to assume that the analysis of the significance of gifts developed by anthropology in seeking to interpret pre-industrial society was not applicable to the study of industrial society. It seems that the gift industry, with its profit margins determined by the numbers of Christmases, birthdays, mother's and father's days it can persuade us to honour, has a rather sharper sense of the multiple significances of gift-giving and exchanging than academic social science. Even while relatively well-heeled academics may jeer at the commercialization of a Christmas not many believe in, few either deny themselves the pleasure of finding and giving the right present or can truthfully deny the sense of feeling cared for as they unwrap the perhaps absurd gift which tells them that its giver has understood some idiosyncratic fancy. We know too, even if they are not large pleasures or large hurts, that it does hurt to be forgotten on one's birthday. Even a birthday card serves to increase and, if forgotten, to decrease, solidarity. And when the card is handmade, how much more is our sense of being loved? Nor is this seemingly trivial example outside social policy, for the poverty studies[2] have long (to their credit) documented the real pain of not being able to buy a small gift to celebrate a beloved child or grandchild's birthday. In our daily lives, even if not in social science, giving and receiving are central, not marginal, to the maintenance of interpersonal relationships.

The divine vocation

Of all the architects of the pre-war welfare state in Britain, Beveridge was one of the most conscious of women's altruism which he calls 'a sense of divine vocation' and describes as follows:

'It means to me that there should be something in the daily life of every man and woman which he or she does for no personal reward or gain, does ever more consciously as a mark of the brotherhood and sisterhood of all mankind.

To take that as their ideal is not idle dreaming. Serving, exhausting oneself without thought of personal reward – isn't that what most women do most of their lives in peace or war?
. . .

The manager of one of our largest war factories told me the other day that the way in which the women in his factories were working was marvellous; they were doing even better than the men. I asked him whether he thought this might be because most women had the habit of working not for pay, but for service in their homes: they never related the amount of their effort to what they were going to get for themselves. He said that very likely that was the explanation.'

(Beveridge 1942: 38–9)

His proposal for restructuring the social security schemes gave pride of place to the housewife and her 'vital, but unpaid work'. The altruistic housewife was a central feature. Benefits were structured in a way which confirmed the priority which *all* married women should give to their 'duties' in the home. Unlike men whose rights to benefit were determined by their relationship to the labour market, women were defined entirely in terms of their marital status. Losing a job gave a man claims to maintenance on the State, losing a husband gave a woman similar claims. (Beveridge wanted to push this to its logical conclusion and give divorced or separated wives a benefit, provided they had not been responsible for ending the marriage, but this was not accepted.)

However, although housewives should not be *paid* for the work they did, they deserved better working conditions. Beveridge had some radical views for improving what he called 'the defective appreciation of the housewife as an unpaid worker' arguing that this would be necessary in 'a social service state':

'Nothing short of a revolution in housing would give the working housewife the equivalent of the two hours additional leisure a day on five days of each week that has come to wage earners in the past 70 years, and nothing but a revolution in holiday accommodation can give to the housewife with children the essence of a holiday, that is, change and release from normal duties.'

(Beveridge 1942: 275)

In order to achieve this, better housing and equipment were needed along with communal services so that: 'Some of what has now to be done separately in every home – washing all clothes, cooking every meal, being in charge of every child for every moment when it is not in school can be done outside the home' (Beveridge 1944: 264). In addition mothers should not be expected to look after their children all the time when they were on holiday because he recognized that too often a holiday 'merely means looking after the children in unfamiliar and less convenient surroundings away from home' (Beveridge 1944: 265). He did not, however, suggest that mothers should be enabled to take a holiday *without* the children.

In Beveridge's scheme of things women were centrally located in the family and there was no question of giving a woman the choice of *not* devoting herself to her family. He was, however, convinced that they needed improved working conditions in order to fulfil their duties the better. In this sense he was rather like the enlightened employer who provided health and welfare services for his workers in order both to increase their efficiency and, therefore, his profits, as well as tying them more firmly into their jobs. However, to be fair to Beveridge, at least he recognized that women were doing socially useful and necessary work. Many of his contemporaries inside government took women's work within the home so much for granted they did not even notice it. For example, Ferguson and Fitzgerald in their official history of the social services during the Second World War comment that: 'When registration of women first began, there had been a belief in government that it would reveal considerable reserves of unoccupied women who had neither jobs nor household responsibilities. But this hope was disappointed' (Ferguson and Fitzgerald 1954: 5).

Mobilizing large numbers of women (between 1939 and 1943 at least three million additional women joined the labour market together with a further one million who did unpaid voluntary work in canteens, nurseries, etc.) meant that families were less able to look after themselves. As a result the home help service had to be expanded. Unattractive occupations such as hospital domestic work which rested on the assumption that women could be expected to go on 'serving, exhausting themselves without thought of personal reward' had to offer better terms because, given the choice, women did *not* want to do them. There were therefore serious staff shortages.

Towards the end of the war when the Royal Commission on Equal Pay reported, some of those who gave evidence were aware that if conditions of employment outside the home became attractive to women they might not 'choose' marriage and motherhood. Equal pay was therefore not an objective to be adopted by the government unless the conditions under which women brought up children were improved. The Royal Commission on the Population echoed these fears four years later in 1948 and just as the early male Fabians had advocated family allowances as a means of improving the status of motherhood, so too did this royal commission and some of those from whom they received evidence.[3] It is clear however that they were not primarily concerned about giving women some access to financial resources within the family in their own right and therefore some measure of economic independence. Eleanor Rathbone's commitment to ending the poverty of women and children within the family caused by the unwillingness of the father to share his resources equally was shared by few policy-makers and politicians. However, largely by her efforts and those of the Co-operative Women's Guild, the government's decision to pay family allowances to the father rather than the mother was reversed in parliament in 1945.

Marriage: the crown of thorns?

Margery Spring Rice, who studied the health of working-class women in the 1930s, understood very well the connections between poverty and women's 'natural' altruism. She writes:

> 'Throughout their lives they have been faced with the tradition that the crown of a woman's life is to be a wife and mother. . . . Everyone is pleased when they get married, most of all the great public, who see therein the workings of Nature's divine and immutable laws. If for the woman herself the crown turns out to be one of thorns, that again must be Nature's inexorable way!'

> (Spring Rice 1981: 94)

Laura Orens's survey of *The Welfare of Labouring Women 1860–1950* (1979) rereads the classical texts of the conditions of poor people and shows how, within the family, resources were distributed unequally between different members of the family. The ideology – and the reality – of the breadwinner in the context of women's weaker access to the better-paid sectors of the labour market was held to justify the man getting the greater share of the necessities as well as such small luxuries as there were. It was unquestioned that if there was not enough meat for all, then the breadwinner had the chief and even exclusive claim. The ideology was so persuasive that even when there was no wage coming in and the entire family was on public or charitable relief the husband was still seen as needing special extras. Wives would accept his needs for some leisure, a little tobacco, the rare glass of beer – needs, real human needs – which they were willing to deny themselves.

Despite the work of Young (1952) and Young and Willmott (1973), whose work has sought to advance the thesis that although the division of resources within the household was unequal in 1952, by 1957 there were moves towards greater equality, and by 1973 equality had been more or less achieved, Orens's world has not gone away. Recent work carried out by Hilary Land (1977), Jan Pahl (1980), and Meredith Edwards (1980) points to the continuing inequalities of resource allocation within the family. Hilary Rose (1978) notes that battered women entering refuges initially find social security as relative riches after trying to manage on the money given them by husbands. Such observations not only illuminate the distribution of resources and altruistic practices within the family but also throw into question research and policy which takes the household/family as the unit for analysis and redistribution. However, poverty studies (which have not had the welfare of women as a specific focus), where they provide sufficiently detailed accounts of resource allocation within the family, reveal the same processes at work. Thus Townsend's *Poverty in the United Kingdom* (1979) acknowledges in the case-histories that resource allocation is unequal. The occasional beer, the small indulgence of tobacco, the little extra, is once more carefully depicted as the recognition of real human needs, the practice of welfare within the family. What is rather less well emphasized is that this 'family' is in reality the mother, who accepts these as real human needs for her children and her husband but does so by denying her own. Her satisfaction is seen to lie in her altruistic practices.

Thus the Nelsons, a family with a painfully ill father and three children, one of whom is delicate, live in a damp, poor house. A window is broken and the family are too poor to get it mended. The wife gave up her job to care for her husband and they live off supplementary benefit. The field interviewer speaks of Mrs Nelson being 'quite the bravest person I have met. This home is full of respect for everyone else and affection.' Mr and Mrs Nelson both deny themselves breakfast so that the children can have porridge. But in this fragile, desperately poor family, held together with affection, consider the self-denial of Mrs Nelson. The income allocation of the weekly benefit is being described. 'The children receive 2½p pocket money apiece. Mr Nelson hands over *his* [our emphasis] benefits to his wife, and when he is well, receives back £2, with which he can buy cigarettes and have an occasional drink in the pub.' And later, 'Mr Nelson walks down to his mother's most evenings if he's feeling well enough. Sometimes she gives him money for half a pint. It does him good.' In this meticulously and tenderly observed account, there is no mention of even the tiniest personal needs of *Mrs* Nelson being met. Willingly and affectionately she meets, from grotesquely inadequate resources, what she can of others' needs (Townsend 1979: 307, 309). The point is, however, that not only do the Nelsons subscribe to the ideology of womanly self-sacrifice, so do the researchers.

The account of the ill-housed Fishers reflects this same ideology and same collusion. They live with their five children in grinding poverty:

'None of the family had had a summer holiday and only the husband had had a night out in the last fortnight at a pub. They eat sparingly but, except for Mrs Fisher, they have a cooked breakfast; and she ensures that the children get enough milk.'

It is where the woman – even in a very small way – goes against the ideology of self-sacrifice that we can really see its power. Thus where women do award themselves little indulgences it seems that the men are critical, in a way that the women are not, nor feel themselves entitled to be. Of two retired people on the margins of poverty, '*Unusually* [our emphasis] she has a cooked breakfast, but he does not. Mr Morgan thinks his wife eats too much. He spends money on the football pool but does not smoke' (Townsend 1979: 334). Even in a situation where there is an element of the man taking over responsibility for some of the household jobs, self-denial is still seen as the woman's special share of poverty.

The three Basnetts, mother, father, and adult son, are disabled, wretchedly housed and poor. They have no holidays, no friends come to the house for a snack or a meal. Only the husband goes out regularly. Mrs Basnett said,

> 'I keep £1 a week for the rates and fuel. I give him something every day. He goes out, spends the day [i.e. 12 noon to 3 p.m.] in the betting shop and comes home in the afternoon with some food for the main meal. He does the shopping [and apparently all the cooking and the cleaning]. I get all my son's books. He [the son] has nothing for himself. I have nothing for myself.'

The altruistic mother

The presumption that women should devote themselves self-lessly to their families is apparent in another report, *The Curtis Report*, which laid the foundation for the post-war services for children in care (Care of Children Committee 1946). Reacting understandably against some of the appalling conditions they had found among children in institutional care, this report favours fostering. Foster care was – and is – also very much cheaper. When discussing how best to recreate a family for the child separated from her or his own family, the question of payment was raised by some of their witnesses. The committee argued that:

> 'There is something to be said for this proposal on the grounds that the mother is doing work for a public authority in caring for the child and that her labour deserves reward. There would

also be the advantage that greater pressure could be put on a paid foster mother to perform her duties efficiently. On the other hand if she receives such pressure she would not be the right type of foster mother, and *some of us feel that the acceptance of payment for the work cuts at the root of the relation between foster mother and the child which we wish to create.*' [our emphasis]

(Care of Children Committee 1946: 156)

In other words, self-sacrifice is an essential ingredient of the mother–child relationship which must be sustained even if the tie is not a biological one.

Payments for fostering are still based principally on reimbursement for the cost incurred in keeping a child rather than on any element of remuneration. An exception to this is made for those prepared to foster 'difficult' children such as handicapped children or disturbed adolescents. The norm of non-reward for fostering is thus still protected, and child care services are cheaper than they would be if there were heavier reliance on adequately staffed institutional care.

But if Curtis was concerned to re-create the mother–child relationship for the child separated from its biological parents, there was still substantial anxiety that the mother–child dyad alone – particularly if the woman was unmarried – could not create the proper setting for healthy development. Denise Riley (1983), in her discussion of Bowlby's influential *Report on Maternal Care and Mental Health* to the WHO in 1951, wrote:

'He recommends, despite his own insistence on the paramount virtue of the mother, that unmarried mothers should be encouraged to submit their children for adoption in the interests of securing a "stable" family for them. However, as long as the mother is married, "children thrive better in bad homes than in good institutions".'

(Riley 1983: 99)

But social policy was not going to leave the development of mothers' altruism to chance; while womanly altruism might be 'natural', nature was not to be entirely trusted. Thus Penelope Hall, discussing the prevention of child neglect, and the need to give the tired mother a rest at a well-run recuperation centre, noted:

'It is important however, that the mother should take her youngest child or children with her, partly because she is likely to settle down better if they are there also, partly because *it should never be suggested to her that her children are a drawback to her happiness* [our emphasis] and third because the aim of such recuperation is not simply to restore the mother to health but to help and encourage her to become a more efficient mother. Education in childcare is thus an important part of the work of the centre.'

(Hall 1959: 223–24)

Much later, the influential Plowden Report was to demonstrate a continuing concern as to whether they could trust a mother to act in the best interests of her child in the matter of pre-school education:

'The extent to which mothers of young children should be encouraged by the provision of full-time nursery places to go out to work raises a question of principle. Some mothers must work because they need the money. The government, for reasons of economic policy, wish to see more women working. But, to work full-time, a mother must expect that her child will attend nursery for extended hours and during school holidays. Our evidence is, however, that it is generally undesirable, except to prevent a greater evil, to separate mother and child for a whole day in the nursery. We do not believe that full-time nursery places should be provided even for children who might tolerate separation without harm, except for exceptionally good reasons.

(DES 1967: 329)

Altruism as indulging in nature

Mildred Blaxter's (1976) study of people with disabilities leaving hospital illustrates very clearly the way in which 'it is taken for granted by all concerned that if female relatives were available no problem would exist'. It was not simply the professionals which made this assumption, it was shared too by caring relatives. She writes:

'It seemed to people that they were caught in a double bind. On the one hand it was a strongly-held cultural norm that families should be responsible for the care of incapacitated members – the patients themselves expected it, and it appears that medical agencies expected it too. They felt that to 'fail' in this elementary duty would have been severely stigmatised. Yet other agencies of society – those concerned with income and employment – not only did not recognise this duty, but appeared to see it as an indulgence to be condemned.'

(Blaxter 1976: 61)

If the naturalness of women caring for disabled relatives is unquestioned, then motherhood is seen simultaneously as a crowning glory and as a form of self-indulgence. Writing in the 1950s, when the ideology of marriage as a team was perhaps at its height, Peter Townsend wrote in his capacity as an adviser on social security to the Labour Party:

'For these reasons it is not easy to justify subsidizing those in old age who have had children. It is obviously right to waive normal contributions during a person's sickness and to credit him with a spell off work. In assessing his pension, his work-span should not be reduced by those periods off work. Such periods in a person's life are periods of adversity, which he *avoids* if given a choice. The years of motherhood are plainly not comparable. . . . The state can be expected to compensate people for time off work only when an adversity is imposed on them against their wishes.'

(Townsend 1975: 245–6)

Compulsory and other altruisms

In the attempt to grapple with the concept of altruism recent work has turned to the anthropological accounts of pre-industrial society with its analyses of altruism and its relationship to reciprocity. The Norwegian sociologist Hilda Ve's important article (1984) draws on the work of Marshall Sahlins (1976), together with that of the feminists Harriet Holter (1984) and Kari Waerness (1984), to develop a model of the altruistic basis of women's interactions with others, so that it better fits the circumstances of capitalist rather than pre-industrial society. She is therefore very directly concerned with women's inter-action patterns in the labour market and the 'meat market' whereas our focus is more centrally on social policy concerns. She identifies three categories of women's altruistic activities. Ve's first category, 'care-giving' work, a term extensively developed also by Kari Waerness, corresponds to what in Britain is usually spoken of as 'caring' or 'caring labour' (Finch and Groves 1983). The carer is an adult woman who cares for a child/ren or an elderly person. The claims of the dependent child and the elderly person are seen as valid, in that denied care they 'may suffer or even perish'. While it is true that many of us feel rather dif-ferently about caring for a healthy child whose helplessness grows into autonomy in a reasonably predictable number of years, as against caring for a very elderly person whose dependency is likely to increase in an open-ended way, both make a moral claim for necessary caring by others which women acknowledge.[4]

Her second category of personal service is seen as taking place between persons who are both capable of self-care, but where the relations of power are unequal between them. In this situation the weaker is required to give in a continuous way more practical and emotional help than she receives. Conversely the Matthew principle holds, and the one with the greater share of the power gets the greater share of the services. This unequal exchange, characteristic of marriage, seems too mildly described by the expression 'personal service', with its English connotation of Seebohm departments, and we will use the term 'compulsory altruism'. In the case of the Morgans discussed earlier, a house-hold living at the edge of poverty, we can see an almost para-digmatic example of compulsory altruism.

Ve's third category of support between friends of approxi-mately equal social power, in which practical and emotional help is offered and received on a mutual basis, shares with her first category something of Sahlin's generalized reciprocity. In this project of mutual aid, there is no invisible accountant balancing the credits and debits between the parties. And, while it is not unlikely that the exchange will be more or less even, this is not predicated by the nature of the relationship.

Titmuss's much earlier study of altruism (1970), while not specifically focused on women, is singularly appropriate for our purposes in that one of its more remarkable features is that it is methodologically without gender bias. His study of blood donors is essentially a search for those who are, in the authentic meaning of the word, donors – that is, someone who has for purely altruistic motives freely chosen to give their blood to the unknown stranger.

But what is especially fascinating to those of us more than a decade on, where the literature on volunteering points unequivocally to it being primarily an activity of women (Baldock 1983), is that, when Titmuss has made some allowance for childbearing as a non-donating period, the gift of blood is made more or less evenly by women and men. His argument is that it is the universalism of the National Health Service, in which need is met, which provides the preconditions in which altruism can freely flower. He writes: 'It [giving blood] is the example of how such relationships between free and equal individuals may be facilitated and encouraged by certain instruments of social policy' (Titmuss 1970: 243). Above all, Titmuss is emphatic that in these circumstances the potential donor is truly free, 'free to give or *not* to give' (p. 239).

Compulsory altruism for some or an altruistic society for all?

Presently the welfare state is in crisis. Its content and form linked to the political economy of mid-twentieth-century capitalist patriarchy, it audibly creaks as it is pushed and pummelled by social and economic forces towards a still uncertain future. Initially the debate launched from the right took the form of a generalized attack on the level of public expenditure. Quite rapidly this generalized attack assumed a clearer form. It was one which talked up the cost of welfare and talked down the cost of military expenditure; which advocated the management of economic restructuring through the deliberate creation of mass unemployment, and the management of social and industrial conflict through confrontation.

Separately, but connectedly, Mrs Thatcher's government described itself as the 'party of the family', while laying siege to the employment and welfare provisions which guaranteed the domestic life of working people. What is true for whites is, because of a deepening racism, even more true for black people. The implications of this for black women, and the kinds of compulsory altruism required from them which specifically flow from their experiences of racism, our paper, criticizably, does not address. Nonetheless Thatcherism, like Reaganomics, is profoundly hostile to women's claims for economic and social independence, and continuously searches for policies which erode such gains as there have been in both public and personal life (David 1983).

In this situation, while the claims of the economy cannot be disregarded, the crisis of the welfare state can be seen as lying equally – if not more – within the political and ideological realms. Thus while it is unquestionably true that the preconditions of the old Beveridge welfare state, with its twin commitment to the (male) full employment economy and the full-time dependent wife-mother, have passed into historical obsolescence, it is also the case that old political alliances falter and new alliances struggle to come into existence. It is commonly understood that the politics of consensus between Labour and Conservative have been breached; what is less well recognized – at least by the dominant discourse within social policy – is the extent to which that consensus also shared masculine values and expressed masculine interests. Nowhere is that more clearly seen than in the debate around the future of the welfare state.

Women have unquestionably gained from the existence of the welfare state, both in terms of employment and also of services, even while its structures seek to constrain them within an enforced dependency and its correlate, compulsory altruism. Women's engagement – with varying degrees of feminist consciousness in the politics of welfare, whether these are located within the family, the statutory services, or the labour market – stems from precisely their lived experience of this contradiction. It has led feminists to defend both specific welfare provisions such as child benefits – which they see as critical to both children's *and* women's needs – and, more generally, to criticize what in Britain are called 'community care' solutions. While accepting that the problems of bureaucratic and insensitive institutions are real, transferring the resolution of those problems to the non-bureaucratic but underpaid or unpaid sector of community care will mean that the costs are to be largely borne by women (Finch and Groves 1983). It is not by chance that the leader of Sheffield, as probably the local authority with the strongest policy commitment towards an effective strategy of community care for elderly people, is on public record as placing relatively low priority on equal opportunity strategies for women.

To argue this is not to be against the expression of free altruism which potentially lies within community care and self-help strategies, but it is to be against social and labour market policies which reconstruct, in new form, the old pattern of enforced dependency and compulsory altruism. Thus the feminist hostility to community care turns partly on the needs and interests of women, which are to be masked once more in altruistic service to others, and partly on the needs and interests of the cared for. In considering the needs and interests of *both*, feminists accept a central insight from *The Gift Relationship*. Titmuss (1970) demonstrated that for the gift to be safe, that is non-injurious to the recipient, it had to be freely given. What is true for the gift of blood is perhaps even more true for that complex and enduring task of caring for another person. For women to be free not to give as well as to give requires that there are good alternative services. Only then will they not feel that they have no choice except to sacrifice themselves for another.

At present, although there are some indications that men are learning to care for others and to take more responsibility for their own and others' children (Lee 1981), the overall picture from the national and international time-budget studies demonstrates that whereas altruistic practices are structured into women's lives they are structured out of men's. To turn this around, to work for a democratic society in which 'the right to give personal care to others' is equally shared between women and men, will require a multiplicity of changes – not least in the dominant values of social policy as it seeks to respond to the crisis of the welfare state.

Notes

1 Sociobiology has been profoundly concerned to reduce altruism, especially that of women, to the implacable biological dogma of the genes. Thus Richard Dawkins (1976) explains away women's greater altruism as predicated by their investment in maintaining their genetic continuity.
2 Peter Townsend's work, from the early *Family Life of Old People* (1957) to the recent *Poverty in the U.K.* (1979), exemplifies this tradition.
3 See for example evidence given by R. F. Harrod in *Papers of the Royal Commission on Population*, 1950.
4 The use of the term 'tending' to describe such care, as Parker (1981) has done, underplays the power of this moral claim made on women by the person for whom they are caring.

References

Baldock, C. (1983) Volunteer Work as Work: Some Theoretical Considerations. In C. Baldock and B. Cass (eds) *Women, Social Welfare and the State in Australia*. Sydney: Allen & Unwin.
Barrett, M. (1979) *Virginia Woolf, Women and Writing*. London: Women's Press.
Beveridge, J. (1954) *Beveridge and His Plan*. London: Hodder and Stoughton.
Beveridge, W. (1942) *The Pillars of Social Security*. London: Allen & Unwin.
—— (1944) *Voluntary Action*. London: Allen & Unwin.
Blaxter, M. (1976) *The Meaning of Disability*. London: Heinemann.
Bowlby, J. (1951) *Report on Maternal Care and Mental Health*. WHO Monograph Series 2. Geneva: WHO.
Campbell, B. (1984) *Wigan Pier Revisited*. London: Virago.
Care of Children Committee (Curtis) Report (1946), Cmnd 6922. London: HMSO.
Chapman, R. W. (ed.) (1979), *Jane Austen's Letters*, 2nd edition. Oxford: Oxford University Press.
David, M. (1983) Thatcherism as Anti-Feminism. *Trouble and Strife* 1.
Dawkins, R. (1976) *The Selfish Gene*. Oxford: Oxford University Press.
Department of Education and Science (DES) (1967) *Children and their Primary Schools* (Plowden Report). London: HMSO
Edwards, M. (1980), Economy of Home Activities. *Aus. J. Soc. Issues* 15 (1) (February).
Eliot, G. (1965) *Middlemarch* (first published 1871). Harmondsworth: Penguin.

Eliot, G. (1979) *The Mill on the Floss* (first published 1860). Harmondsworth: Penguin.

Ferguson, S. and Fitzgerald, H. (1954) *Studies in the Social Services*. London: HMSO.

Finch, J. and Groves, D. (eds) (1983) *A Labour of Love*. London: Routledge & Kegan Paul.

Gaffin, J. and Thomas, D. (1983) *Sharing and Caring*. Manchester: Co-operative Union.

Gaskell, E. (1982) Household Advice to an Aspiring Woman Writer (first published 1862). In Murray (1982).

Gilligan, C. (1982) *In a Different Voice: Psychological Theory and Women's Development*. Cambridge, Mass.: Harvard University Press.

Hall, P. (1959) *The Social Services of Modern England* (first published 1952, revised 1959). London: Routledge & Kegan Paul.

Holter, H. (ed.) (1984) *Patriarchy in a Welfare Society*. Bergen: University of Bergen Press.

Land, H. (1977) Inequalities in Large Families: More of the Same or Different? In R. Chester (ed.) *Equalities and Inequalities in Family Life*. Oxford: Pergamon.

Lee, R. (1981) The Effects of Flexitime on Family Life – Some Implications for Managers. *Personnel Review* 10 (3).

Murray, J. (ed.) (1982) *Strong Minded Women and Other Lost Voices from Nineteenth Century England*. Harmondsworth: Penguin.

Nightingale, F. (1982) *Cassandra* (first published 1852). Quoted in Murray (1982).

Orens, L. (1979) The Welfare of Labouring Women, 1860–1950. *Feminist Studies* 5 (1) spring.

Pahl, J. (1980) Patterns of Money Management. *J. Soc. Pol.* 9 (3).

Parker, R. (1981) Tending and Social Policy. In E. Goldberg and S. Hatch (eds) *A New Look at the Personal Social Services*, Discussion Paper No. 4. London: Policy Studies Institute.

Riley, D. (1983) *War in the Nursery*. London: Virago.

Rose, H. (1978) In Practice Supported, in Theory Denied: An Account of an Invisible Social Movement. *J. Int. Urban & Reg. Res.* 2 (autumn): 521–37.

Royal Commission on the Population (1952) *Memoranda*, vol. 5. London: HMSO.

Sahlins, M. D. (1976) *The Use and Abuse of Biology*. Ann Arbor, Mich.: University of Michigan Press.

Spring Rice, M. (1981) *Working-Class Wives; Their Health and Conditions* (first published 1939). London: Virago.

Titmuss, R. (1970) *The Gift Relationship*. London: Allen & Unwin.

Townsend, P. (1975) *Family Life of Old People*. London: Routledge & Kegan Paul.

—— (1975) *Sociology and Social Policy*. London: Allen Lane.

—— (1979) *Poverty in the United Kingdom*. Harmondsworth: Penguin.

Ve, H. (1984) Women's Mutual Alliances: Altruism as a Premise for Interaction. In Holter (1984).

Waerness, K. (1984). In Holter (1984).

Woolf, V. (1929) *A Room of One's Own*. London: Hogarth Press.
Young, M. (1952) The Distribution of Income within the Family. *B. J. Soc.* 3 (4) (December).
Young, M. and Willmott, P. (1957) *Family and Kinship in East London*. London: Routledge & Kegan Paul.
—— (1973) *The Symmetrical Family*. London: Routledge & Kegan Paul.

PART TWO
WELFARE AND
THE MARKET

5
Markets and neo-liberal political economy*

DAVID WHYNES

The modern welfare state is an unequivocal attempt to patch up capitalism. More formally, its evolution throughout the post-war period can be interpreted as a progressive compensation for the various types of 'market failure' recognized by economists from the time of Adam Smith onwards. There exist circumstances, it is argued, which inevitably prohibit the free market mechanism within the economy from delivering the socially optimal solution and there will accordingly be a case for government intervention. Over the past few decades governments have been expected to manage the level of aggregate economic activity, to regulate externalities or 'neighbourhood effects', and to provide forms of insurance against the adverse consequences of ill fortune, illness, and poverty. As a direct consequence of the extension of government activity in western economies the share of public expenditure in total output has risen consistently over time. In the UK it rose from 32.6 per cent to 44.6 per cent between 1960 and 1980;

*In preparing this paper I have benefited greatly from discussions with Geoff Reed and Chris Ennew.

the rise for the OECD economies as a whole was from 28.5 per cent to 39.4 per cent (Heald 1983: 30–1).

Not everyone has applauded the growth of the welfare state. Marxists, for instance, have seen it as an invidious attempt to extract further surplus value from the proletariat whilst simultaneously acting to subvert the revolutionary potential of that class. More recently, another group of thinkers has objected on the grounds that, important though government intervention might be, the modern welfare state has displayed a tendency to outgrow its usefulness. Such people argue that, first, the government's zeal to rectify instances of market failure has, almost by its own momentum, led it into areas where markets are manifestly not failing and where interference is unjustified. Second, government provision in place of market failure is no guarantee of success *per se*. Government provision can, in itself, be imperfect in an economic sense and the consequences of 'government failure' could be worse than those of the market failure which the policies were intended to ameliorate.

Since the 1970s, this belief that the welfare state has grown too extensive has become more and more acceptable in the western economies. The prevailing structure of welfare provision is, it is now more widely felt, in need of an overhaul. Although the intention of creating a secure and fair society was certainly laudable at the outset, it seems to some that the initial seed of the welfare state has matured into a sprawling giant which smothers human initiative, inhibits individual freedom and choice, imposes intolerable tax burdens, and is, pure and simple, inefficient. Welfare provision, such people believe, needs to be reappraised and the market principle must be reintroduced in circumstances where it is more appropriate – hence the current interest in returning nationalized assets to private ownership, in breaking public-sector monopolies, in 'contracting out' to private agencies work formerly done by public ones, and in introducing charges for certain public services.

The view that the market society is both just and efficient has a long and illustrious history. The kernel of the idea is contained in the work of Thomas Hobbes and John Locke, and the theme is regularly visited by the philosopher-economists of the eighteenth and nineteenth centuries. In its modern guise, however, the market philosophy owes most to post-war German, American, and British neo-liberal thought.

Amongst the many contributors to the movement the name which surely stands out is F. A. Hayek. As founder-president of the 'Mont Pelerin' society in 1947 Hayek brought together market-orientated economists in an international forum, whilst his tenure of a chair at the University of Chicago from 1950 undoubtedly helped to mould that form of Chicago neo-liberalism associated with the names of Knight and Friedman. The foundation of the influential Institute of Economic Affairs (IEA) is traditionally dated to 1945 when Anthony Fisher read Hayek's *The Road to Serfdom* and was subsequently persuaded by the man himself to establish a research organization (Seldon 1981: 247). Certainly a number of contributors to the IEA's list of publications were pupils of Hayek when he taught at the London School of Economics during the 1930s and 1940s.

The IEA claims, and with some justification, to have 'created the post-war focus for the demonstration that market analysis was indispensable for understanding and solving economic tasks and problems' (Seldon 1981: xvii). Since its foundation well over 300 books and pamphlets have been produced and it has recently begun to publish a journal. The IEA's influence on UK government policy can scarcely be doubted when the present prime minister assures its members: 'All policies are based on ideas. Our policies are firmly founded on those ideas which have been developed with such imagination in your *Journal*.'[1]

In view of its prestige in official circles at the present time 'market' is in grave danger of joining the growing list of 'hurrah' words (which includes 'democracy', 'peace', and 'efficiency'), that is, words which describe indisputably good notions that no one could possibly oppose. Social scientists should, I feel, be more than a little troubled by unqualified approbation for any slogan along the lines of *market good, non-market bad* (or, for that matter, the contrary proposition), because a market is actually an exceedingly complex social institution. It is not simply a matter of sale and purchase, for exchange is just the tip of the iceberg. Implicit within the market principle lies a deeper moral and economic argument. Before, therefore, the 'market' is removed altogether from the agenda for debate an exploration of the argument would seem necessary. With this in mind the purpose of the present paper is, first, to explore some logical foundations of market structures and, second, to suggest that the wider implications of the use of markets in place of government intervention lead us down some intriguing and ill-explored paths.

The market model

The market is one amongst a number of possible forms of social organization. In order to prove that it is the most appropriate form (politically acceptable and economically efficient) it is necessary to establish a logically prior theory of human nature. As we shall see, this further requires a theory of property and a theory of government.

Following the style of MacPherson (1964) we can construct our model of the market economy from a series of axioms, each derived on an empirical, a tautological, or a transcendental basis:

1. Individuals exist and it is they who initiate actions.
2. Actions are initiated rationally, with the view of attaining ends.
3. The individual is his/her own best judge of the merits of any given end.
4. In pursuit of an end individuals are necessarily constrained by the means available to them, as well as by the prevailing adequacy of information about both means and ends.
5. Of that which is preferred, more is preferred to less.

Human nature is accordingly about 'being oneself' and the essence of being oneself (i.e. that which preoccupies one's existence) is 'personal development'. Mill's metaphor about human nature, in *On Liberty*, is justly famous – he likened it to a growing tree, counterposing this image against that of a fabricated mechanism constructed from a set plan and designed to perform a set task. Implicit within the notion of being oneself is, therefore, a conception of freedom as an absence of external constraint upon one's progress. From the axioms above it can be inferred that the expression of selfhood involves, first, the exercising of free choice over courses of action and, second, the directing of one's efforts according to one's own subjectively assessed criteria. Individuals are, in other words, responsible and there is no *a priori* reason to expect all to behave alike. Naturally, as axiom 4 accepts, some constraints to freedom are bound to exist – individuals will never possess perfect knowledge and certain ends might be precluded by physical impossibility. However, we can hardly regard our present inability to defy the law of gravity as an *illegitimate* constraint upon us!

In order to make our model more plausible we must now posit the existence of a number of individuals coexisting with a given physical space. This immediately generates a potential problem because the physical space will define the quantity of resources available to the individuals for use as means to attain ends. Given axiom 5, means will be scarce relative to ends for the group as a whole. There exists, therefore, an 'economic problem' and this will lead to the violation of our earlier axioms. In the first place, choices will be limited because any one individual's ability to use resources now depends upon the extent to which such resources have already been appropriated by others. Second, the pre-emptive use of resources, coupled with the particular form of use another envisages, could effectively coerce an individual into following a course of action not otherwise of his/her choosing.

Under such conditions the problem of scarcity cannot be overcome although it can be satisfactorily accommodated by the adoption of an additional axiom:

6. Given scarcity there will exist conflict, coercion, and insecurity in use. Therefore it is legitimate to establish a set of rights and duties specifying which individual is entitled to employ which resource, and also the manner of such employment.

In our collectivity of individuals we are accordingly required to institute a system of property rights. Of necessity this system must be comprehensive. It must specify, in each case, the right-holder, the right-regarder and the object of the right, that is, that which is owned. It must, again in every case, define the characteristics of ownership, for example specific rights regarding consumption, transfer or modification of things owned, including possible duties to forbear from certain uses.

Each individual has accordingly been endowed with a bundle of rights and, in the achievement of ends, each will use the resources entailed as he/she sees fit. The interesting use from the present point of view is exchange. If two right-holders are willing freely to exchange rights then the implication to be drawn from our axioms is that they expect the new, post-exchange distribution of rights to be preferable to the old, pre-exchange distribution. Any voluntary exchange which takes place must therefore be moving the individuals concerned nearer to their espoused ends. In fact, exchange is to be expected in view of the likely differences in property holdings and different attitudes to personal development. For any given rights distribution, free exchange can only enhance the welfare of all participating individuals.

One final piece of the jigsaw remains. We have established a system of rights and duties but we have not yet specified any reason why individuals would abide by such a system. Why should an individual exchange when it would appear feasible to expropriate? The solution is to add a final axiom:

7. In order to prevent violations of rights, and to arbitrate in cases of dispute, it is legitimate to create an institution of government whose will, regarding such matters, is sovereign over all other wills.

We now possess an umpire for our game and, within the framework of a given distribution of rights, individuals can enter into exchange contracts to secure that which, for them, constitutes the most valued resources. We have arrived at an essentially Hobbesian conception of society and it is a conception which lies at the root of modern neo-liberalism. The relevant image is conveyed in the phrase *free economy, strong state* (coined by the German neo-liberal, Alexander Rüstow) and the epithet does highlight the dual role the state (as government) is expected to play. In matters concerning the proper rules of conduct the power of the state must be absolute; if it is not then rights are not enforceable. Beyond the basic rules, however, state power must be nonexistent because, in terms of our model, a powerful and coercive state must violate the earlier axioms relating to the freedom to choose one's own development path, a path realized by the use, including the exchange, of one's property (Friedrich 1955). Seen in these terms we can interpret the present neo-liberal critique of the welfare state as being about misplaced power. In certain areas, it is argued, the government presently has control where such control is illegitimate.

How does one appraise the market model as an operational system of organization for a real-world economy such as that of the UK, judged in terms of our earlier criteria of acceptability and efficiency? One possible approach would be an examination at the philosophical level. We might choose to question the transcendental axioms, for example, whether individuals really are the best judges of their own welfare or whether the exchange relationship is indeed the determining bond between persons. Alternatively, we could consider the empirical circumstances. Would there exist, in the specific economy, conditions we might expect to give rise to market failures, thus indicating the inadequacy of the market? Markets generally under-supply goods with public characteristics, for example, with the result that, to the extent that individuals manifest a preference for such goods, they will have to be provided, in some degree, in a non-market manner (Whynes and Bowles 1981).

The case for a complete system of markets would be weakened if either of the above tests was to be failed. Even so, all forms of social organization are vulnerable to dispute at the metaphysical level and very few pro-market writers seriously countenance the prospect of a *pure* market economy as outlined above. Friedman (1962), for example, advocates a considerable extension of market forces in western economies yet accepts the case for government involvement on the grounds of technical monopoly, neighbourhood effects, and the necessity of caring for the irresponsible, in addition to the 'umpiring' role.[2]

In that which follows, however, neither of these two lines of appraisal will concern us. We shall instead remain firmly within the context of the market to appraise it from its own point of view. This will involve the exploration of some broad corollaries following from the acceptance of the market model, corollaries which appear to have been somewhat neglected in contemporary policy debate. Before venturing further, let us briefly note a few logical fallacies involving claims popularly made in favour of markets.

First, it is often argued that the creation of a market for a good or a service will necessarily make its provision more efficient (for instance, if the government were to consider replacing socialized medicine with a purely private scheme). However, the point is that the efficiency case does not rest on the existence of a market *per se* but on the existence of a competitive market. When the buyer is confronted by several sellers the latter are obliged to reduce their costs in order to lower the offered prices necessary for the securing of the established contract. In the case of pure monopoly, where many potential buyers confront a single seller, no competitive pressure or cost-reducing incentive exists. However, following our earlier theory of human nature, we have no reason to expect a private monopoly to behave any different from a public one, for both are operated by the same sorts of human being. If we thought that, for a given industry, there would exist an inherent tendency towards monopoly then a change in ownership would not necessarily counter the declining incentives to efficiency unless a regime of competition were to be artificially maintained, presumably by the government. In cases where the monopoly tendency arises for reasons of economies of scale or size (Friedman's technical monopoly), such a regime of competition could only be maintained at the *expense* of efficiency!

Second, the freedom dimension within the market model is often interpreted in an unqualified manner, implying that a situation of choice is *always* better than one offering no choice. Such a view is behind the approval of policy measures to encourage new suppliers to enter into areas formerly the domain of institutional monopolies. However, the unqualified proposition holds only in conditions of perfect information, and the less the information available then the more dubious does it become. At the lowest level, it is difficult to see how choice can be made rationally when one is ignorant of the implications of choosing. In conditions of uncertainty, choice is something individuals might be willing to forgo, preferring instead to defer to the judgement of those they believe to possess superior information. If one is ignorant of matters medical one will solicit help from a qualified physician. The possibility of having a number of qualified physicians to choose from will, in this instance, be of little consequence because one's ignorance of the matter precludes the establishment of criteria to judge others' expertise beyond their equivalent qualifications.

Third, markets are often judged superior to government-managed schemes because of their ability to summarize and communicate information rapidly. Markets send price signals to manufacturers to indicate the existence of excess demand or supply, and manufacturers are themselves willing to provide information to consumers in order to encourage them to buy. This communicative ability of markets is a great virtue and, indeed, is recognized by planning theorists such as Kantorovich. However, there do exist instances where the market is actually poor at disseminating information. The need to persuade, for instance, can encourage the deliberate propagation of inaccurate information. Fraud will eventually be exposed in competitive markets but society might regard the costs as prohibitive – it could take quite a number of deaths before the demand for an incompetent physician's services fell such that he/she was forced out of business. Also within a market context, it is difficult to see who would have any incentive to discover and propagate dissuasive information. Would anyone have any substantial private incentive to point out the harmful effects of cigarette smoking, excessive alcohol intake, or debilitating working conditions, for example?

Finally, support for the extension of markets derives from the mistaken belief that, because exchange can move individuals from a less-preferred to a more-preferred state of affairs, it is *only* exchange which can bring about welfare gains. This view receives reinforcement from the particular manner of income accounting employed in western economies. The technique values production in terms of prices, and many non-traded goods are therefore omitted from consideration altogether. In hiring the services of a housekeeper or child-minder I pay monies to such persons and thus add to the wage element of national income. However, if I or my wife undertake such domestic production no wages are paid and no addition is made to national income. Non-market services, such as health care and education, are included in the accounts as financial costs of input, not value of output, with the result that, in accounting terms, they never appear to contribute to value added. All our economic performance indicators, in sum, are biased towards marketed goods.

Three corollaries

As has been appreciated since the time of Hobbes, the 'free economy, strong state' model contains one central weakness, relating to this question – under what conditions would a collectivity of individuals, whose concern is the achievement of private objectives with the minimum of constraint, voluntarily accept a government with what appears to be absolute power? For such a community to exist, it would seem, it would be necessary for it to remain in the shadow of the Leviathan and to run the risk of being coerced. Hobbes himself resolved the contradiction by arguing that, in the case of the individual believing his or her liberty to be infringed, rebellion against the state was legitimate. For obvious reasons, it would also be somewhat futile. Hobbesian social order would, most likely, be highly unstable.

Subsequent generations of liberal theorists have appreciated that, to a considerable extent, the key to the resolution of the problem lies with the form of government. The individuals in the 'free economy' will only accept the 'strong state' if certain safeguards can be built into the system. Not surprisingly, those features regarded as desirable in markets as the protectors of economic freedom find parallels in the design of the acceptable form of government. More specifically:

1. The government would have to be accountable. The rational individual would not be willing to transfer power to the government on a permanent basis. As government policy operated, each individual would appraise his or her changing circumstances. In conditions of deterioration, Hobbesian rebellion can be side-stepped by giving individuals the opportunity to 're-negotiate their contracts' with the government. A facility would have to exist to permit governments/umpires perceived as good to be substituted for those perceived as bad. Individuals, in other words, would

only be willing to yield their sovereignty if, on occasions, they were able to re-exercise it by means of an acceptable election procedure.

2. The government would have to be limited. Individuals would not hand over power to government unless they were confident that such power would only be exercised in the 'proper' manner.

3. Government would have to be dispersed. The larger the community then the more probable it is that there will exist variations in local conditions. Government policy, however, has 'public' characteristics; it is applied equally to all. A likely consequence is the effective coercion of individuals in all circumstances other than for those for which the policy is precisely appropriate (Breton 1974). It follows that as government dispersion (i.e. localization) increases, coercion should correspondingly decrease.

4. Government would have to be insulated. Individuals in market society are concerned to reduce coercion applied by others. They would therefore be unlikely to accept a government if they felt that other individuals had a disproportionate influence on the outcome of its decisions.

Contemporary pro-market thinkers such as Hayek and Friedman are well aware of the corollary about the theory of government. Indeed, Hayek devotes the final volume of his *Law, Legislation and Liberty* trilogy to discussions of this nature (Hayek 1979). A theme of the work is a sustained critique of modern western democratic structures in terms of the categories derived above. Hayek talks, for example, of the 'tragic illusion' that the 'adoption of democratic procedures made it possible to dispense with all other limitations on government power' (p. 3). Important though this component is, *democracy* is not only a question of electoral systems. Hayek in fact argues that democracy 'is increasingly becoming the name for the very process of vote-buying for placating and remunerating those special interests which in more naïve times were called "sinister interests"' (p. 32). 'The result is a distribution of incomes chiefly determined by political power' (p. 13). A parallel hostility to contemporary structures can be detected in the work of Friedman. The prevailing system, he writes, 'tends to give undue political power to small groups that have highly concentrated interests' and 'to give greater weight to obvious, direct and immediate effects of government action than to possibly more important but concealed, indirect, and delayed effects' (Friedman and Friedman 1980: 292).

In the light of remarks such as these, certain commentators (such as Gamble 1979) have interpreted the neo-liberal theoretical position as undemocratic. Only on the narrow basis that contemporary political structures are criticized would this perhaps be the case, for the neo-liberal rejection of the *status quo* follows from the observation that current 'democracy' is not *sufficiently* democratic. The central theme of Hayek (1979) is the consequence of the merger of legislation and administration – 'today legislatures are no longer so called because they make the laws, but laws are so called because they emanate from legislatures' (p. 4). It follows that one vital control over arbitrary government action – the independent constitution – has disappeared, a feature which sets all modern polities along the road to serfdom.

Summarizing this stage of the argument, it would seem that any western government seriously committed to the philosophical principles behind the market model ought to be similarly committed to a fairly radical reform of political institutions. In the UK, for instance, the market case could be used to justify new forms of electoral procedures and to legitimate institutions which counterbalance the present autocracy of the House of Commons. Furthermore, the necessary devolution of power to local government is indicated; Friedman (1962) judges that, in the case of the USA, if 'government is to exercise power, better in the county than in the state, better in the state than in Washington' (p. 3). Strangely enough in view of its ostensible support for the pro-market philosophy, none of these reforms seems to have been on the UK government's political agenda in recent years.

For the sake of argument, let us suppose that the citizens of our market society are governed in a manner they deem acceptable. Their affairs will now consist of a series of exchanges dictated by the perception of opportunities to exchange less-valued resources for more-valued ones.[3] For the economy as a whole the rates of exchange between all items can be represented as a vector of prices, or exchange equivalents, and each price clearly has two determinants. First, the higher my subjective valuation of an item then the more would I be prepared to give up in order to obtain it, *ceteris paribus*. Going back to the theory of human nature outlined earlier, I should be prepared to pay more to follow a more-preferred development path. Second, the higher my initial resource stock available for exchange then the more can I afford to pay to obtain another's resource, *ceteris paribus*.

To understand the significance of these determinants, consider a simple economy which consists of a nobleman and a jester. If we start off by giving the nobleman all of the society's alienable resources he will probably be happy to purchase the one resource remaining, the jester's labour power, for entertainment purposes. The jester will receive a wage dependent upon the nobleman's pleasure derived from watching the jester's antics and his willingness to pay for such pleasure. Now we shall reverse the distribution; the jester shall have all the alienable resources. Unfortunately for our aristocrat, jesters do not need the services of noblemen and no exchange will take place. Our destitute nobleman will be obliged to seek sanctuary elsewhere. Clearly, the two outcomes are not symmetrical.

The consequence of market activity is thus conditioned by the specific set of valuations of participants and on the initial distribution of property rights amongst them. Using the term 'equilibrium' to signify a state of affairs where no further voluntary exchange in an economy will take place, it would seem that there ought to exist an equilibrium for each possible set of valuations and each possible distribution of property rights.[4] From our earlier model, it is also clear that an equilibrium state must be preferable to non-equilibrium, but which of the many possible equilibria is the optimum? Clearly, we need not discuss the personal valuation issue because our model has already established that whatever individuals think is best *is* best. We must accordingly conclude that the optimum equilibrium is the one which results from the 'most appropriate' distribution of property rights and property as such between the members of our community. The second corollary of our market model is therefore the necessity of a theory of distributive justice.

One specific conception of distributive justice is, of course, implicit within the market model anyway. Because voluntary exchange of property is legitimate, owners must be entitled to whatever they hold as the result of such exchange. Nozick (1974) is perhaps the best-known articulator of this proposition. In addition to a procedural theory of distribution, however, we need a structural theory, to provide answers to two questions. First, what is to determine the initial property endowments of individuals prior to exchange? Second, is it not possible that rights acquired legitimately at some time in the past, and perpetuated throughout by legitimate exchanges, might turn out to be unjust in structural terms for a changed social situation (Becker 1977)?

The best-known attempt to derive a structural theory of justice from liberal axioms is that of Rawls (1972). Rawls sets up the problem by asking what distributive principles rational individuals would need to see in a society before they were willing to become members, and such a question is directly analogous to that asked about the desirable characteristics of government. Rawls argues, first, that these principles would comprise 'equality in the assignment of basic rights and duties' and, second, that socioeconomic inequalities would only be tolerated if they resulted in 'compensating benefits for everyone, and in particular for the least advantaged members of society' (pp. 14–15). The logic behind the derivation of the principles is straightforward – individuals could not be expected to participate voluntarily in a social arrangement which they had reason to believe could confer disadvantage upon them. Faith in the virtues of market society, and a willingness to abide by its dictates, are direct functions of the expected benefits to be derived. The greater one's prospective command over resources then the greater will the perceived benefit be, and it is the position of equality in endowment of rights which, in effect, maximizes the aggregate acceptability of participation (Pattanaik 1968).[5]

It should be noted that Rawls's first principle calls for equality of rights and not equality in property holdings. Nevertheless there must, in any real-world economy, exist some degree of correspondence between rights in principle and rights as actualities. In the example above, the nobleman could hardly be expected to enter into a market society with the jester if he was aware, in advance, that he would possess no rights of ownership over alienable resources. One suspects, however, that he would have been equally unwilling to participate had he known that, whilst being permitted to own resources in principle, he was actually going to be endowed with none. In the market context participants require both the rights and the means to participate and, with exchange, the means are income and wealth. As Rawls implies from his second principle, equality in rights will *tend* to be paralleled by equality of holdings although the provision for externalities consequent upon inequality gives scope, in reality, for a wide variety of potentially acceptable distributions.[6]

Even if one feels unable to accept Rawls's conception at face value the central point remains, namely, that it is necessary to subscribe to *some* structural theory of distribution. It is, moreover, necessary to make a judgement about the acceptability of the existing real-world income distribution because a belief in the desirability of 'letting market forces operate' is, from the point of view of our market philosophy, only valid if one simultaneously accepts the legitimacy of the prevailing distribution. The entitlement theory within the market model yields a powerful conclusion here – if the initial distribution is considered illegitimate then the consequent distribution resulting from the untrammelled operation of free market forces will still be illegitimate. Within the modern economy, therefore, the extension of market forces is not, in itself, sufficient to guarantee automatic economic improvement.

Again for the sake of argument, let us suppose that the *ex ante* distribution of wealth and income has been deemed fair. Within the market society exchange will now take place and many of the services currently provided without charge to users in the modern welfare state will be subject to private exchange arrangements. The security functions of the welfare state (insurance against unemployment and illness) will be taken over by commercial enterprises, with individuals buying as much or as little insurance as they think they require. Altruistic tendencies will be catered for by private charity. Having set up such a system it might appear that government would never need to intervene in distribution again, yet the writers so far discussed (with the exception of Nozick) all support the existence of a 'social minimum' or 'safety net'. Rawls's government is expected to interfere with procedurally legitimate principles which violate desired structural outcomes (pp. 274–84). Hayek argues that there is 'no reason why in a free society government should not assure to all protection against severe deprivation in the form of an assured minimum income, or a floor below which nobody need to descend' (1976: 87).

At first sight, the requirement of a safety net would seem tantamount to admitting to the inadequacy of market solutions. In fact, a case for state involvement is not too hard to engineer. First, there might exist in society persons (such as those handicapped from birth) who, through no fault of their own, are unable to survive in market society by virtue of having nothing to exchange. It would be quite consistent with Rawlsian principles to permit the state to provide income for such persons. Second, using Friedman's technical monopoly argument, insurance systems might actually function better at a nationalized, rather than at a private and competitive, level, because the effectiveness of any system at risk-spreading is, *ceteris paribus*, a function of the number of those insured. Finally, given that all real-world decisions are made under conditions of uncertainty (including ignorance about risk, which accordingly precludes the rational estimation of the amount of insurance which it is appropriate to purchase), individuals might plausibly accept a government safety net to protect them from the vagaries of the economy or cases of plain 'bad luck'.

Agreeing to the existence of a social minimum is one thing; estimating its size is another. Here our theorists are far less precise. Hayek says:

'So long as such a uniform minimum income is provided outside the market to all those who, *for any reason*, are unable to earn in the market *an adequate maintenance*, this need not lead to a restriction of freedom, or conflict with the Rule of Law.'

(Hayek 1976: 87, emphasis added)

How adequate, we need to ask, is adequate? Friedman supplies the apparent solution: 'I see no way of deciding "how much" except in terms of the amount of taxes we – by which I mean the great bulk of us – *are willing to impose upon ourselves* for the purpose' (1962: 191, emphasis added). Rawls arrives at not dissimilar conclusions via a more formal route (1972: 285–6).

This issue needs careful consideration. Within a functioning market economy, it seems, the 'adequate' social minimum will be maintained by private charity payments supplemented by government transfers. In view of the structure of the modern democratic process, however, it remains unclear whether such government supplements would occur at all. If individuals are willing to pay up to and including, say, £x as alms for the poor, why should they then vote for a government committed to taxing away from them any sum in excess of £x to finance precisely the same charitable activity? People have to pay taxes but they do not have to vote for prospective governments which will commit them to paying high taxes. Under the process of political competition, prospective governments offering a package in which the tax take is regarded as being too high will be outcompeted by prospective governments offering the 'correct' tax take. Such government supplements could thus occur only if (a) governments were autocratic and monopolistic (and liberal individuals would probably consider such governments as illegitimate) or if (b) individuals subscribed to the view that the government 'knows best' on this issue (which comes close to violating axiom 3 and which prompts the question – if governments know best here, why not elsewhere?).

Friedman himself sees the problem as a 'public goods' issue, that is, your helping the poor relieves my distress at seeing poverty and we therefore have an incentive to attempt to 'free-ride' on each other's contributions. Unfortunately, the device (government) designed to remedy market failure is the outcome of a quasi-market process which is itself subject to failure. This argument has affinities with that of Downs (1960) – whilst tax burdens are felt at the individual level the benefits of expenditure are diffused and are accordingly perceived as relatively low by taxpaying voters. Public sectors will inevitably be 'too small', Downs argues.[7]

This market failure argument suggests that decisions made by individuals under Rawlsian conditions (i.e. in ignorance of the precise circumstances of one's future social existence) are likely to be very different from those made when individuals are aware of their actual circumstances. The handicapped and the unemployed will both be well-defined disadvantaged minority groups in market society, for example. Making decisions behind the 'veil of ignorance' one might consider it quite acceptable that guaranteed adequate provision for members of such minorities existed, on the grounds that one might be chosen by lot, as it were, to fall into one of these categories. However, the present knowledge on the part of the majority of individuals that they themselves are neither handicapped nor unemployed, and that they are not particularly likely to become either, would probably lead to the decision not to subsidize either group to any great extent. Whether the level of provision regarded as adequate by the donor is similarly regarded by the recipient remains a moot point; there is no necessity for any equivalence. Of course, individuals might be willing to subsidize the disadvantaged on altruistic grounds although, in such circumstances, they would hardly require a government to effect the transfers for them.

Pro-market ideology

The preceding section examined three corollaries of the market model. In view of the present interest being shown in the market in several western countries, notably the UK, we might presume that such corollaries would be areas which supporters of the market would be subjecting to the most rigorous scrutiny at the present time. Certainly in the UK, however, this appears not to be the case. Far from wishing to devolve power, the present government appears concerned with centralization and the constraining of local government. Discussions about the 'appropriate' distribution of income and wealth scarcely seem to have emerged.[8] Although it would appear that there are grounds for believing the government sector to be 'too small' in a mixed economy, present concern seems to be focused exclusively on the inevitability of it being 'too big'.

The reason for these apparent contradictions is that the contemporary ruling ideology in the UK has not emerged as a rational construct from logical foundations; rather, it consists of an amalgam of influences. The result is a 'particularly rich mix. It combines the resonant themes of organic Toryism – nation, family, duty, authority, standards, traditionalism – with the aggressive themes of a revised neo-liberalism – self-interest, competitive individualism, anti-statism' (Hall 1983: 29). As with the development of most practical ideologies the component ideas were not integrated wholesale. Particular features of the market model were accepted or rejected depending upon whether or not they meshed with other themes adopted from outside the strict neo-liberal philosophical position.

A number of factors combined to give rise to the pro-market economic ideology which emerged in the 1970s in the UK. First, there came into being an almost axiomatic belief in the existence of economic decline. Casual empiricism coupled with a deep-seated conviction convinced the ideologues that this decline had arisen from the strangulation of healthy capitalism by, amongst other things, a militant working class and a welfare state which protected the weak at the expense of the strong (Bleaney 1983). Second, by the 1980s a substantial body of anti-government economic theory had become established. Models of budget-maximizing bureaucrats and power-maximizing politicians all contributed to a picture of the government as rapacious and inefficient. These theories lent support to calls for tax reductions and private provision in place of public-sector provision. Third, theoretical worries appeared to have empirical substance because the share of government expenditure in total output rose sharply in the mid-1970s at the same time as economic problems worsened.

With the benefit of hindsight we can now see that certain elements of the pro-market ideology have rather insubstantial foundations. A belief that a growing public sector is a sufficient condition for the retardation of economic progress is hard to maintain when one appreciates that the taxation/public expenditure circumstances of the UK over the past thirty years have been essentially similar to those of West Germany, the 'model' industrial state. Since 1960 the shares of government spending in GDP have been virtually identical and, in both cases, annual expenditure growth has outstripped annual income growth by 1 per cent. In the mid-1970s the share of government spending in GDP rose sharply in both countries due not to increases in public-sector activity *per se* but rather to the maintenance of spending levels coupled with the sudden fall in GDP precipitated by the 1973 oil crisis (Alt and Chrystal 1983). Recently, criticism of the 'economics of politics' literature has arisen, on the grounds that its preconceptions about behaviour tend to make the demonstration of inefficiency and government failure almost inevitable (Heald 1983). It is not difficult, further-more, to demonstrate that this particular theoretical approach can prove to be a double-edged weapon. If one argues that private provision ought to replace government provision on efficiency grounds then one is obliged to accept that activities which, by general agreement, must remain the province of government (e.g. technical monopolies, the maintenance of law, arbitration in disputes) will be provided inefficiently. If one now responds by arguing that there might exist alternative methods of ensuring efficiency for such activities then this is equivalent to accepting that the existence of a market is not a necessary con-dition for efficiency. An important part of the pro-market argument is therefore refuted. On the other hand, if one agrees to accept the inevitability of inefficiency within the government sector, then second-best theory would suggest that the criteria for efficiency in the non-government sector are by no means as clear-cut as the market economists appear to believe.

Interpreting the prevailing ideology as authoritarian populism (Hall 1983), it is easy to appreciate why the market model appears so appealing. The ideologue can immediately accept the 'strong state' principle supportive of views about nation, duty, and tradition although not, of course, the corollaries about legiti-mate forms of government. If one is concerned to reduce tax burdens one can latch on to the market notion that the economic sphere of government ought to be limited. Expenditure cutbacks similarly find legitimation, although it is necessary to ignore the corollary that substantial transfer payments could be necessary to generate an acceptable income distribution prior to exchange. Convincing people that the individual is the essential economic actor permits the government to eschew intervention and to disclaim responsibility.

Some sixty years ago the economics whipping-boy of the past

decade – John Maynard Keynes – delivered a lecture entitled 'The End of Laissez-Faire'. Clearly, the lecture was given prematurely, and it is both intriguing and sad that its message remains fresh. The lecture opened with a summary of the economic basis of the *laissez-faire* philosophy of the late nineteenth/early twentieth century. Keynes next remarked: 'This is what the economists are *supposed* to have said. No such doctrine is really to be found in the writings of the greatest authorities. It is what the popularisers and the vulgarisers said' (Keynes 1926: 17). Towards the end of the lecture Keynes re-iterated his theme: 'It is *not* a correct deduction from the Principles of Economics that enlightened self-interest always operates in the public interest. Nor is it true that self-interest generally *is* enlightened' (p. 39).

Keynes ultimately went on to argue for an organizational structure we should nowadays recognize as indicative planning, although this is not the point presently at issue. In his lecture Keynes was saying that the contemporary ideology advocating a *laissez-faire* approach to economic affairs had been concocted by means of a judicious selection of ingredients in terms of whatever, in his own words, 'happened to suit'. Precisely the same thing, it would appear, has occurred in the case of the pro-market ideology of today. The notions of the 'greatest authorities' of more recent times have been stripped of caveats and blended into a *mélange* of economic dogma (on occasions, it should be said, with the obvious approval of such authorities). In common with all economic dogma, the pro-market ideology contains certain intellectual strengths hand in hand with practical contradictions and unanswered questions. We depart from a rationalist critique at our peril.

Notes

1 Taken from a letter from the prime minister to *Economic Affairs* (formerly the *Journal of Economic Affairs*), reprinted in a centrefold to the October, 1983 edition.
2 It follows that, accepting this argument, the question of the economic significance of government now becomes a wholly empirical issue; the greater the economies yielded by monopoly production, the greater the observed exter-

nalities and the larger the number of persons deemed 'irresponsible' (e.g. children, the insane) then the more pervasive will be the state sector.

3 Asymmetry of subjective valuation is presupposed. In saying that we are willing to exchange my A for your B, the implication is that I value B more highly than A but you value A more highly than B.

4 Whilst such a view is intuitively plausible, it should be noted that economists remain some way from a generalized existence proof for equilibria under all economic conditions. The problems involved are discussed by Arrow and Hahn (1971) and Hahn (1982), the latter having much to say on the problems of markets in general.

5 Although nested squarely in the framework of the market model, Rawls's conception of justice does not exhaust all possibilities. One criticism commonly made, for example, concerns Rawls's necessary assumption of risk aversion. Rawls's individuals are not risk averse in the sense of avoiding risk – they are quite willing to take fair risks and it is such behaviour which gives rise to the distribution principles. They will certainly not pay for the privilege of taking risks, however, and should such a delight in risk-taking be a feature of any real-world society the principles would require revision (Tucker 1980).

6 Hayek's vision of the Good Society is not too dissimilar. It would be one which did not offer 'delectable plums to a few but offered better prospects to the great majority' (Hayek 1976: 132).

7 Friedman's individuals are paying to relieve their own distress at seeing poverty in others, not others' distress as such. They are not, therefore, altruists and many modern social economists (e.g. Culyer 1980) would dispute this behavioural assumption. An intriguing implication of Friedman's position is that, were government supplements actually to occur, donors to charity would presumably contract their private payments by a corresponding amount, that is, the policy would be self-defeating. Further problems with the Friedman view, especially with respect to insurance strategies, are discussed by Sugden (1982).

8 Two contributors to the IEA's *festschrift* (Seldon 1981) independently criticize the IEA for an inadequate emphasis on the importance of income distribution.

References

Alt, J. E. and Chrystal, K. A. (1983) *Political Economics*. Brighton: Wheatsheaf Books.

Arrow, K. J. and Hahn, F. H. (1971) *General Competitive Analysis*. Edinburgh: Oliver & Boyd.

Becker, L. C. (1977) *Property Rights: Philosophic Foundations*. Boston. Routledge & Kegan Paul.

Bleaney, M. (1983) Conservative Economic Strategy. In S. Hall and M. Jacques (1983): 132–47.

Breton, A. (1974) *The Economic Theory of Representative Government*. Chicago: Aldine.

Culyer, A. J. (1980) *The Political Economy of Social Policy.* Oxford: Martin Robertson.

Downs, A. (1960) Why the Government Budget Is too Small in a Democracy. *World Politics* 12: 541–63.

Friedman, M. (1962) *Capitalism and Freedom.* Chicago: Chicago University Press.

Friedman, M. and Friedman, R. (1980) *Free to Choose.* London: Secker & Warburg.

Friedrich, C. J. (1955) The Political Thought of Neo-liberalism. *American Political Science Review* 49: 509–25.

Gamble, A. (1979) The Free Economy and the Strong State. *Socialist Register 1979*: 1–25.

Hahn, F. H. (1982) Reflections on the Invisible Hand. *Lloyds Bank Review* 144: 1–21.

Hall, S. (1983) The Great Moving Right Show. In S. Hall and M. Jacques (1983), 19–39.

Hall, S. and Jacques, M. (eds) (1983) *The Politics of Thatcherism.* London: Lawrence & Wishart.

Hayek, F. A. (1976) *Law, Legislation and Liberty: The Mirage of Social Justice.* London: Routledge & Kegan Paul.

——— (1979) *Law, Legislation and Liberty: The Political Order of a Free People.* London: Routledge & Kegan Paul.

Heald, D. (1983) *Public Expenditure.* Oxford: Martin Robertson.

Keynes, J. M. (1926) *The End of Laissez-Faire.* London: Hogarth Press.

MacPherson, C. B. (1964) *The Political Theory of Possessive Individualism.* Oxford: Oxford University Press.

Nozick, R. (1974) *Anarchy, State and Utopia.* Oxford: Basil Blackwell.

Pattanaik, P. K. (1968) Risk, Impersonality and the Social Welfare Function. *Journal of Political Economy* 76: 1152–69.

Rawls, J. (1972) *A Theory of Justice.* Oxford: Oxford University Press.

Seldon, A. (ed.) (1981) *The Emerging Consensus.* London: Institute of Economic Affairs.

Sugden, R. (1982) Hard Luck Stories: The Problem of the Uninsured in a Laissez-faire Society. *Journal of Social Policy* 11: 201–16.

Tucker, D. F. B. (1980) *Marxism and Individualism.* Oxford: Basil Blackwell.

Whynes, D. K. and Bowles, R. A. (1981) *The Economic Theory of the State.* Oxford: Martin Robertson.

6

On being right or wrong about the welfare state

A. J. CULYER

Economists trained in the 1960s find it very hard to understand the 1980s. Ideas which appeared to be intellectually obsolete at this earlier time seem to have been seized upon by a new generation of politicians, academics, and publicists, and welded together into a grand philosophical outlook labelled 'neo-libertarianism' or, more popularly, the 'new right'. Although amorphous at the best of times, this outlook does have one or two recognizable policy predilections, for instance, a *laissez-faire* view of the role of government. In the context of the elaborate provision of all forms of social welfare in western European economies – health care, education, housing, social security, and so forth – it favours a radically different allocation mechanism from that employed in many countries at present. The new right argues that, in general, the provision of social welfare goods and services could be far better accomplished by replacing the modern 'welfare state' approach with the market principle.

Before we all begin the systematic destruction of the welfare state we need to develop satisfactory answers to two questions. First, is the case made by the 'marketeers' convincing? Would the public really be better served by the extension of markets for welfare? Second, if, as is being suggested, the welfare state is an inferior good, how do we explain its existence and, indeed, its expansion over the past few decades? Have grave mistakes been made in all the western economies?

I shall be concerned with aspects of both questions in this chapter. I shall begin with an examination of the case made by the marketeers, both in terms of their own image of market mechanisms and in terms of their objections to the present welfare allocation mechanisms. Comparison of this case with the realities, as opposed to the images, of markets suggests that, even at the level of abstraction, the marketeers' case remains 'not proven'. Finally, I shall address an issue which seriously weakens the marketeers' case but, it must be said, also that of many of the modern welfare state's most devout supporters – the substitution of ideology for empiricism, of assertion for evaluation. The pervading – and perversion – of scholarly argument about the welfare state was one of the sorriest features of the earlier round of debate about social policy. This chapter tries to show that there is an alternative that is both substantive and exacting and it entails the possibility that arguments can actually be shown to be *wrong* rather than merely ideological.

Having been charged in my time both with being a member of the 'new right' and with being a pretty wet liberal socialist, whereas – so far as I can tell – I have hardly changed my mind on any of the major issues (though I hope to have cultivated it somewhat over the years!), I take it that, in thus being all things to all men, my impartiality is well established! Further, in being consistent in my attitude to the welfare state, the sense of *déjà vu* that the reader might feel in looking through what follows is only to be expected.[1]

The case for the market

The marketeers' image of the market is that the inherent rivalry of private interests can be reconciled by voluntary contracting between interested parties. If such contracting takes place, upheld by a system of enforcement, then resources will have been allocated in an efficient fashion, a fashion such that any further improvement in someone's lot could be done only at the expense of someone else. The institutional counterpart to this image is that the right to use resources in specific ways may be exchanged between individuals if suitable compensation is forthcoming, and that free production and exchange will produce an outcome in which all resources have been transferred to their most valued uses. At that point, the economic cake can be differently distributed but its size cannot be larger; indeed, it may become smaller.

From this general image flow directly a number of specific images of how a service (social or otherwise) ought to run. First, services should not be provided free. This imperative follows from the proposition that the resources used by services are scarce and also from the law of demand. If services are free then more will be demanded than is warranted. Resources will be drawn into the care system away from other wants whose marginal value is higher and the outcome is an inefficient allocation. Within a market, however, at the going price demanders will get as much as they demand and this will be as much as suppliers want to supply. The sector will be of an appropriate size. There will be no queues and rationing will be on the basis of price (rather than at the whim of someone in authority determining 'need'). The market procedure will minimize the role of those who like arranging other people's lives – 'life-arrangers' – and therefore will be conducive to freedom. To a charge that the market could deny access to those with insufficient income, the marketeers' retort will be that an unjust income distribution can be remedied by an appropriate income transfer, without having to destroy the market. Alternatively, if the distribution is just, then so is any consequential inability to obtain services.

Second, there should be no regulation. According to the marketeers, regulation is a simple way of accomplishing either of two objectives, each of which is undesirable. Regulation gives power to the life-arrangers to determine what is to happen. The marketeers reject the idea that those with superior information or 'noble motives' should be placed in a position to arrange the lives of others; the correct solution to the problem of inadequate information is the provision of more information. The other objective of regulation is the granting of monopoly power to particular groups. Those ostensibly regulated, argue the marketeers, capture control of the regulatory mechanisms and turn them to their own advantage – professional licensing is a classic case. The proper answer is to allow competitors to expose fraudulent claims and incompetence, to permit markets in relevant information to develop, and to allow recourse to the courts in cases of fraud or negligence.

Third, insurance should not be made compulsory. Most people are risk averse and, in a market, insuring agencies will emerge to bear the financial risks of an individual's falling sick or becoming unemployed. Those for whom the financial prospect of, say, being ill next year is worse than the prospect of paying a sure premium will therefore insure; those for whom this is not true will not. However, to force the latter group to insure is to make them worse off, for their costs will exceed their perceived benefit.

Fourth, profit-seeking should be encouraged. Marketeers allow that certain non-profit agencies might naturally arise within markets (e.g. charities) and, if they are successful in competition with profit-making concerns, then well and good. However, should they fail to compete there is no case for public support in the form of subsidies or tax exemptions. Lacking owners who can signal approval or disapproval of the agencies' work, and lacking strong motives to improve efficiency, managers of non-profit agencies are likely to perform inefficiently. Accordingly, non-profit activity will tend to be high-cost and therefore relatively unimportant in the market, although individuals must be permitted to offer their labour on a 'voluntary' basis if they so wish.

Finally, the market ought not to be used to rectify 'bad' income distributions, because the distortion of the market produces inefficiency and harms freedom. Thus, this 'solution' to any problem creates further problems. Actually, the marketeers argue, insurance can minimize distributional problems because individuals will pay only insurance premia; they will not be obliged to face medical bills or to face a loss of income as a result of becoming unemployed. With risk pooling by insurance agencies, relatively high risks are subsidized by relatively low risks. If the poorer members of the community are exposed to the highest risks, as most evidence suggests, then insurance helps to reduce the inequality problem.

The marketeers' image of the socialized welfare system flows directly from their image of the market. This image includes the following elements:

1. One objection to free services is that, by abolishing prices, the necessary evidence to weigh value against cost is lost. The result must be a sector of arbitrary size. Users will always demand more than is supplied, leading to waiting lists and to rationing by suppliers. Marketeers have mixed attitudes, on the whole, as to whether welfare services provided free of charge will be too large or too small. Some argue that ignorance by taxpayers of the tax price which they pay leads them to underestimate the cost of services to them, while being fully aware of the manifest benefits of a free service as and when they need it; the predicted outcome is a budget that is too large. Others argue that the system will be too small but all agree that only a fortuitous accident could give rise to a service of the correct size.

2. A basic condition for efficiency is that whatever is produced should be produced at minimum cost. Those who are most successful at minimizing costs are also those who will compete most successfully for consumers by keeping prices low. Competition is absent from socialized welfare systems such as that of Britain and the characteristic marketeers' conclusion is that 'the British do not get their money's worth for their tax dollars. They have less care and a lower quality of care than could be achieved for the same amount of spending' (Goodman 1980: 52).

3. Part of the inefficiency of the services such as the NHS is said to lie in the incentives facing managers, incentives that are thought to produce the wrong mix of services. Of demanders of health care it has been said:

   'They demand pleasant surroundings and prompt attention by their physician. They demand privacy in their hospital accommodation and answers to their questions about health. Even when well, they seek reassurance about troubling symptoms and ailing relations. Because it is not observed, this sort of medical care output will be given less attention in government medical care budgets. If financed, budgeters would have no way to verify that the resources were used for the purposes intended, so they are not even budgeted. Bureaucratic managers in their turn will devote fewer resources to providing this type of care because it cannot be counted and does not therefore reflect favourably on their recorded performance as managers.

(Lindsay 1980: 56)

4. Another aspect of inefficiency will be reflected in procedures and costs. Since the returns from capital expenditure may not become apparent until after a government has left office, this form of expenditure will be pared back. Of course, there will be relatively little capital spending anyway in residential services (such as hospitals and homes for the elderly) on televisions, furnishings, personal telephones, and so on, since these constitute services that no one in the socialized services will have any reason to supply. On the other hand, clients will be allowed to remain in the institution for relatively long stays because client days are a quantifiable measure of the system and because longer stays lower the cost per client per day. As a result, average cost per case might well be higher and the number of cases lower.

5. Waiting in queues will be an inevitable result of the absence of prices. We all know (don't we?) that in the NHS people just wait and wait. They wait for appointments, they wait in doctors' offices, they wait to see a specialist. If they are in line for serious medical treatment then the waiting *really* begins. Patients scheduled for operations can end up waiting for years. Thus even under a 'free' system, the service is not really free, even to users. Those who actually receive care are those who have been willing to wait longer and to bear more inconvenience than others. (This is a paraphrase from Goodman 1980.)

6. As the monopsony power of a national service as an employer becomes effective so professional salaries are likely to be

squeezed, especially when compared with those who sell their labour in a less-monopolized market. In health care, for example, this will induce a net emigration of physicians and a shortage of individuals seeking training. Doctors trained in foreign countries with lower incomes may be willing to supply medical services at lower prices than locally trained doctors, that is, foreigners may be hired to replace the locally born doctors who are emigrating. Such foreign-born doctors, however, will probably offer a lower-quality service (especially in respect of the intangible characteristics mentioned above). The same could be true for all types of medical personnel. Thus, while a national health service might be able to operate at a lower *per capita* expenditure rate it can do so only at the cost of underpaying its manpower and offering inferior quality of service.

7. One aim of public intervention in welfare services is the achievement of equality in consumption for those with similar needs. However, need is such a vague concept that equality can scarcely be made operational as an objective. The geographical distribution of resources is therefore unlikely to be related to any defensible concept of need, nor will it approach the ideal of equal availability for all persons. Wage earners pay a higher price for waiting in physicians' surgeries than do salary earners, and salary earners pay a higher price than those that need not work for a living. Furthermore, the higher social classes are more articulate in making their demands effective. In sum, therefore, the chances are that a socialized system will tend to redistribute resources *away* from the poorer members of the community and *towards* the better off.

Markets and realities

This case for the market would appear to relegate socialized welfare systems to a poor second place. Indeed, it would seem that such systems must fail by their own criteria and the rolling back of government in the provision of social services must therefore be the appropriate policy. Image and reality are two different things, however, and in this section I shall examine the marketeers' arguments a little more closely, specifically in the context of medical care provision.

THE REALITIES OF INSURANCE AGAINST HEALTH EXPENDITURES

Insurance is equivalent to a price subsidy on health care. Suppose you are fully insured against the financial burden of whatever health care you may receive in the event of your falling sick. This means that when you fall sick, the price you confront is effectively zero. A fully insured person is thus in precisely the same position as one in a 'free' health care system. Since the demand for all forms of health care rises (though not proportionately) as price falls, a health system with insurance suffers from the same difficulty as a zero price system does. The main difference is that in an NHS-type system, whether the extra care demanded will be supplied depends upon the rationing method used, whereas in the market system the suppliers will be reimbursed by an insurance company. There is thus a built-in propensity for over-supply in an insurance-based system.

Another force also works towards over-supply: if one is insured, the financial burden of sickness is relieved, hence there is no urgent incentive to avoid a sick state. The probability of falling sick will therefore rise in so far as an individual's health state can be – if only in part – influenced by his own actions. This applies too in 'free' health systems. Both these effects are usually referred to by the quaint name of 'moral hazard' and they apply equally in a market with insurance, and in the NHS. A paradox begins to emerge as *the reality of the market* converges on the marketeers' *image of the NHS*.

Markets do evolve methods of mitigating moral hazard. All involve financial penalties for insured parties and hence reduce the benefits (for risk-averse people) of being insured, namely *fixed indemnity* (a maximum level of benefit), that does nothing to affect behaviour leading to any expense less than this; *deductibles* (akin to the 'excess' in British motor vehicle insurance), which have little effect so long as expected expense exceeds the deductible; *co-insurance*, whereby the insurance company pays only a certain proportion of the medical bill above the deductible, and that clearly erodes the benefit of insurance. In general, then, the more complete one's insurance the more one is in the position leading to the inefficiency complained of by the marketeers. The more effectively moral hazard is curtailed the less the benefits of insurance: moral hazard is zero when co-insurance is 100 per cent but this is where one has no insurance at all!

Another difficulty with health insurance in the market is called 'adverse selection'. Insurance companies assess the probability that an individual will fall sick and make a claim upon broad classes of experience across groups of the population (so-called 'community rating'). Any individual who feels that the probability of his needing care is higher than that on which his insurer is assessing him will have an extra incentive to insure. Take a population of 100 people, 50 of whom on past history may be expected to pay £100 in medical fees, and 50 of whom may be expected to pay £300. The insurer offers premiums on the basis of the average risk, so (ignoring the insurer's own operating costs) the premium will be set at £200 since £200 × 100 will just cover the expected pay-out of £100 × 50 + £300 × 50. This will seem an excessive premium to those expecting only £100 expenses, who will therefore not buy insurance unless they are quite extraordinarily averse to bearing the risk themselves. The insurer is left with the high risk cases insured at a risk calculated actuarially too low. In a pure market we therefore expect to see insurance agencies being forced away from community rating and having to tailor individual premiums more to individual risks.

In the USA, Blue Cross/Blue Shield originally adopted community rating such that all families of a given size paid the same premium. When commercial insurers entered the market they used 'experience rating' thereby offering probable low users more favourable premium terms than Blue Cross/Blue Shield who, in response and in order to maintain market shares, had to modify their community rating basis for premium calculation.

This illustrates well the problem that competition creates in markets: it is less a problem of efficiency (for efficiency requires that premiums be proportional to risk) than of equity, for if premium averaging becomes impossible by pooling risks, the premiums for high risk groups, the chronic sick, etc., are likely to become sufficiently high for major distributive questions to be raised. Specific health subsidies for these groups will be demanded and with them the whole panoply of regulation, state finance, monitoring, and audit.

THE REALITIES OF MONOPOLY AND REGULATION

Conducting health service policy on the assumption that monopoly and regulation will be swept away by appropriate policies is a doubtful procedure. It is enormously difficult either to prevent the growth of monopoly or to push it back once it has grown. But if it should not prove possible to eliminate monopoly and regulation for the sake of the regulated, then the rest of the marketeers' programme has to be called in question.

An obvious example occurs in the case of the medical profession, though as Dennis Lees has pointed out (Lees 1966) the granting of professional licences has continued apace in Britain in many spheres including many ancillary to the doctors themselves (dentists, chiropodists, physiotherapists, dietitians, and lots more). The same appears to be true of all developed countries. It seems that a strongly organized professional monopoly that controls entry to the profession, terms of service, permitted forms of advertising, disciplinary procedure, etc., is a *universal* characteristic of all developed countries (wherever they lie on the liberal-collective spectrum). But if that is so, to advocate the market in *the rest* of health care activity no longer becomes an obvious logical corollary of the search for either efficiency or freedom. At the least, further regulation may become warranted (e.g. to limit and monitor abuse). Moreover there is at the least a *prima facie* case for introducing a countervailing bargaining power, in the form of the state, in the determination of wages and salaries.

Another good illustration comes from the history of the relationship between Blue Cross and the hospitals in the USA. Blue Cross was originally created by hospitals and the American Hospitals Association in the 1930s. The Blue Cross plans were quickly successful in gaining charitable status and exemption from state taxes in many states as well as from federal tax. This gave them an immediate competitive advantage over commercial insurers and it is not surprising that Blue Cross had 60 per cent of the hospital insurance market after the Second World War. This large proportion also enabled Blue Cross to negotiate favourable 'quantity discounts' with the hospitals.

A code of practice was at the same time established by the American Hospitals Association that patients should be free to receive care in the hospital of their choice, that any plan licensed to use the Blue Cross insignia had to have written agreements with at least three-quarters of the non-federal hospitals in its area, and that Blue Cross cost reimbursements to hospitals could vary according to what the costs happened to be. This effectively removed competitive incentives for hospitals to provide efficient (i.e. least cost) care. Blue Cross, with its implicit subsidies via its charitable status and the bulk discounts, was able for a long time to fend off commercial competitors even though actual costs must have been higher than a fully competitive system could have achieved. The regulated had again effectively captured the regulatory mechanism (in this case they invented it!) and used it to destroy competition.

The theoretical advantages of a private property system depend upon the existence of an appropriate economic environment. Without that, the differences in efficiency to be expected between, say, privately owned and publicly owned institutions begin to look rather small in terms of *efficiency* of their operation. What may not be at all similar, of course, is the resultant distribution of wealth. A monopolized insurance industry, a monopolized pharmaceutical industry, a regulated hospital industry, and regulated medical professions are all likely to generate much higher wealth for their members in a market system that has failed than in a truly competitive market system or in a publicly owned system. That, of course, is why it pays them to monopolize and regulate. But this reality is a far cry from the image of the marketeers' ideal markets.

THE REALITIES OF FREEDOM

The robust individualism of the marketeers betrays a naïve faith in the capacity of individuals to resolve their own problems and neglects two crucial aspects of the demand for health care, both of which are illustrated alike in market and non-market health systems. These are two aspects of what seems to be a fact: that there is a demand for 'life-arranging'. The first aspect of this rather special kind of demand is that individuals demand the services of professionals to advise them and act for them as agents – interpreting both their needs and arranging for them to be met where possible. The second aspect is that individuals are manifestly not uninterested in the health of their fellow citizens. Let us examine each aspect in turn.

The 'agency relationship' between a professional and his client has been much discussed in the literature and there has been no settled empirical conclusion to the question whether (in either the market or the NHS) the nature of this relationship enables physicians so to manipulate consumer demand to their own financial benefit (see e.g. Newhouse 1981). This power is evidently more exercisable where there is (as there invariably is) a strong professional monopoly that both controls entry to the profession and limits competition between professionals and information about the quality of one's competitors. For this reason alone, every society has seen the necessity to regulate the professional to protect the public from abuse. It seems clear that the incentive to induce (or discourage) demand depends upon the mode of payment of physicians. For example, fee-for-service payments provide a direct incentive to provide more services. A salaried form of employment provides no such incentive. A combination of part-time salary in the NHS *plus* private practice provides a direct incentive to generate NHS waiting lists in order to bolster demand for care in private beds. These distortions exist in *all* systems. Research (of which there is not enough in this territory) has not yet provided satisfactory answers to questions about the magnitude or desirability of the consequences of the behaviour changes induced by these employment conditions. What is clear is that the marketeers' image of a prototypical consumer shopping around for the best-quality care at the least price, and getting it, is not a phenomenon that is anywhere actually going to be observed.

The second aspect of the 'life-arranging' argument casts

further fundamental doubt on the adequacy of the marketeers' image. It will be recalled that the root of the marketeers' claim that the market will promote the efficient outcome depends upon the notion that marginal value and marginal cost will be brought into equilibrium in the market. Now suppose, however, that the value of a person's health, or of his health care received, is not only that which he himself places upon it. Suppose that others too place a value upon an individual's health – or consumption. (If this were not the case, who other than the very poor would ever advocate subsidizing the health care of the very poor? The remarkable fact is that almost the only people who do not actively advocate such subsidies are the poor themselves!) It immediately follows that the market will *under-supply* health (and/or health care) by failing to allow for the additional value placed upon it by people other than the direct consumer. Therefore, even within its own efficiency claims the market image fails, for a part of the value of health or health care must lie in the collective value placed upon the individual's health or health care consumption, and this value is *over and above* the value ascribed to the consumption by the direct consumer himself. The various forms this collective interest may take in the consumption of an individual have been explored recently (Culyer and Simpson 1980) and applied in a wider context (Culyer 1981). There is, of course, no reason to suppose that those features of markets that tend to produce over-supply will do so in a manner appropriate to the efficient internalizing of any relevant externalities.

DISTRIBUTIONAL QUESTIONS

The theoretical advantages of private insurance from the distributional point of view are, as we have seen, likely to be eroded by actual insurance practice. With monopoly in the hospital industry and insurance industry too, these advantages will be further eroded by premium 'loading', that is, the addition to premiums of costs of administration and the costs of the inefficiencies that monopoly makes possible.

A marketeer's response to such difficulties would characteristically be to arrange public subsidy for insurance premiums via tax deductions, vouchers, etc. For the chronic sick and uninsurable, special programmes may have to be devised. The state really has little option but to become involved not only in health care financing but possibly also in its provision. To the extent that it does *not* engage in the latter, it will have to finance services billed at inflated cost thanks to the effects discussed above: one has state interference *and* inefficient markets.

The implications of caring

I believe that the majority of individuals who think about or work in the social services actually care quite a lot about their work. They do not, in other words, regard the potential solutions to the problems of poverty or illness simply as amusing brain-teasers in the manner of crossword puzzles. Whilst we might wish to applaud noble sentiments, concern does pose a considerable problem. It has a great facility for clouding reason. A great many of the pro- and anti-welfare state arguments currently in circulation are based on considerable fancy and precious little fact. Since *caring* is subtle, and hard to measure empirically, it is easy for the new right to claim that it doesn't exist. It is just as easy for the wets to argue that it is omnipresent. My own view is that here is a classic case in which the quantified drives out the important.

Here I shall concentrate on just one instance of confronting ideology with evidence. Let us return to the marketeers' case examined earlier. The proof that freely functioning markets can produce optimal resource allocations is well established and not to be quibbled with. However, this proof requires the fulfilment of a number of conditions. Should one or all of these conditions remain unsatisfied we might well reach the conclusion that the market mechanism represents an inferior allocation system. One obstacle to the reaching of a neat solution in the basic market model is the presence of an externality.

Consider the concept of 'caring'. Here is a clear instance of externality because, if I care about some aspect of your welfare, *your* pleasure or pain, protection or exposure, use or non-use, health or sickness, influences *me*. How would we want to run an economy *if* people cared about one another?

To begin with, let us root the question in fact. What evidence do we have on the issue? There are three ways of dealing with the problem of evidence.

The first of these, introspection, appears to be what has led some observers, like Titmuss, Tobin, and Buchanan, to postulate the presence of caring preferences. My own introspection accords with theirs: I am indeed prepared to sacrifice my own consumption that others may have more, to do so both voluntarily by acts of (often tax-subsidized) giving to charity and perhaps less voluntarily by acquiescing in my contribution via taxation to the welfare of others. Moreover, I care more about some individuals than others and more about some aspects of their circumstances than others. I care more, for example, about poverty in Britain than about poverty in Bangladesh, despite the fact that poverty here may appear as a relatively affluent state when viewed from there. Similarly, I care more about the quality of education for British students than for Bangladeshi. This is not to say I care nothing for people in distant lands, only that I care less for them. Moreover I cannot find a moral justification for my feelings: *they seem to be matters of preference rather than of morals*: at least of *my* preferences rather than *my* morals since the latter lead me to hold that I ought not to discriminate in the way I do.

An appeal to introspection is flawed, however, by the evident possibility that while the introspections of some may reveal such sensibilities, the introspections of others may not. As a basis for empirical support for the caring postulate, therefore, this procedure cannot be held to be at all definitive. Even if one were to mount a survey designed to elicit directly the preferences of individuals it would be subject to the difficulty that most people would naturally seek to appear to possess sensibilities they think will win approbation, particularly if they are not asked to contemplate the possibility of sacrificing some of their *own* wealth for the sake of others.

The second line of attack seems more promising as a way of establishing the truth or otherwise of the caring postulate: this is to seek to establish the motives underlying ostensible acts of unselfishness. While there is no space here for an exploration, social history provides a suitable testing ground for this type of enquiry (see e.g. Knapp 1981).

The third kind of evidence does not seek *directly* to investigate preferences but tests for their nature by looking at what a postulated *general* form implies for behaviour and choice of social institutions. One of the most striking things that has repeatedly been observed either by introspection or by historical review is the *specific* nature of the caring concern. This is consistent with the specific nature of the transfers in kind and specific subsidies offered by the welfare state, whether to publicly owned or to privately owned institutions providing appropriate services. It is also consistent with the fact that general cash subsidies are given only to the very poor – where the empirical evidence (quite apart from common sense) tells us that they will be primarily spent on such basic necessities of life as food and clothing. It is also consistent with the kind of financial reform of the welfare state that has been increasingly frequently proposed, even by those who are often opposed to the welfare state – a reverse income tax to benefit the very poor and specific vouchers for specific consumption purposes by the poor and non-poor, such as education, health and housing. The combination of vertical redistribution (mostly in untied cash) between income classes, and horizontal redistribution (mostly tied in one form or another) within income classes seems very characteristic of the welfare state (and suggests, incidentally, that an exclusive emphasis on its vertical redistribution characteristics may miss a large part of its purpose).

If the welfare state in its complexity of individual and institutional subsidies and varying types of institutions for providing services did not have these redistributive characteristics but was, say, either distributively neutral so that each received roughly what he contributed, or merely concerned with the *vertical* redistribution of purchasing power, then the caring postulate as put forward here would have been decisively refuted by the evidence. But it is not. Moreover this is telling evidence against the view that redistributive caring is concerned only – or even mainly – with cash redistribution from rich to poor. That may be the kind of redistribution *preferred* by some liberals and socialists but the evidence suggests it is not that preferred by the *median* voter who determines, on the assumptions, the redistribution that will *actually* take place.

But in addition to these rather obvious implications of the caring hypothesis, there are less obvious ones. The postulated presence of caring externalities implies that the consumption (or characteristics) of others is 'public' in the sense that if one caring person sees the poverty (or whatever) of another being mitigated, so do other caring persons. *Anyone* who cares benefits, in this sense, from the measures taken by another who sacrifices his own resources to benefit someone else. This 'jointness' in consumption provides an incentive for each who shares in the external benefit to 'free-ride' at the expense of others. For example, if I care about the reduction of poverty, rather than simply about what *I* am doing about it, then I benefit from the relief of other people's poverty even when *you* are paying for it. In the limit this would appear to imply that no one would ever voluntarily give to others, choosing to leave it to the others who share in the external benefit. Since, however, the same incentive to free-ride confronts everyone, no one would contribute – despite the fact that all stand to benefit by some appropriate rate of transfer. Even caring individuals can fall victim of what, in game theory, is called the prisoner's dilemma.

This extreme implication of the public good phenomenon is not observed in practice. Individuals *do* contribute individually to the welfare of others; they *do* form groups and clubs for making joint transfers; intermediary organizations like fund-raising charities *do* emerge and thrive. The reason is surely clear – it is in the interest of all caring individuals to try to devise a set of arrangements that produces their jointly preferred level of transfers. There are lots of formal and informal mechanisms to help in this battle against the free-rider. The most pervasive is, perhaps, the high social approbation attached to acts of giving to 'good causes', and the cultivation of a moral climate whereby there is a duty to make a contribution – just as many people regard it as a moral (*as well as* a legal) obligation to repay debts, carry out the agreed terms of a contract, and so forth. The cultivation of a moral climate for the transaction of affairs seems to be a common complement to the use of legally enforcible sanctions in all societies *and it has the great advantage of using up relatively few resources*. Morals are cheap, so we expect to see them cultivated. Another commonly observed technique, related to this, is the provision of means of identifying givers (and hence non-givers) via the sporting of lapel badges, the naming of buildings and trust funds after their benefactors, the recording of the names of donors on plaques, subscription lists, and so on. Sometimes direct rewards are arranged as in the pay-offs to participants in unfair (in the actuarial sense) lotteries (raffles, tombolas, bottle stalls, etc.). This does not imply that the reasons why benefactors give are selfish, only that we see fit to harness selfish motives so as to reinforce unselfish actions, paradoxically to *harness* self-interest in order to prevent it from destroying generosity.

In other cases clubs may be formed, membership of which requires the payment of a contributed share of the cost of the charitable activity. Voluntary hospitals prior to the NHS had this characteristic: subscribers were entitled to use the facilities (and their names were made known) but the main activity of such hospitals was in giving care to non-subscribers – or at least to those making only nominal contributions. The churches are another important example of 'clubs' in this sense. It is striking that nearly all fund-raising charities organize their collections from small, organized, committed groups, who themselves give their money and their time in organizing shops, collections, and fund-raising events. In small voluntary groups free-riding is hard to get away with.

Such efforts are unlikely to eliminate the free-rider problem completely, but they are responses that arise only in the presence of a problem that *itself* arises only in the context of the publicness of caring sentiments: one does not sport badges or have one's name recorded for public edification when one makes *personal* purchases of goods. Such phenomena, then, are consistent with the caring postulate. Their absence would refute it.

Other phenomena too are implied. One is that in view of the imperfection of the kind of device just discussed yet other devices will be resorted to so as to encourage charitable giving. An obvious stratagem that has already been mentioned is to seek ways of reducing the price of giving on the presumption that, at the margin, a preference for the consumption of others declines much in the same way as a preference for one's own consumption. Given the publicness of caring sentiments we would expect to see social arrangements that had this effect. One that does precisely this is the income tax relief afforded on charitable giving.

Consider a further implication: the 'club' solution to the free-rider problem is subject to the severe restraint that individuals may still free-ride by not joining the club. Suppose, however, that sufficient numbers feel that the activities of the club are of such merit that the opportunity to free-ride by not joining ought to be reduced as far as possible to zero. An obvious way of doing this would be to make membership *compulsory*. This will admittedly be rough justice for those who do not share the view about the merits of the club's activities, but the element of unfairness may be considered a price worth paying for the increased scale of activity that compulsory membership makes possible. Where the caring externality extends across a whole nation, and is not merely local in nature, a natural extension of this is to the government itself. The public sector becomes, by analogy, a kind of national club, with compulsory membership fees in the form of taxes, and its charitable output the provision and subsidy of activities subsumed in the welfare aspects of the public sector. The government can thus be seen as the board of trustees of a kind of national charity. Compulsion is the other obvious solution to the free-rider problem.

In the public sector we have a complex of services provided for both unselfish and selfish reasons. The fact that I care about my own health and that of my nearest and dearest is not sufficient to explain the NHS, but if I care for others *as well* then something like the NHS *is* implied, providing for me and mine as well as for others, regardless of willingness or ability to pay. The welfare state in general can be seen, I suggest, as essentially a product of this dual nature of man, representing both the dismal *and* the noble sides of his character. It isn't *only* caring that matters. It isn't *only* the meeting of one's own needs, current or prospective, sure or uncertain. It is *both* of these things that gives the modern welfare state its chief characteristics.

That at least is *my* theory. Whether it is right or wrong is evidently something I care about. But I care almost more about the manner in which the discussion of the welfare state is to be conducted. I have tried to set it up in such a fashion that it can become a proper topic for social science: the development and empirical testing of hypotheses rather than the mere assertion of conflicting ideologies (with the occasional descriptive fact or two to lend weight to one's prejudices).

With the resurgence of the ideological debate about the welfare state we are sorely in need of a more satisfactory means of tackling the basic issues than our particular politics can provide. A priorism, on which I focused in the first part of this essay, is one means. Hypothesis development and testing is another. Whatever the ideologues might get up to, I hope that serious students of the welfare state will join me in working through this *real* agenda that confronts us. It is one that defines a research programme having social science at its very heart. It also puts us all at risk of being shown to have been wrong rather than merely wicked.

Note

1 This article indeed draws heavily on two recent pieces by me, namely, Culyer (1982, 1983).

References

Culyer, A. J. (1981) *The Political Economy of Social Policy.* Oxford: Martin Robertson.
—— (1982) The NHS and the Market: Images and Realities. In G. McLachlan and A. Maynard (eds) *The Public/Private Mix for Health.* London: Nuffield Provincial Hospitals Trust.
—— (1983) Economics without Economic Man. *Social Policy and Administration* 17: 188–203.
Culyer, A. J. and Simpson, H. (1980) Externality Models and Health: Rueckblick over the Past Twenty Years. *Economic Record* 56: 222–30.
Goodman, J. C. (1980) *National Health Care in Great Britain: Lessons for the USA.* Dallas, Tex.: Fisher Institute.
Knapp, M. (1981) Productivity Relations for Old People's Homes. PhD thesis, University of Kent at Canterbury.
Lees, D. S. (1966) *Economic Consequences of the Professions.* London: Institute of Economic Affairs.
Lindsay, C. M. (1980) *National Health Issues: The British Experience.* Rockville, Md.: Roche Laboratories.
Newhouse, J. P. (1981) The Demand for Medical Care Services: A Retrospect and a Prospect. In J. Van der Gaag and M. Perlman (eds) *Health, Economics and Health Economics.* Amsterdam: North-Holland.

7
Welfare: who pays?

ALAN MAYNARD

Introduction

The welfare state was created as a mechanism to mitigate the effects of Beveridge's five giants: want, disease, ignorance, squalor, and idleness. To combat want, Beveridge advocated the creation of a national insurance system which, in conjunction with public assistance, created an income maintenance system. To combat disease, Aneurin Bevan implemented legislation to create the NHS. Ignorance was mitigated by Butler's Education Act and a variety of crude policy instruments were used to over-invest in the housing stock and mitigate squalor. The adoption of Keynes's principles contributed to a period of minimal idleness (unemployment) which, when it was reversed in the late 1970s, led to renewed levels of considerable idleness and the questioning of all the other welfare state policies initiated in the 1940s.

The objective of this chapter is not to review the financial mechanisms of this broad range of services but to analyse the impact of payment systems on providers and demanders specifically in health care systems: similar arguments can be used to analyse other parts of the welfare state, for example the education system (see Maynard 1982). In the first section there is a brief examination of tax and insurance mechanisms as methods of generating revenues to finance health care. The common characteristics of these systems, 'moral hazard' and third-party-pays, generate perverse incentives and inefficient behaviour.

The characteristics of efficient behaviour are elaborated in the second section and there is an explanation of ways in which public and private health care systems may improve incentives in a way which would induce suppliers to provide care more efficiently.

Whilst decision-makers in public (tax-financed) and private (insurance-financed) health care systems confront the same problem of improving efficiency in provision, they seek dissimilar distributional goals. The differences in these goals are set out in the third section and their implications for the design of health care systems in particular, and the welfare state in general, are examined.

In the final section it is concluded that socialists and liberals alike should welcome improvements in incentive systems, competition of one sort and another, which generate increased efficiency. However, the differences in distributional goals are more difficult to narrow and are an inevitable derivative of the competing ideologies, socialist and liberal. Debate about the welfare state is confused by misconceptions about disagreements on the supply side, where liberals and socialists might agree, and as a result there is a failure to confront the essential question of whether health care and other welfare state services should be distributed on the basis of willingness and ability to pay or on the basis of need, as defined, in the case of health care, below.

Tax or insurance financed?

Any comparison of the effects of tax and insurance mechanisms as a means of financing health care is complex. The NHS is basically tax-financed, i.e. 97 per cent of its revenues are derived from general taxation (85 per cent) and NHS contributions (12 per cent). The effects of direct and indirect taxes are well described in any public finance textbook. Increases in indirect taxes, such as excise taxes and value added tax, tend to be passed on to consumers in the form of higher prices. The problem emphasized in any discussion of income taxes (including national insurance contributions which are, in effect, proportionate income tax surcharges) is the impact of reduced real rewards for labour on incentives to work, save, and take risks. The usual argument is that higher marginal tax rates reduce these incentives to the detriment of economic growth. However, the empirical evidence is not so clear-cut (see e.g. Brown 1980; Godfrey 1975) and it may be that some workers (particularly perhaps the more affluent professionals) respond to higher marginal tax rates by working harder.

However, whilst it may not be conventional wisdom to argue that higher tax rates may generate greater activity and higher rates of growth, it is accepted generally that these taxes are cheaper to collect, especially for a government which uses the employer as a tax collector. Hence the nature of the tax mechanism which finances the bulk of NHS expenditure is well known even if its precise effects are a matter of dispute.

These tax revenues are allocated by cabinet to the three component parts of the health care system: the hospitals, family practitioner services, and personal social services. The hospital budget is cash limited and distributed by the four national agencies (in England the DHSS) according to a similar but not identical resource allocation formula (in England it is called RAWP). The local government budget which finances personal social services (PSS) is rate-capped and expenditure is controlled tightly by the central government. The expenditure on family practitioner services (FPS) which finances the provision of primary care, is an open-ended, demand-determined contract.

The constituent parts of the health service have different budgeting arrangements and incentive structures which often lead to inefficient strategic behaviour at the margins or boundaries of the component parts of the system, in particular, cost shifting. Such inefficiencies are compounded by problems of moral hazard and third-party-pays. The consumer (patient) is provided with care which is zero priced at the point of consumption. Thus, in the absence of user charges (e.g. a payment for hotel accommodation in hospital) there is no financial incentive to economize.

In terms of *Figure 7.1*, a market with no insurance and no NHS would generate a consumption decision of Q_1 (where the marginal cost equals the marginal benefit (demand) for health care). The creation of an NHS with zero prices leads to demand increasing to Q_2. The supply of care, determined by cabinet, is likely to be to the left of Q_2 generating 'excess demand' and non-price rationing.

If, instead of an NHS, the 'free' market for health care was replaced by an insurance system, the outcome would be similar. Payment of the premium would create moral hazard, or access to benefits and the abolition of the price barrier. With no economic (payment) incentive to cost minimize, consumption would rise to Q_2. Both the insurance system and the NHS create the problem of moral hazard or the abolition of the price barrier which leads to over-consumption and welfare losses equal to the shaded area in *Figure 7.1*.

These outcomes can be complicated by a simple elaboration of *Figure 7.1*. The market for health care is characterized by an asymmetry in information between providers and patients. The primary provider on the supply side is the doctor who is the gatekeeper to the health care system: he decides who will get what health care when, or to be more emotive, he determines who will live and who will die and who will live in what degree of pain and discomfort. This provider is the 'expert' whilst the patient is ill-informed generally about diagnosis, treatment, and prognosis. As a consequence of this asymmetry in knowledge, the patient may delegate to the doctor the role of agent who, on behalf of the patient, decides how to care for the patient.

This 'agency relationship' gives the doctor an unusual role: it is he who determines demand and controls the supply of health care. Such a situation creates the possibility of 'physician-induced demand' by doctors who seek to maximize their interests (especially income) rather than provide the efficient level of care (see e.g. Maynard 1983). Thus the downward-sloping demand curve in *Figure 7.1* can be reinterpreted as the doctor's view of the marginal product of health care. The efficient level of care would be at Q_1 where the benefit (product) of health care is equal to its cost at the margin. Because the cost of health care is borne neither by the doctor nor the patient, there is no incentive for either of these parties to select Q_1. The cost of care is met by third parties; by the exchequer in the NHS and by insurers such as BUPA in a private system, who tend to act as bankers, paying on demand.

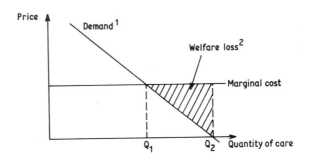

Notes:
1. Demand: this can be interpreted as either
   (a) the marginal benefit curve for health care for the patient – consumer
   or
   (b) the marginal product curve of health care as seen by the doctor – agent.
2. For any consumption past Q_1 the marginal cost exceeds the marginal benefit. The total loss to society due to over-consumption to Q_2 is the shaded welfare loss area.

Figure 7.1 The problem of moral hazard

As a consequence of the agency relationship and third-party-pays, health care systems, public and private, tend to produce inefficient outcomes. In terms of *Figure 1* the efficient level of provision is Q_1 where marginal cost equals margin benefit to the consumer (or in the second version the marginal product as perceived by the doctor). To consume less than Q_1 means that benefits exceed costs at the margin. To consume more than Q_1 means that the costs of an additional unit of care exceeds its benefits.

These attributes of health care systems encourage inefficient use of scarce resources. Providers (doctors), consumers (patients), and funders have little incentive to pursue efficiency. Inefficient behaviour by providers keeps people on waiting lists and increases costs. Inefficient behaviour by consumers has the same effect. However, neither party stands to gain from reductions in such inefficiencies. The funding agencies either pass on the expenditure consequences of decision-making by doctors and patients in the form of high taxes and insurance premiums or seek to control aggregate expenditure, by cash limits and cost containment programmes, with all too little regard to allocative efficiency at the micro-level.

Efficiency in provision

The common problem faced by all health care systems, public and private, is that the incentive structures inherent in these systems are inadequate or perverse. As a consequence economy in the use of resources is a problem to which lip service is paid but which is not achieved.

Why should we be concerned with efficiency? The ubiquitous nature of scarcity means that rationing is unavoidable; all decisions have opportunity costs. A decision to provide more care for the elderly means that there is less to spend on the mentally handicapped. A decision to spend over £9,500 million on Trident leaves less for the NHS and the education system. A decision to spend £2.5 billion on the police leaves us with less to spend on roads.

Scarcity generates an imperative to be efficient, by which is meant choice of those alternatives which are cheapest (minimum input per unit output) and which generate the highest level of benefits (maximizing the value of output per unit of input). Minimizing costs and maximizing benefits creates the maximum amount of benefits or social welfare from the available, inevitably limited, budget.

Without efficiency many ethical problems are created. Inefficiency means that potential patients who could benefit from treatment are deprived of access to health care. Such inefficient behaviour is surely unethical. It is, however, consistent with the individual ethic of the medical profession, to do all that is possible for the patient in care. The role of the economist is to point out that this ethic may result in the commitment of resources to patient 'x' with little benefit and, as a consequence, deprivation of a patient on the waiting list for care from which the benefit might be substantial.

For instance, a doctor may treat a patient in the labour force with low back pain with little effect but substantial cost, particularly in terms of his scarce time, and leave an elderly person with only five years of life left in great pain and discomfort due to the non-provision of a hip replacement procedure. The costs and benefits, in terms of some crude measure of quality adjusted life years (QALYs), of these alternatives need to be quantified and compared. It will be necessary for doctors to give up procedures which are relatively unproductive (e.g. ineffective treatment of low back pain) and this change in behaviour would be efficient and more ethical in terms of the social ethic of the cost-benefit value of alternatives to society.

However, the successful pursuit of greater efficiency is a difficult process. The decision rules for efficient resource allocation are: (a) total benefits exceed total costs, and (b) marginal cost equals marginal benefit. Any project or activity that fails these tests should be abandoned. The first problem for any health care financer or provider who wishes to have efficient practices in his health care system is to identify the costs and benefits, total and marginal, of alternative modes of care. The majority of health care therapies in use today have not been rigorously evaluated and most decision-makers do not know accurately or even approximately the cost-benefit attributes of their behaviour.

As a consequence an essential ingredient into the process of increasing efficiency is the evaluation of options in health care, prevention, and health promotion. Such work is complex and expensive as good clinical trials are difficult to design and execute. However, without this work the stock of knowledge about the relationships between inputs and outcomes will remain inadequate and inefficient practices will continue.

The results of evaluative work will accrue over time. Whilst the stock of input-output knowledge increases what can be done to apply other data to the process of increasing efficiency? Most health care systems seem to collect data they do not use for management (or any other) purposes. In England the Hospital In-Patient Enquiry (HIPE) and Hospital Activity Analysis (HAA) provide data sets which can be manipulated to ask questions about the processes of care (e.g. variations in staffing and lengths of stay) and some of its outcomes (e.g. mortality rates). The use of such data to formulate questions enables managers to probe the unexplored mass of medical practice occurring in health care systems today. The answers to such questions can often only be discovered by clinical trials but if the use of such crude data increases the pressure for such trials they will have proved their worth.

In some areas, for instance primary care, the outputs of the activity are unclear. The bulk of the general practitioner's case-load consists of upper respiratory infections, vomiting and diarrhoea, and depression. Often these complaints are either not very amenable to medical intervention and correct themselves. The average GP with the average case-load gets each year few cancers, few heart attacks, and few examples of other serious illnesses.

How is the general practitioner's efficiency to be evaluated? The inevitable answer is, with difficulty! If it is not possible to analyse input–output links, it is necessary to evaluate input–process links. For instance, what is the appropriate treatment of a patient presenting with a sore throat? If peer group consensus can determine the process of care thought to be the best, this standard can be used as a yardstick by which practices can be evaluated. Only if there is systematic and extensive evaluation of practices can the input–output and input–process links of alter-native patterns of care be identified. Without such work it will be impossible to grope towards the identification of efficient practice. This evaluation of alternative patterns of care is an essential part of the process of identifying efficient practice.

However, while inefficiency may be unethical and its reduction is dependent on the results of careful evaluation of the costs and benefits of clinical practice, such results alone will not improve efficiency. Evaluative work may make it possible to identify efficient practice but how is the behaviour of prac-titioners to be altered in such a way that 'best practice' is adopted by all? You can lead a horse to water but to get it to drink is another matter! In order to persuade inefficient practitioners to adopt the most efficient method of treatment it is necessary to create incentive systems which reward the efficiency-seeking and penalize the inefficiency-supporting.

Such incentives are not easy to identify. Remuneration systems appear to affect behaviour and these effects may or may not be efficiency-inducing. Payment by fee per item of service may increase doctors' work rates (e.g. surgical activity) but such responses may serve their desire to maximize income rather than social welfare (unnecessary surgery may be carried out). Payment by capitation fees may induce the leisure-maximizing physician to ration his patient contact time (e.g. to four or five minutes for a GP consultation). Whether such a consultation period is too long or too short is unclear, but the outcome is consistent with simple theory. Salary systems may create incentives for on-the-job leisure and this can be achieved by the appointment of assistants (junior doctors) who may take some of the consultants' load. The simple conclusion is that utility (satisfaction) maximizing labourers, be they doctors or grave-diggers, do appear to respond in predictable and not necessarily efficient ways to incentives. As a consequence incentive structures have to be created with care in order to achieve outcomes consistent with the goals of the organization.

If a goal of a health care organization is efficiency, what characteristics should be inherent in the incentive system? Answers to this question can only be based on hypothesis because no body of systematic knowledge is available. Once again there is a need for evaluation and this evaluation could be based on innovative experiments.

One such radical innovation available at the level of a complex hypothesis is the labour-managed firm, a US variation of which in health care is the Health Maintenance Organization (see e.g. Luft 1981; Brown 1983). Applying this notion to general practice in Britain we could envisage patients selecting their preferred group practice (PGP) and in exchange for a fee, paid by the state or the insurer, the managers of the PGP would issue an annual contract offering comprehensive health care (carefully defined to include or exclude such things as coronary artery surgery and renal dialysis). The PGP would provide primary care itself and would buy hospital care as and when it was necessary.

What would be the effects of such an arrangement at the level of hypothesis? The income of the PGP would be determined by its ability to attract customers (patients). Any surplus of income over expenditure would be profit for use by the members of the PGP to develop the practice or increase its practitioners' income. This direct cash nexus would create incentives for the managers of the PGP to cost minimize. Thus they would evaluate and monitor each other's performance: inefficiency would reduce the incomes available to them. The PGP doctors would evaluate and monitor hospital stays. Such peer review would increase the pressure to minimize hospital costs (longer lengths of stay cost the PGP money) and, in conjunction with the PGP's ability to 'shop around' amongst competing private and public institutions, would put considerable pressure on hospitals to be efficient. Another potential virtue of the PGP would be that with an annual contract unsatisfied customers could leave at the year's end if they were not satisfied and take their custom elsewhere to a competing PGP.

All these outcomes are mere predictions. Although there is evidence about outcomes for the USA (see Luft 1981) these cannot be transplanted to the UK and are subject to dispute. What are the predicted problems associated with PGP-type structures? First, in an effort to reduce costs, the managers of the PGP may reduce quality. This outcome requires careful evaluation. Second, like the NHS now, the managers of PGPs will ration demand with queues. Will these outcomes be worse than now? Third, how will the customer fee be determined? In some areas (e.g. the countryside) there will be no competition and the PGP, as a monopoly, could inflate its fees. In other areas where there are many PGPs competing for customers, their managers may collude and rig prices. The state can either regulate prices, and experience of state regulation suggests that this is never very satisfactory, or regulate to ensure competition by making advertising legal and encouraging the generation of information to inform customer choice.

Like all proposals the PGP is not without its problems. Its potential virtue is that by creating internal cost-minimizing incentives it may generate evaluation, peer review and greater efficiency in resource usage. Such proposals require elaboration and experimentation with careful evaluation. Only with experimentation and evaluation can the hypotheses inherent in the PGP idea be tested.

The PGP may generate greater efficiency by increasing competition, for instance between the providers of hospital care. To increase efficiency, the use of the weapon of competition is unavoidable. Thus the Conservative government's use of the private tendering option may identify potential economies. The potential drawbacks of this programme are that it may reduce the incomes of people who are already poorly paid and it may be difficult to enforce a private contract and monitor quality. However, if the objective is cost minimization, the inevitable consequence may be the creation of unemployment and reduced provider income. Such outcomes should be mitigated by sensible policies elsewhere, in particular macro-policies of reflation. Any failure to get the desired quality of provision is a reflection on management and such outcomes can be avoided if public use of private cleaning, catering, and laundry firms is monitored and evaluated efficiently.

The main criticism which can be made of the Thatcher government's use of such competitive policies is the conservative way in which they have been used. Why not privatize pathology and pharmacy services? Why not buy in cold surgical services from the private sector? Such private options would give the NHS manager relative cost information which would be invaluable in controlling his labour force (especially the professionals), his costs, and seeking out efficient options.

It is sad that the rhetoric of some socialists prevents them from discovering that competition within a state-financed and controlled health care system is not inconsistent with socialist goals: Lange's advocacy of the use of the price mechanism and competition to direct resource allocation in a socialist state seems remote from many socialists today (Lange and Taylor 1938). It is sad that the rhetoric of some liberals (conservatives) prevents them from using competitive policies more imaginatively to challenge the monopoly rents and unethical inefficiency of many (often highly paid) practitioners. For those interested in efficiency the use of competition to control the monopolistic tendencies of providers, public and private, is consistent with socialist and liberal goals.

Distributional justice

Whilst there may be some agreement between liberals and socialists about the need for efficiency in the provision of health care, there tends to be no such agreement about the rules by which health care should be distributed amongst competing demanders (patients).

Hayek (1976), a liberal much read by politicians, rejects the notion of social or distributional justice as meaningless:

'in a society of free men whose members are allowed to use their own knowledge for their own purposes the term "social justice" is wholly devoid of meaning and content [and] attempts to enforce it (social justice) in a society of free individuals must make that society unworkable. . . . [The] phrase "social justice" is not, as most people probably feel, an innocent expression of goodwill towards the less fortunate, but . . . a dishonest insinuation that one ought to agree to a demand of some special interest which can give no real reason for it. If political discussion is to become honest it is necessary that people should recognise that the term is intellectually disreputable, the mark of demagogy or cheap journalism which responsible thinkers ought to be ashamed to use because, once its vacuity is recognised, its use is dishonest.'

(Hayek 1976; 96–7)

This sharp conclusion is derived from the liberals' belief that freedom should be the supreme goal of any social system. From the pursuit of this goal flows decision-making in decentralized and competitive markets and the minimal state whose role is merely to defend the citizen from foreign and internal law breakers and to enforce contracts. The nature of liberal attitudes to personal responsibility, social concern, equality, and freedom is summarized in *Table 7.1* and is adapted from Donabedian (1971).

This table also summarizes what Hayek believes is the

intellectual dishonesty of socialists. Their primary goal is reduced inequality, a means to a more equitable distribution of the ability to choose and thrive in society. To achieve this, redistribution policies are necessary and this requires the state to circumscribe freedom (e.g. by taxation) so that previously disadvantaged individuals can achieve greater ability to choose and reach greater freedom.

The nuances of the component points of the liberal and socialist positions are complex and closely interlinked. In the political debate they are confused often but in the intellectual debate they are clearly distinguishable in this century in the work of people such as Hayek (1976) and Tawney (1964). Such distinctions have not reconciled the contending normative beliefs of the two parties. Political fashion, influenced by economic events and greater awareness of the weaknesses of the current system of belief as it is translated into policy, fluctuates and this has led to a resurgence in liberal values, set forth so clearly by Hayek, and attempts to 'roll back the state' or privatize the welfare state.

The causes of the reaction to the welfare state merit closer analysis. The destruction of full employment by the oil price hike in the early 1970s coincides with an increased awareness that the efficiency of the component parts of the welfare state in increasing equality was less than satisfactory. The work, for instance, of Atkinson (1969) and subsequently Atkinson, Maynard, and Trinder (1983), showed that the income maintenance system was a less than satisfactory remedy of cross-section poverty and that the effects of the welfare state on intergenerational mobility appeared to be very small. The work of Halsey (e.g. Halsey, Heath, and Ridge 1980) has shown how education inequalities have survived. The work of Sir Douglas Black and his colleagues (DHSS 1980, reprinted in Townsend and Davidson 1982) brought together a body of literature which had accumulated since the late 1960s and which indicated that significant inequalities in health and health care remained over thirty years after the creation of the NHS.

Health is a stock whose initial value is determined by genetic endowment. Over the life-cycle a variety of factors such as income, education, housing, work environment, diet, and exercise, affect that stock and determine health status. The supply and demand for these factors depends on endowments, tastes and costs: low income groups have limited willingness and ability to pay and acquire tastes which affect their perception of costs and benefits at the margin. Thus, the poor tend to smoke more than the rich and this may be in part due to the lack of access to knowledge of substitutes (e.g. Mozart or hill-walking) and discount rates which make it sensible to choose benefits now (smoking) for costs a long way in the future. Equalizing policies might thus concentrate on the factors that determine time preference or discount rates (Fuchs 1982).

Equalizing the use of efficiently produced health care must also take account of time preference, differential endowments and differences in costs. The time costs of using NHS facilities differ between social classes (e.g. a Rowntree's worker will lose wages if he goes to Outpatients, whilst an academic's wage will be unaffected) and may generate the observed class differences in access to and use of the NHS. Countervailing these and other effects may require radical policies which favour the disadvantaged. One characteristic of the NHS has been a reluctance to target policies at least advantaged groups. Such policies in the USA (e.g. Medicare and Medicaid), despite their incompleteness of cover, have, for those covered, proved to be very effective ways of increasing the utilization rates of disadvantaged groups such as blacks and poor whites. More careful targeting of NHS care might mitigate the inequalities shown to exist in the Black Report.

The causes and cures for these inequalities require careful investigation because all too little is known about their characteristics. For instance, the work of Klein and Collins, using General Household Survey (GHS) data concludes that the use of primary care between the social classes shows only minor differences. Le Grand's work (1982) criticizes these findings but they have been repeated in further work by Collins and Klein (1984). The data sets, for instance, the GHS, are less than perfect and results, such as those of Le Grand (1982) which showed that in 1972 an average person in social class I (the rich) for an average illness consumed 40 per cent more NHS resources than an average person for the same illness in social class V (the poor),

Table 7.1

	Liberals	*Socialists*
Personal responsibility	Personal responsibility for achievement is very important, and this is weakened if people are offered unearned rewards. Moreover, such unearned rewards weaken the motive force that assures economic well-being, and in so doing they also undermine moral well-being, because of the intimate connection between moral well-being and the personal effort to achieve.	Personal incentives to achieve are desirable, but economic failure is not equated with moral depravity or social worthlessness.
Social concern	Social Darwinism dictates a seemingly cruel indifference to the fate of those who cannot make the grade. A less extreme position is that charity, expressed and effected preferably under private auspices, is the proper vehicle, but it needs to be exercised under carefully prescribed conditions, for example, such that the potential recipient must first mobilize all his own resources and, when helped, must not be in as favourable a position as those who are self-supporting (the principle of 'lesser eligibility').	Private charitable action is not rejected but is seen as potentially dangerous morally (because it is often demeaning to the recipient and corrupting to the donor) and usually inequitable. It seems preferable to create social mechanisms that create and sustain self-sufficiency and that are accessible according to precise rules concerning entitlement that are applied equitably and explicitly sanctioned by society at large.
Freedom	Freedom is to be sought as a supreme good in itself. Compulsion attenuates both personal responsibility and individualistic and voluntary expressions of social concern. Centralized health planning and a large governmental role in health care financing are seen as an unwarranted abridgment of the freedom of clients as well as	Freedom is seen as the presence of real opportunities of choice, and although economic constraints are less openly coercive than political constraints, they are nonetheless real, and often the effective limits on choice. Freedom is not indivisible but may be sacrificed in one respect in order to obtain greater

	Liberals	Socialists
	of health professionals, and private medicine is thereby viewed as a bulwark against totalitarianism.	freedom in some other. Government is not an external threat to individuals in the society but is the means by which individuals achieve greater scope for action (that is, greater real freedom).
Equality	Equality before the law is the key concept, with clear precedence being given to freedom over equality wherever the two conflict.	Since the only moral justification for using personal achievement as the basis for distributing rewards is that everyone has equal opportunities for such achievement, then the main emphasis is on equality of opportunity, and where this cannot be assured, the moral worth of achievement is thereby undermined. Equality is seen as an extension to the many of the freedom actually enjoyed by only the few.

tend to be quite old. The more thorough investigation of existing data sets and the development and analysis of new data sets are essential if the nature and causes of inequalities in health and health care are to be more fully understood.

Whilst there may be agreement between liberals and socialists to investigate the characteristics of inequality, the policy prescriptions of adherents of the competing ideologies will differ. The liberals will elect for minimal redistribution, preferably by private agencies (see *Table 7.1*), or for minimal redistribution by fiscal means (Friedman 1962). In all cases the term 'minimal' tends not to be defined in any precise fashion and no vehicle to advance and maintain such payments within existing political mechanisms is put forward. The definition of 'minimal' in cross-section, life-cycle and inter-generational terms needs to be confronted more rigorously by liberals and socialists!

Even if some definition of 'minimal' and 'adequate' residual support for the indigent could be arrived at, the use of the price mechanism in the health care market has to be appraised with care. The liberal uses the price mechanism to allocate health care on the basis of willingness and ability to pay. A substantial body of evidence (see e.g. Maynard 1979) has shown that quite small user charges (co-insurance and deductibles) do affect the demand for health care.

Thus, the price mechanism is an effective rationing device in health care markets. The Rand social experiments have shown that by putting a maximum limit on user contributions (e.g. pay the first £250 after which care is free at the point of consumption), health care can be rationed and the financial burden placed on low-income groups mitigated (Newhouse *et al*. 1981). However, the effect of user prices on demand for the input health care is only one part of the story. What is the effect of user prices on the utilization of inputs and what is the effect of changed patterns of utilization on health; the desired outcome? The results of the Rand experiment are complex and disputed. Prices may cut consumption of health care which has little impact on health status. Prices may also cut the consumption of health care whose marginal product is substantial (Brook 1983).

What is the role of user prices in a socialist health care system? The answer to this question must depend on the objectives of that system. Rather than maximizing freedom in decentralized markets like the liberal, and allocating resources on the basis of willingness and ability to pay, the socialist is seeking to allocate resources on the basis of need. Need can be defined as those who can benefit most, in terms of improvements in health status, from health care regardless of willingness and ability to pay.

This definition requires careful analysis. It means that if the choice is to care for a forty-year-old social class I (rich) person over a forty-year-old social class II (not so rich) or V (poor) person, and the use of scarce resources generates more quality-adjusted life years (QALYs) for the social class I person, he will live and the others may die or be left in pain or discomfort.

An obvious objection to this is that this outcome may be the result of inter-generational and life-cycle inequalities which favoured the rich person. Only if those inequalities are mitigated would some socialists accept the preceding decision. If this decision is reversed and the poor person is kept alive, this generates less QALYs and the lost QALYs are an efficiency payment to compensate for preceding inequalities in life chances. How far should such a trade-off be taken?

Looking at health care alone, a decision to follow this socialist rule of maximizing QALYs regardless of willingness and ability to pay may ensure efficiency in the use of resources and implies no role for user prices in the NHS. Indeed, to reduce the time costs to utilization, the use of negative prices (subsidies) may be efficient if they improve access to and use of the NHS by the poor. The idealized and actual characteristics of the NHS and the market are outlined elsewhere (McLachlan and Maynard 1982; Maynard and Williams 1984).

Thus the implications of the liberal and socialist attitudes towards distributional justice are clear. Hayek advocates a minimal state with little role for the NHS, a view reiterated by Minford (1984). The socialist prefers, as a means to his ultimate goal of greater equality, a health care system allocating on the basis of maximizing health status improvements regardless of willingness and ability to pay. This disagreement about ends and means permeates all health care debates and cannot be resolved on scientific grounds. The choice is clear: normative decisions have to be made!

Conclusions

Who pays for welfare? The answer to this question is that it all depends on your ideology.

The liberal, as always seeking to maximize freedom in decentralized and competitive markets with a minimal state, will advocate payment by market mechanisms (i.e. out-of-pocket payments or insurance) with no 'lame duck' subsidies to suppliers or insurers and only the indigent somehow defined, receiving state-financed health care. The socialist, seeking to increase equality and allocate health care to the needy or on the basis of the individual's ability to benefit from care, will advocate payment by the state from tax revenue so that resources are used in a manner consistent with the maximization of improvements in health status regardless of willingness and ability to pay.

The liberal and the socialist may agree on the role of competition and effective incentives to ensure efficiency in the production of health care. However, they will disagree on the use of price (incentive) rules on the demand side of the market. The liberal will use user prices to curb the effects of moral hazard and make consumers be cost minimizers. The socialist, recognizing the problems of physician-induced demand, may advocate the use of the price mechanism to control producers but will accept only a muted role for user charges.

There tends to be a lack of clarity in the ends and means of the competing ideologies. This creates much confusion in public debate and wastes scarce intellectual resources in fruitless arguments which reinvent the wheels of disagreement. Once the goal is chosen, liberal or socialist, it would seem sensible to use such resources to remedy the many defects of the means that exist to achieve that preferred goal but maybe that is the naïve optimism of an academic outside the political arena!

References

Atkinson, A. B. (1969) *Poverty in Britain and the Reform of Social Security.* Cambridge: Cambridge University Press.

Atkinson, A. B., Maynard, A. K., and Trinder, C. G. (1983) *Parents and Children: Income in Two Generations.* London: Heinemann.

Brook, R. (1983) Does Free Care Improve Adults' Health? Results from a Randomized Controlled Trial. *New England Journal of Medicine* 309 (8 December) (23): 1426–33.

Brown, C. V. (1980) *Taxation and the Incentive to Work.* Oxford: Oxford University Press.

Brown, L. (1983) Health Maintenance Organization. Washington, DC: Brooking Institute.

Collins, E. and Klein, R. (1980) Equity and the NHS: Self Reported Morbidity, Access and Primary Care. *British Medical Journal* 281: 1111–15, 6248.

—— (1984) Self Reported Morbidity, Socio-economic Factors and General Practitioner Consultations. Mimeograph, University of Bath.

Department of Health and Social Security (DHSS) (1980) *Inequalities in Health* (The Black Report). London: HMSO.

Donabedian, A. (1971) Social Responsibility for Personal Health Services: An Examination of Basic Values. *Inquiry* 8 (2): 3–19.

Friedman, M. (1962) *Capitalism and Freedom.* Chicago: University of Chicago Press.

Fuchs, V. R. (1982) Time Preference and Health: An Explanatory Study. In V. R. Fuchs (ed.) *Economic Aspects of Health*. Chicago and London: National Bureau of Economic Research, University of Chicago Press.

Godfrey, L. G. (1975) *Theoretical and Empirical Aspects of the Effects of Taxation on the Supply of Labour*. Paris: Organisation for Economic Cooperation and Development Press.

Halsey, A. H., Heath, A. F., and Ridge, J. M. (1980) *Origins and Destinations*. Oxford: Clarendon Press.

Hayek, F. A. (1976) *Law, Legislation and Liberty*: volume 2 *The Mirage of Social Justice*. London: Routledge & Kegan Paul.

Lange, L. and Taylor, F. M. (1938) *On the Economic Theory of Socialism*. Minneapolis, Minn.: University of Minnesota Press.

Le Grand, J. (1982) *The Strategy of Equality*. London: Allen & Unwin.

Luft, H. S. (1981) *Health Maintenance Organisation*: Dimensions of Performance. New York: John Wiley.

McLachlan, G. and Maynard, A. (eds) (1982) *The Public–Private Mix for Health*. London: Nuffield Provincial Hospitals Trust.

Maynard, A. (1979) Pricing, Insurance and the NHS. *Journal of Social Policy* 8: 157–76.

—— (1982) Privatisation and Market Mechanism. In A. Morris and J. Sizer (eds) *Resources and Higher Education*. Research in Higher Education, Monograph 8. Guildford: Society for Research into Higher Education.

—— (1983) The Production of Health and Health Care. *Journal of Economic Studies* 10 (1): 31–45.

Maynard, A. and Williams, A. (1984) Privatisation and the National Health Service. In J. Le Grand and R. Robinson (eds) *Privatisation and the Welfare State*. London: Allen & Unwin.

Minford, P. (1984) State Expenditure: A Study in Waste. *Economic Affairs* (April–June supplement).

Newhouse, J. P. (1981) Some Interim Results from a Controlled Trial of Cost Sharing in Health Insurance. *New England Journal of Medicine* 305 (25): 1501–507.

Tawney, R. H. (1964) *Equality*, 4th ed. London: Allen & Unwin.

Townsend, P. and Davidson, N. (1982) *Inequalities in Health*. Harmondsworth: Penguin.

8

Welfare, redistribution, and inequality – disillusion, illusion, and reality*

MICHAEL O'HIGGINS

Economic prosperity and optimism about the beneficial effects of more extensive social programmes were the Siamese twins of the post-war consensus in British social politics. Not only was increased social expenditure the product of sustained economic growth – leading to Klein's description of the welfare state as the 'residual beneficiary of the Growth State' (1980: 29) – but, for many people, the rationale for the pursuit of growth was the facilitation of the achievement of social aims such as greater equality. Thus, Tony Crosland argued that 'a rapid rate of growth . . . so far from being inconsistent with socialist ideals, is a pre-condition of their achievement' (1956: 288). Given this symbiosis, it is not surprising that recession, or the arrival of the Slow (or No) Growth State, should have caused strains in social spending programmes.

These strains have fairly clear economic and political com-

*This paper draws on research carried out as part of a larger project funded by the Anglo-German Foundation, to whom my thanks are due. In this research I am grateful to Jenny Church of the UK Central Statistical Office for data access, and to Sara Horrell for research assistance.

ponents. On the economic side, the absence of growth eliminates the increment of resources from which increased social expenditure (and thus, it was assumed, increased redistribution) could be financed without cutting into pre-tax living standards. Without growth, redistribution requires real losses for some. Recession compounds this difficulty by increasing claims on social welfare services (most obviously because of increased unemployment) at the same time as it reduces the capacity of income support systems to maintain benefits without increasing tax or social insurance contribution rates on those still in work. The current recession coincides with a period when the effects of an ageing population are further increasing the claims on income maintenance and health and social services in the UK.

This twofold economic effect is mirrored by the impact of recession on political responses to redistribution and social security. The economic insecurity which accompanies recession may reduce the willingness of taxpayers to accept tax increases in order to fund welfare. Perhaps more importantly, however, the social welfare system may itself come to be seen as a cause of recession if it is believed to contribute to slower economic growth because of disincentive effects or a reduced willingness to adapt to technical change.

It might have been expected that these greater difficulties would have led to discussion and re-evaluation of how to make progress towards equality and other social aims despite a static economy. This indeed was the response of Crosland, for so long previously synonymous with the 'Redistribution through Growth' thesis. He considered the question of 'what could be advanced within the framework of reduced public spending?' (1982: 357) and argued that the appropriate strategy was to '(1) choose and *announce* limited number of priorities; (2) create sense that still have a *vision* despite constraints' (1982: 306).

In other quarters, however, the economic and political stresses appear to have been accompanied by what may be termed an intellectual crisis of belief in the effectiveness and impact of state social welfare and, in particular, an egalitarian scepticism about its redistributive impact. Writing in an international context, Delcourt specifically identifies the parallel natures of the fiscal and intellectual crises:

'Two complementary explanations of what some call the crisis of the welfare state and others call its change of character, are increasingly accepted. One lies in the now chronic imbalance between social expenditure and available receipts. The other may be deduced from the mounting criticism of the effectiveness of social policy as regards both delivery and redistribution and of what economists and sociologists call its perverse effects.'

(Delcourt 1982: 61)

In Britain, this 'mounting criticism' is reflected in Taylor-Gooby's conclusion that: 'a growing body of academic work shows increasing disillusion with the achievements of state welfare and pessimism about its potential for achieving redistribution to those in need' (1982: 345).

Some of this British disillusion arises from a general concern with the failure of state services to equalize opportunities for control or participation (e.g. Hadley and Hatch 1981), although it may be argued that this failure simply reflects the relative neglect of participation in the Fabian tradition of thought on egalitarianism and welfare (Gutmann 1980). Green links this concern to more traditional criticisms of state activity: 'state provision of services [*funded through taxation*] prevents the emergence of a wide variety of organisational types. Taxation compels people to pay for a method of providing services selected by the government and thereby denies them the resources which make self-organisation possible' (1982: 38).

More particularly, however, British egalitarian critics focus on the redistributive impact of the state. Townsend and Davidson note that 'despite more than thirty years of a National Health Service expressly committed to offering equal care for all, there remains a marked class gradient in standards of health' (1982: 15) and suggest that in certain respects these inequalities had increased rather than diminished. Taylor-Gooby, after reviewing the evidence, argues 'it is in the area of cash benefits if anywhere that we should look for evidence of welfare state redistribution. The evidence that we have indicates that the egalitarian dreams of post-war reformers have been rudely shattered by reality' (1983: 109). Le Grand (1982) documents evidence suggesting that spending on free or subsidized public

services (health, education, housing, and transport) benefits the
rich more than the poor, and may even fail to reduce inequality.
Thus, the strategy of equality – the pursuit of equality by
redistribution through social services – is said to have failed.

These intellectual critiques of state social expenditure and
redistribution appear to be mirrored in recent British survey
evidence of popular perceptions on redistribution. When asked
who got the 'best value for money from the system of taxes and
benefits taken as a whole', non-manual workers, high income
earners and Conservative supporters were more likely to respond
'low income groups'; manual workers, lower income groups and
Labour supporters plumped for high income groups. As Taylor-
Gooby reports, 'there was . . . a strong relationship between
household income and a tendency to think that the state welfare
system as a whole benefits other income groups' (1982: 337–38).
At a time of significant fiscal stress, therefore, the basis of support
for state welfare spending appears peculiarly weak: it is
ideologically vulnerable from both left and right and it cannot
rely on the perceived self-interest of either rich or poor for its
defence. Yet, as this chapter demonstrates, much of this
egalitarian critique is misplaced, both conceptually and
empirically. Whilst the welfare state may not, in Westergaard's
terms, achieve 'substantive equality of condition' it brings about
a significant measure of 'diffuse redistribution' (1978: 84–93). In
particular, the distribution of resources through state welfare is
markedly more equal than the distribution of market-generated
income.

This paper first outlines and discusses the conceptual weaknesses of the egalitarian critique of state welfare and continues by
presenting the most recent empirical evidence on welfare and
redistribution. This then provides a basis for a concluding consideration of the likely distributive impact of a variety of possible
initiatives to reduce the role of the state in welfare by
privatization.

Welfare and equality: disillusion and illusion

Before considering new empirical data on the distributive impact
of welfare it is important to specify why the conventional

egalitarian analyses and conclusions are deficient. In a previous paper (O'Higgins 1983) I suggested three possible sources of deficiency – interpretational inadequacies, inappropriate counter-factuals, and illusory expectations – and this discussion expands and elaborates on that argument.

First, many analyses of distribution and redistribution do not take account of the different compositions of the income units – the fact that an income unit such as a household may consist of such varied elements as a single pensioner, a couple with children or four adults sharing a dwelling. Since the size of the income unit consistently increases with the income of the unit the top half of the distribution of income units generally consists of between three-fifths and two-thirds of the individuals in the households (O'Higgins 1983: 174–75). The explanation therefore, for the conclusion cited by Taylor-Gooby, that 'benefits in kind (education, housing, the NHS) provide more in absolute terms to the better off' (1983: 106), is that the conclusion is based on the amounts being received by the bigger income units, who are not necessarily those with higher living standards. In fact, the distribution of education benefits across households closely mirrors the distribution of children, whilst the distribution of NHS benefits is more favourable to lower income households than would be the case if it were allocated purely by household size (because of the predominance of pensioners, who make greater use of the NHS, in lower income households) (O'Higgins 1983: table 1; 1985: tables 6 and 7).

Taking account of household size and composition affects not only conclusions about the degree of redistribution in the fairly straightforward manner suggested above. It also significantly alters the rank order of households and individuals in any measure of economic welfare, and therefore renders suspect, particularly for policy evaluation or planning, any measures of redistribution based upon a rank ordering of unadjusted income. This point is illustrated in *Table 8.1* which is a matrix of households organized by deciles of unadjusted and of equivalent market income.

The data indicate that less than half of all households remain in the same decile when their economic welfare is measured by equivalent as compared to unadjusted income. There is rela-

Table 8.1   *The distribution of households by deciles of unadjusted and of equivalent market household income, 1982*

deciles of equivalent market income

	1	2	3	4	5	6		8	9	10	% of households All
1	9.84	0.16	0	0	0	0	0	0	0	0	10
2	0.15	8.70	1.16	0	0	0	0	0	0	0	10
3	0	1.16	7.14	1.64	0.05	0	0	0	0	0	10
4	0	0	1.56	4.28	2.03	0.90	1.02	0.22	0	0	10
5	0	0	0.15	2.85	2.36	2.07	0.58	1.00	1.00	0	10
6	0	0	0	0.96	3.47	1.88	1.83	0.77	0.66	0.43	10
7	0	0	0	0.26	1.44	2.73	1.70	2.50	0.46	0.92	10
8	0	0	0	0.01	0.51	1.75	2.68	1.49	2.92	0.62	10
9	0	0	0	0	0.13	0.61	1.72	2.68	2.19	2.67	10
10	0	0	0	0	0	0.05	0.47	1.33	2.77	5.37	10
All	10	10	10	10	10	10	10	10	10	10	100

deciles of unadjusted market income (row axis label)

Source: Analyses of Family Expenditure Survey data.
Note: An equivalence scale value was calculated for each household by assigning a weight of 0.6 to the first adult in each household, 0.4 to each subsequent adult and 0.3 to each child. The household's equivalent income was then calculated by dividing its income by this equivalence scale value.

tively little change in the bottom two deciles, but a full two-thirds of all other households are affected; in the fifth to the ninth deciles less than one in four households is in the same income decile on both measures. These sizeable differences mean that criticisms of the redistributive impact of social welfare based on analyses of unadjusted income data may be quite misleading and unnecessarily pessimistic.

A second possible source of egalitarian disillusionment is that there is a confusion about the precise nature of the egalitarian objectives of particular parts of the welfare system. In particular, the different forms of equality which might be policy objectives are inadequately distinguished and thus the possible conflicts between them are left unresolved. This can be illustrated by reference to Rae's distinction between marginal and global egalitarianism where marginal implies distributing a particular good or service equally, whilst global implies distributing it unequally in order to counteract pre-existing inequalities and thereby achieve a more equal overall distribution of resources

(1981: ch. 3). Since some of the major elements of state welfare, such as the NHS, child benefit and parts of state education, are designed to promote marginal egalitarianism they will not, therefore, seem particularly effective if judged by criteria of global egalitarianism.

In this connection it is particularly relevant to return to Crosland's original arguments for public expenditure as a vehicle to social equality. Whilst emphasizing his view that the primary purpose of social services is the relief of distress, he defines social equality as an 'important subsidiary objective' (Crosland 1956: 88) and is explicit about the egalitarian impact he expects from state welfare services:

'If the state provides schools and hospitals, teachers and doctors, on a generous scale and of a really high quality, then *the result will be, not indeed a greater equality of real incomes, but certainly a greater equality in manners and the texture of social life . . .* the fact that people of every class go to the same school and use the same hospital facilities . . . is an immensely important influence in creating a sense of social equality and lack of privilege.'

(Crosland 1956: 85, emphasis added)

The NHS, in other words, is expected to promote equality by reducing social differentiation not by equalizing incomes. One may disagree with this strategy of equality but with around 95 per cent of the population using the NHS it can hardly be argued to have failed in its own terms. Global egalitarianism neither was nor could be the policy objective of the NHS: to expect it to promote equality, other than in access to health care, is to expect something for which it is neither designed nor capable.

This directly leads to the third possible explanation of welfare disillusionment, which is that it may reflect no more than the illusory nature of some previous expectations about the scope for increasing equality through welfare spending. This explanation follows Klein's argument: 'the disillusion of the Left is largely self-inflicted: it rests on an inadequate analysis of the political and economic framework of social policy' (1980: 25). Welfare spending may thus be conspicuously egalitarian in its impact but it is only one element of people's incomes. Income from the market, with its inegalitarian distribution, is still the major source of income for most households. The impact of welfare can only be reasonably evaluated, therefore, within the context of and by comparison to the inequalities generated by market incomes.

Having argued that these three factors of interpretational inadequacies, inappropriate counter-factuals and illusory expectations may have contributed to a distorted and unduly pessimistic interpretation of the impact of social expenditure on equality, the next section is duly wary of these factors in presenting and examining the empirical evidence on the distribution of market and welfare incomes.

Income inequalities in 1982

Table 8.2 sets out the most recent available data on the composition of the income distribution and the shares of various income sources going to different parts of the distribution. All of the income data are equivalent income: that is, they have been adjusted to take account of differences in household size and composition, and so measure (approximately) the living standards experienced by different households. Although the households, and hence the quintiles, still differ in size and composition, the effect of the adjustment is such that the individuals and households in each quintile would have similar living standards if each quintile had an equal (20 per cent) share of equivalent income.

The rank ordering of the households, from which the five quintiles are constructed, is based on their equivalent market income – in other words, it reflects the order of living standards arising from the distribution of rewards through the market. This is not to say that this is what the distribution would have been if social welfare programmes did not exist. In the absence of state redistribution through, for example, social insurance, people would make other arrangements to provide for contingencies such as retirement, sickness, and unemployment. Similarly, market incomes include salary and job pensions paid by the state; if doctors, teachers or civil servants were privatized the

Table 8.2   *Income inequalities in the UK in 1982*

equivalent quintile shares (%) of:	quintiles of equivalent market income						
	bottom	2nd	3rd	4th	top	av. nos	as % of av. gross income
children	12.4	25.2	34.3	20.0	8.1	0.7	
adults who are:	14.9	19.3	22.5	22.9	20.5	2.0	
working	0.6	11.7	25.3	30.9	31.5	1.10	
unemployed during year	9.7	33.1	28.2	19.2	9.9	0.11	
long-term unemployed	55.7	18.8	13.5	8.8	3.2	0.05	
retired	45.8	31.6	10.3	7.5	4.8	0.39	
unoccupied	20.8	25.0	27.1	17.9	9.2	0.35	
primary earnings	0.1	6.7	19.2	26.7	47.3		57.1
other earnings	0.0	2.6	12.1	29.6	55.8		15.0
investment income	3.9	15.6	11.6	20.7	48.3		4.6
occupational pensions	4.6	30.4	19.2	20.6	25.3		4.2
retirement pensions	49.7	32.6	8.2	6.0	3.5		9.2
child benefit	13.1	24.0	33.1	20.8	9.1		1.7
unemployment benefits	22.6	34.0	21.3	14.7	7.4		0.9
supplementary benefits	79.4	12.9	4.5	2.3	1.0		3.0
market income	0.6	8.0	17.5	26.5	47.5		81.7
cash benefits	48.0	28.2	11.7	8.0	4.2		18.3
gross income	9.3	11.7	16.4	23.1	39.6		£7,309
direct taxes	0.2	5.4	16.2	26.6	51.7		18.5
disposable income	11.3	13.1	16.5	22.3	36.9		81.5
indirect taxes	11.6	15.0	17.9	23.2	32.4		20.6

Source: Analyses of Family Expenditure Survey data.

Notes:
1. The households are ranked on the basis of household equivalent market income, the value of which, like all other income and tax values, is derived by dividing the unadjusted figure by an equivalence scale value. The calculation of this value is explained in the footnote to *Table 8.1*.
2. Market income is all cash income apart from social security benefits. Gross income is original income plus these cash benefits. Disposable income is gross income less direct taxes.
3. Working adults are self-employed or employed for at least nine months in the year prior to interview; correspondingly those 'unemployed during year' were away from work for more than three months of that year. An unoccupied adult is one who is under the minimum pension age and is not seeking employment or has been out of paid employment for more than five years.

distribution of market income would be unlikely to remain unaltered. Nonetheless, the distributional differences between market and welfare incomes are a reasonable indicator of their relative priorities, and the rank order locations of different types of individuals in *Table 8.2* describes the pattern of 'gainers' and 'losers' arising from the current operation of the market.

The data indicate starkly the extent to which working adults are more likely than any other individuals to be found in the households with higher living standards. Almost two-thirds of all working adults were in the better-off 40 per cent of households, whilst less than one in eight were in the bottom 40 per cent. Conversely, more than half the long-term unemployed and almost one half of retired adults were in the bottom fifth of households. Children are under-represented in the top quintile, but they are particularly concentrated in the middle and lower middle parts of the distribution, rather than at the very bottom.

The distribution of market incomes

The data in *Table 8.2* show the extent to which all sources of market income primarily benefit better-off households. This is particularly true of earnings, about half of which go to house-holds in the top quintile with a little more than a quarter to the next quintile and the remainder (slightly less than a quarter) to the bottom three quintiles. Within earnings, the distribution of primary earnings (that is, income earned by the household member whose earnings are highest) is slightly less skewed towards better-off households than the distribution of other earnings, indicating that such secondary earnings are especially important in explaining inequalities in living standards. Many of the best-off households, in other words, are those with two or more earners.

The distribution of investment income over the five quintiles is somewhat less unequal than that of primary earnings; although the top quintile receives a marginally greater share of the former, households in the bottom two quintiles fare better, and those in the third and fourth worse from investment income than from primary earnings. Over the bulk of households, therefore, investment income serves to reduce the inequalities generated by earnings. (If the discussion related to income bands narrower than quintiles, such as deciles or semi-deciles, this conclusion would have to be more heavily qualified at the top of the distribution.)

The other major source of market incomes is occupational pensions. Since the passage of the Social Security (Pensions) Act 1975 occupational pension schemes are an explicit part of public policy about welfare, with membership of either the state earnings-related pension scheme or an approved occupational pension scheme being mandatory, and occupational pension schemes subject to both regulation and subsidization by the state. The implications for inequality of this interaction and of possible changes in it are further discussed below. While this legislation will render it increasingly less appropriate to regard occupational pensions simply as market incomes, the data presented in *Table 8.2* relate to occupational pensions already in payment and, therefore, are mostly not specifically affected by this legislation. They show that all quintiles except the bottom significantly benefit from this income source, with the greatest impact being in the second quintile.

Occupational pensions are, therefore, particularly important in determining which pensioners have living standards above the level of the bottom quintile of households. However, while their dis-tribution is more egalitarian over the quintiles than that of other market income sources, it is sharply inegalitarian when compared to the distribution of retired adults which represents, albeit imperfectly, the group of individuals who might receive these pensions. Thus, although the second quintile receives a large share of the living standards funded by occupational pensions, the top quintile receives five times as great a share as the bottom, despite having only around one-tenth as many retired adults. Occupational pensions, therefore, serve to reduce the average inequality between retired and non-retired adults but increase inequality amongst the retired.

Earnings are the dominant source of market incomes; primary earnings alone account for about 70 per cent of all market incomes while for total earnings the figure is close to 90 per cent. The overall distribution of market incomes is therefore very similar to the earnings distribution, and constitutes the basic pattern of inequality against which to examine the impact of income transfers from welfare.

The distribution of transfer incomes

The distributive impacts of the other major components of the cash benefit system, as well as of all cash transfers in aggregate, are also shown in *Table 8.2.* The pattern for each of the components is largely explained by the benefit target group. The shares of retirement pensions and of child benefit are determined by the quintile shares of retired people and of children. The distribution of unemployment benefit is broadly similar to that of shorter-term unemployment, since those unemployed for more than a year are ineligible for this benefit. The income source the biggest share of which goes to low-income households is supplementary benefit, which is means-tested.

These and other components contribute to a distribution of cash benefits which is almost exactly the reverse with respect to quintile living standards as that of market incomes. Almost one half of equivalent cash benefits go to the bottom quintile, just as almost a half of equivalent market incomes go to the top; the second from bottom quintile receives just over a quarter of cash benefits, as does the second from top of market incomes; the reverse shares are exactly equal in the fourth quintile (cash benefits) and the second (market incomes). The symmetry is only slightly flawed by the fact that the top quintile is more favourably treated by cash benefits than the bottom by market incomes.

That these cancelling patterns do not lead to quintile equality in equivalent gross income shares is due, of course, to the much greater share of gross income accounted for by market incomes as against cash transfers, the latter amounting to just 18.3 per cent of average gross income in 1982. Nonetheless, the inclusion of cash benefits gives the bottom quintile of households a 9.3 per cent share of equivalent gross income, as against a share more than four times as large, 39.6 per cent, for the top quintile. Moreover, a more detailed examination of the income distribution over a period of years indicates that, whilst market inequality increased significantly during the recession, the effect of cash benefits sharply limited the extent to which gross incomes became more equal: while the top quintile share of equivalent market income increased by more than 3 percentage points between 1976 and 1982 the increase in its gross income share was just over 1 percentage point (O'Higgins 1985: table 8).

Cash benefits do not, therefore, go anywhere close to bringing about global equality, in Rae's sense, of living standards but they are markedly global egalitarian in their impact. This conclusion is in sharp contrast to that reached by Taylor-Gooby (see above p. 164).

The interpretation offered here suggests that this conclusion is based on illusions – or dreams – about the impact of welfare in a mixed economy. Transfer incomes are markedly more egalitarian than income distributed through the market, but the market – and employment in particular – is still the major determinant of inequality. A substantial reduction in inequality therefore requires either a reduction in the role of the market or a reduction of inequalities within it.

Inequality and welfare privatization

The analysis thus far has suggested that the major in-kind welfare services, the NHS and most of the education system, are generally marginal egalitarian in their impact – that is, they are used equally by individuals at different income levels – whilst cash benefits are, overall, highly redistributive towards lower income groups. Any form of welfare privatization which simply took the form of a reduced role for the state and an increased role for the market, with their relative distributive impacts unchanged, would, therefore, clearly increase inequality.

The major possible forms of welfare privatization are, however, unlikely to have such a simple incremental character, and the following analysis suggests that both the subject and form of privatization and the nature of the distributive target need to be carefully specified before any conclusions can be reached. In particular, the provision, financing, and regulatory roles of the state need to be distinguished. It is also necessary, as I have argued in detail elsewhere, to separate services in kind such as education and the NHS from cash services like social security in order to examine the implications of welfare privatization (O'Higgins 1985: 129–30).

For welfare services, privatization may be broadly defined as *an increase in the proportionate role of either or both private production or private finance.* According to Crosland's social differentiation perspective on the egalitarian role of these services, neither increase need automatically be inegalitarian: provided that, for example, the contracting out of certain NHS services (within the ambit of the NHS) or the use of higher or more extensive charges to finance part of the NHS do not reduce the proportion of the population currently or prospectively relying on the NHS for their health care they are not inegalitarian developments by this criterion.

On the other hand, any privatization of health or education services which took the form of requiring a significant proportion of the population to purchase these services privately while leaving residual state services for the remaining, poorer, part of the population would be judged inegalitarian by this standard. By a distributive criterion, however, such residual state services would now be significantly more redistributive towards lower income groups (since only they would now benefit from these state services), so that such privatization would appear to be a shift from a marginal to a more comprehensive global egalitarian approach to welfare. This apparent clash between differentiation and distributive criteria is, however, likely to be eliminated once distributive criteria are applied to the overall distribution of health or education services. While this form of privatization might increase the egalitarian impact of state spending, it would probably increase inequality in access to and the distribution of total health care or education provision, since the increased role for the very much more unequal market sector would be expected to outweigh the increased redistributive focus of the state sector. (It is not, however, certain that this would always be the case; if it were not then distributive and differentiation criteria of egalitarianism would be in conflict.) The redistributive impact of state services is one policy criterion, but it is part of and cannot properly be examined except in the context of the wider distribution of services and resources, whether through the state or the market.

This point applies equally to the rather different case of social security, where privatization options relate only to the quantity or source of income to be transferred. Elsewhere, in an analysis upon which the following draws heavily, I identified four forms of social security privatization: benefit erosion, benefit inadequacy, compulsory private insurance and mandated third-party coverage (O'Higgins 1984). The first three of them may be dealt with briefly. The first two forms – reducing the real value of benefits or failing to increase them in line with public expectations, thereby increasing the pressure for private market benefit arrangements – would, following the earlier distributive analysis, be expected to increase inequality. The effects of the third form, compulsory private insurance, could not be predicted without knowing the pattern of benefits payable and the nature and degree of credit or subsidy, if any, offered to low-income individuals in order to allow them to acquire coverage.

The fourth option, mandated third-party coverage, is worth dealing with in more detail since it is the most relevant to recent and prospective British experience of social security privatization, is closer to the conventional interpretation of privatization in the context of services in kind and, by suggesting circumstances where privatization might increase equality, emphasizes the importance of separating issues of the structure of provision from those of distributive impact in the analysis of welfare, whether public or private.

Mandated third-party coverage describes situations where the government may require third parties, usually employers, to organize or provide income security coverage. The two major examples of this policy in the UK are sick pay, where a degree of privatization was brought about from April 1983 onwards by requiring employers to pay specified levels of benefit for the first eight weeks of sickness, and earnings-related pensions, where the 1975 legislation mentioned earlier required provision for all employees but left a choice as to whether it would be private (occupational pensions) or public (the state earnings-related pension scheme). It has been argued that social security privatization should be extended by reducing the state's involvement with earnings-related pensions (Adam Smith Institute 1982).

Technically it is possible that the privatization of either sick pay or earnings-related pensions could increase *or* decrease the overall degree of income inequality. Prior to privatization in 1983, many employees were entitled to occupational sick pay as well as the state sickness benefit, but the distribution of occupational benefit entitlements closely resembled the distribution of market incomes: in general, higher paid or higher status employees were entitled to have a higher proportion of their normal earnings reimbursed for longer periods of sickness and with fewer conditions about length of service. Privatization could have been used to require higher minimum levels of benefit for all employees thus diminishing the degree of inequality in the distribution of occupational benefits.

The current structure of earnings-related pensions facilitates the coexistence of state and private pensions through a compromise which offers to those on higher incomes quite significant benefits from public funds because of the underwriting by the state of the guarantees of index-linking of pension values offered to those who are contracted out of the state scheme. This underwriting significantly increases the prospective cost of the scheme to the state and reduces its redistributive impact (Creedy 1982: ch. 6; Hemming and Kay 1982). State responsibilities or spending could be reduced by weakening those indexing guarantees or shifting more of their costs onto occupational pension schemes; this in turn might lead to less generous occupational provision for those contracted out. Privatization and public spending cuts may therefore be compatible with an increase in egalitarian distributive impact.

These arguments refer only to what is technically possible, not to what is actually likely to occur in particular political economies. In the case of sick pay, privatization was intended not to decrease the inequality of unregulated private welfare but simply to reduce the role of the state. Egalitarian options were not pursued, not because they never exist with privatization but because the political values generating the pressures for privatization are not seeking egalitarian impact. There is no reason to believe this conclusion will apply to any less an extent to the outcome in practice of any attempt to privatize pensions.

The existence, however technical, of such egalitarian options through privatization nonetheless demonstrates that where public and private income sources coexist and interact, a focus only on the state or the distributive impact of state services is inadequate. Policy impacts can be properly examined only within the context of the total distribution of resources.

Within that context, as this analysis has shown, state services are broadly egalitarian and state cash benefits markedly redistributive towards lower income groups. This does not suggest an uncritical defence of all aspects of current spending or provision: some parts are not particularly vertically redistributive, and it would even be possible to increase egalitarian impact by some forms of privatization. It does demonstrate, however, that in terms of restricting inequality, welfare services are performing as well as might reasonably be expected in achieving the somewhat confused aims set for them. More importantly for the future, perhaps, it suggests a need for greater clarity about both the definition of welfare objectives (including distributive and other aspects of equality and the possible conflicts between them) and the identification of how best to pursue them. If the continuation of a high degree of inequality is the product not of the failure of welfare services but of the magnitude of market inequalities, then the defence of welfare objectives requires more than a simple defence of welfare services. It requires that social policy analysis and formulation focus upon means of achieving these objectives through both the market and the state.

References

Adam Smith Institute (1982) *Privatising Pensions*. London.
Creedy, J. (1982) *State Pensions in Britain*. Cambridge: Cambridge University Press.
Crosland, C. A. R. (1956) *The Future of Socialism*. London: Jonathan Cape. Page references are to the revised 1964 edition.
Crosland, S. (1982) *Tony Crosland*. London: Jonathan Cape.

Delcourt, J. (1982) Social Policy – Crisis or Mutation? *Labour and Society* 7 (1): 61–89.

Green, D. (1982) *The Welfare State: For Rich or For Poor?* London: Institute of Economic Affairs.

Gutmann, A. (1980) *Liberal Equality.* Cambridge: Cambridge University Press.

Hadley, R. and Hatch, S. (1981) *Social Welfare and the Failure of the State.* London: Allen & Unwin.

Hemming, R. and Kay, J. (1982) The Cost of the State Earnings-Related Pension Scheme. *Economic Journal* 92 (366): 320–40.

Klein, R. (1980) The Welfare State: A Self Inflicted Crisis? *Political Quarterly* 51 (1): 24–34.

Le Grand, J. (1982) *The Strategy of Equality: Redistribution and the Social Services.* London: Allen & Unwin.

O'Higgins, M. (1983) Issues of Redistribution in State Welfare Spending. In M. Loney, D. Boswell, and J. Clarke (eds) *Social Policy and Social Welfare.* Milton Keynes: Open University Press, 171–82.

—— (1984) Privatisation and Social Security. *Political Quarterly* 55 (2): 129–39.

—— (1985) Inequality, Redistribution and Recession: The British Experience 1976–1982. *Journal of Social Policy* 14 (3).

Rae, D. (1981) *Equalities.* Cambridge, Mass.: Harvard University Press.

Taylor-Gooby, P. (1982) Two cheers for the Welfare State: Public Opinion and Private Welfare. *Journal of Public Policy* 2 (4): 319–46.

—— (1983) The Distributional Compulsion and the Moral Order of the Welfare State. In A. Ellis and K. Kumar (eds) *Dilemmas of Liberal Democracies: Studies in Fred Hirsch's Social Limits to Growth.* London: Tavistock: 98–121.

Townsend, P. and Davidson, N. (1982) *Inequalities in Health.* Harmondsworth: Penguin.

Westergaard, J. (1978) Social Policy and Class Inequality; Some Notes on Welfare State Limits. In R. Miliband and J. Saville (eds) *The Socialist Register 1978.* London: Merlin, 71–99.

PART THREE
CONSUMERS
AND VICTIMS

9
Social welfare and the Thatcher administration
ROBERT PINKER

Key trends and issues in social welfare

In June 1983 under the leadership of Mrs Thatcher the Conservative Party was returned to office with an increased majority in the House of Commons. The Labour Party suffered almost the worst electoral defeat in its history and the Liberal-Social Democratic Alliance failed to win more than a handful of seats even though it polled nearly as many votes as Labour.

In this essay I will discuss some of the implications of this second consecutive victory of the Conservative Party for the future of the British welfare state. Since 1979, radical changes have occurred in British industry while the basic structure of the statutory social services – apart from housing – has remained substantially unchanged. There are now clear signs that these services are about to be subjected to a searching review, with the possible introduction of fundamental changes which would profoundly affect the long-term relationship between work and welfare in our society.[1]

The government is ideologically committed to the promotion

of private and voluntary welfare initiatives, while insisting that it wants to preserve a statutory welfare system, and it has to find a way of reconciling these two objectives. The substantive issues would be the same for any government. First, there is the already massive and still rising cost of pensions and other social services for the growing proportion of elderly people. Second, there are all the costs and other claims relating to over three million registered unemployed people. Third, there is the problem of decayed inner city areas suffering from multiple deprivation. Fourth, there is the problem of poverty and low wages among a substantial minority of families in the United Kingdom. All these claims emerge in the context of an economy which has experienced a severe recession.

The government claims that its policies are beginning to achieve results, despite obvious setbacks. During 1981 many manufacturing companies became more competitive, raising output per worker by an impressive 10 per cent. As this was achieved by reducing the work-force and cutting labour costs, such companies are unlikely to jeopardize their prospects for recovery by taking on more workers in the future. Higher productivity is seen as the only road to recovery, although for some people the personal costs are bound to be high. The government also draws attention to its success in forcing down the average level of pay settlements in the public sector during the past year and on having maintained a generally tough line with the trade unions. Those who have jobs will benefit if the rate of inflation continues to fall. Despite signs of a gradual improvement, however, there are doubts that the rate of recovery will be sufficient to reduce the level of unemployment over the next year, and the more pessimistic analysts are predicting further recession (Hutton 1983).

The option of raising tax levels would probably be limited even if we had a different government, but Mrs Thatcher's administration is committed to the reduction of taxes over the next five years. It is a central tenet of government thinking that further increases in taxation would reduce incentives, discourage economic recovery, and thus have indirect but adverse effects on the poor. In addition social welfare claims on the public purse have to be set against those of defence, which are considerable and certain to rise over the next few years. Despite these problems Mrs Thatcher reiterates that she does not intend to cut welfare expenditure and that in particular 'The National Health Service is safe in our hands'.

Several factors contribute to the continuing popularity of the Thatcher administration. There is no doubt that in relative terms a large minority of British citizens are poor – poorer than they were in 1979. But the majority are not poor. As it was in the 1930s, the real distinction is between those who have jobs and those who do not. Inflation is the other major threat to welfare. Although it is under control for the time being, there is, as there was at the time of the general election, widespread anxiety about the likely consequences of economic reflation, fuelled by a new round of increases in public expenditure.

Furthermore the collectivist and redistributionist welfare policies which were almost bipartisan throughout the 1960s and 1970s have lost some of their electoral appeal. Some indication of the present political mood is given by Brian Walden (a former Labour MP), writing in the *Standard*: 'The third evil of the Welfarist Ideology [out of a list of six] is to implant in the minds of some the belief that the gratification of their material needs is, in all circumstances, a moral imperative for their society' (Walden 1983).

A government may impose welfare cuts because it believes that they are a necessary if regrettable short-term expedient. When economic conditions improve, it can then increase welfare expenditure as resources permit. Alternatively it may take the view that the recovery of economic prosperity has occurred *because of* cuts in welfare budgets, and that it would therefore be sensible to safeguard future prosperity by making *further* cuts in public expenditure – to the point at which selectivity becomes the rule rather than the exception, and the broad framework of universalist services is effectively dismantled.

How far the government is determined to go in these directions remains a matter of debate. In September 1982 the cabinet debated a major policy document on the social services prepared by the Central Policy Review Staff (the 'Think Tank'). The gist of this confidential report was that for the foreseeable future public expenditure will continue to absorb 45 per cent of gross domestic product – only 1 per cent less than it did in the highest year during the last Labour government. The report argued that more radical cuts required more radical policies and it outlined proposals for major reductions in public spending on education, health care, and defence; it also recommended that the link between social security benefit levels and the rate of inflation should be abandoned.

The contents of the report were leaked to the press. It appears that the cabinet had been sharply divided, with possibly a majority of members opposing the proposals, which is not surprising, since the implications of the proposals would affect every home in the country. One of the features of universalist services is that the better services are used as much by the better off as by the poorest – if not more. Since the report was leaked the prime minister has denied any such radical intentions (*Economist* 1982), adding that the report was merely a discussion paper.

Having won a second term of office, the government announced in the House of Commons in July 1983 that it would undertake a major review of the British welfare state, starting with social security. A comprehensive survey is long overdue; we have not had one since the publication of the Beveridge Report in 1942. The review will undoubtedly provoke intense debate on the aims of social policy, the relationship between social policy and economic policy, and the extent of collective obligation with regard to the effects of social change, particularly in the case of vulnerable individuals and minorities. Conflicts of opinion on these issues are bound to become increasingly polarized now that the Conservative and Labour parties are both moving away from the central ground of British politics.

There is, for example, a basic disagreement between institutionalists (who want social policies to serve radically redistributive ends) and residualists (who do not). In general terms the social services of any society reflect differing views about the relationship between collective provision and individual forms of self-help as well as the criteria of eligibility for collectively financed help. These questions of proportion and degree arise in *all* complex industrial societies. There are no instances of any such society completely refusing to make any collective provision. Similarly there are no instances of any such society minimizing the importance of voluntary service or individual self-help. As social policies tend to develop over time in a largely piecemeal manner, few welfare systems are un-equivocally institutional or residual in character, although there are times in every nation's history when governments make radical attempts to change the established pattern.

There is also conflict between the view that social policies ought to be inclusive, meeting an agreed range of needs or states of dependency without reference to the cause of need or dependency, and the view that there should be discrimination between 'deserving' and 'undeserving' cases, judged according to whether the need or state of dependency could have been avoided through personal forethought and self-help.

The moral implications of the latter approach are examined in Titmuss's defence of the principle of universality in *Commitment to Welfare*. He points out that:

'If the causal agents of need cannot be identified or are so diffuse as to defy the wit of law – as they so often are today – then is not the answer "no compensation and no redress"? In other words, the case for concentrated selective services resolves itself into an argument for allowing the social costs or diswelfares of the economic system to lie where they fall.'

(Titmuss 1968: 133)

Titmuss, however, is not content to let the costs lie where they fall. He suggests that, because social change invariably inflicts costs or losses on some people, social services 'represent partial compensations for disservices, for social costs and social insecurities which . . . are part of the price we pay to some people for bearing part of the costs of other people's progress', and consequently that the 'hundred-and-one socially generated dis-services . . . are socially caused diswelfares; the losses involved in aggregate welfare gains' (Titmuss 1968: 133). He therefore con-cludes that society has a moral obligation to compensate the relative losers 'for bearing part of the social costs of other people's progress' (Titmuss 1968: 159).

The issue of avoidable dependency affects both the 'agents of diswelfare' and their 'victims'. In the case of environmental pollution, for example, victims can seek legal redress, although it may be difficult to prove liability, and the cost of legal action can be prohibitive. In the case of unemployment, however, an employee may lose his job for a variety of reasons, which adds contemporary relevance to Titmuss's argument that 'Non-discriminating universalist services are in part the consequence of unidentifiable causality' (Titmuss 1968: 134).

In social policy the purpose of discriminating between avoidable and unavoidable states of dependency is to establish moral grounds for treating some people less favourably than others. Relief provided to the less-deserving recipient is associated with stigma even though it may also affect his 'innocent' dependants, and that is the inconsistency in basing policies of discrimination on personal accountability. This is not to suggest that the issue of personal responsibility is absent from the universalist approach, but it is not treated as a matter of overriding importance. When three million people are unemployed it is hard to believe that there is all that much scope for self-help unless we are convinced that the major cause of unemployment is a widespread preference for idleness.

Welfare in social policy

In reviewing the government's response so far to these issues of redistribution, the determination of responsibility for states of dependency and the treatment of dependent people, it is important to compare the trends in social policy with those in economic policy. The phenomenon of mass unemployment has shifted attention from the customary trench warfare of the statutory social services to the blitzkriegs of rapid manufacturing decline and closure and the social casualties of structural unemployment. No hard-and-fast lines can be drawn between these casualties because today's recipient of social security is yesterday's redundant worker. Nevertheless there is recent evidence that some redundant workers receive much more generous compensation than others, and are therefore *initially* less dependent on the statutory social services.

Within the statutory social services government policy is more consistent. Every effort is being made to impose stringent limits on public expenditure, despite the inevitable rise in the social security budget which 'has grown 26 per cent in real terms over the period 1978–79 to 1983–84', compared with 16 per cent in the health and personal social services (Treasury 1984: 8). The current review of social security will focus on four main areas of service provision – benefits for children and young people, housing benefit, supplementary benefit, and pensions, with disablement as a possible fifth. The government green paper, *The Next Ten Years*, sets the ideological context in which this review will be conducted when it states that:

> 'It would, of course, always be open to the government to decide, once the virtuous circle of lower taxes and higher growth had been established, to devote some of these resources to improved public services rather than reduced taxation. There should, however, be no general presumption that higher public spending is inevitable if provision in these areas is to be improved, given the scope for switching from public to private sectors, and for improved efficiency within the public sector.'
>
> (Treasury 1984: 20–1)

The recent Fabian Society response to the social security review reminds us that the linkage between pensions and income levels is already broken (so that flat-rate pensions increase only in relation to price rises), that the number of citizens primarily dependent on statutory sources for their income is in excess of 17 million, and that 3.7 million children – or one in four – are living in families whose income is at or below the poverty line, taken as 140 per cent of supplementary benefit income (Fabian Society 1984).

Local authority personal social services are faced with the prospect of stringent cuts. The origins of the proposed legislation on rate-capping local authority expenditure go back to the 1979–80 government white paper on expenditure, which argued the case for a reduction of 7 per cent in local authority personal social service budgets. Despite this injunction, spending on these services continued to rise in real terms, although there were variations between local authorities. The government attempted to control the 'high spenders' by enforcing the grant-related expenditure assessments formula (GREA), but the exercise revealed that the offenders included Conservative as well as Labour local authorities, some of which were 'overspending' by as much as one third above the approved level (Townsend 1984).

The Rates Bill currently before parliament will effectively deprive local authorities of their right and powers to fix their own rate and expenditure levels, although the present system of government penalties for 'high spending' has caused many local authorities to increase rates as the only way to save their services. As John Stewart points out:

> 'The proposed legislation means that a local authority will no longer be able to make its own decisions on its level of expenditure even though it is willing to raise the level of taxes. For the Government is proposing to take powers to limit the level of rates that a local authority can raise.'
>
> (Stewart 1984)

The ultimate decision in fixing the rate levels and hence the expenditure levels of local authorities will rest with the Secretary of State. The government's view is that the local authorities are currently budgeting to overspend by 7 per cent above the level laid down by the Rate Support Grant Order. The green paper on *The Next Ten Years* states that 'local authority current spending has risen since 1978–9 by 9 per cent in real terms in England and 15 per cent in Scotland' (Treasury 1984: 9).

The local authority personal social services are critically important in the provision of community and residential care for the frail elderly, the mentally or physically handicapped, and the mentally ill. Cuts in these services must have serious implications for the National Health Service, especially when the proportion of the very old is rising so rapidly. Very frail elderly patients who are physically ill or mentally confused, or both, occupy a disproportionately large number of hospital beds. Roughly one in four of all hospital beds is occupied by a mentally ill patient and two in three of all admissions to mental hospitals are re-admissions from the community, where support services are generally inadequate.

In 1983–84 the government budgeted for a 4.9 per cent growth in NHS expenditure in cash terms but this increase was more than cancelled out by inflation and salary and wage increases.

The net effect has been 'a 1 per cent cut in the main NHS budget, comparing planned spending for this year with actual spending in 1982/83' (*New Statesman* 1983). The government's plans for 1984–85 provide for a budget increase of 5.3 per cent but once again likely trends in inflation and wage settlements will leave about a 1 per cent real increase in resources, which will be slightly in excess of demographically determined increases in demand. The success of this holding operation will be contingent on the members of NHS unions accepting an average pay rise of 3 per cent – which will mean a real cut in their wages unless the rate of inflation falls to an extent which is not anticipated.

During the past financial year the government imposed cuts of £80 million and nearly 5,000 staff on some sectors of the NHS. A recent *Guardian* survey suggests that these economies are affecting some regions more directly than others; nevertheless the most consistent losers are the elderly, the mentally ill, and the mentally handicapped. The survey was based on only 36 per cent of the UK health authorities but 'nearly all' the administrators who responded were highly critical (to put it mildly) of current policies (Heake 1984). These cuts have had the effect of closing hospital wards, reducing furniture stocks, bedding, and linen services, and curtailing the development of community care provision.

We know from the findings of the Black Report that serious class-based inequalities of access and care persist in the NHS, with markedly higher rates of infant mortality, accident, and illness among the poorest section of the community (Black *et al.* 1980). As waiting lists grow longer, marginal cuts are being made in the number of NHS beds and staff at all levels, while nearly 10,000 qualified nurses and midwives and roughly 3,000 doctors are out of work (October 1983).

Welfare in economic policy

These attempts to hold down public expenditure are only part of the government's general strategy for reviving Britain's economy, which also includes increased reliance on the free play of market forces, stricter application of market principles in the public sector and, where appropriate, the privatization of nationalized industries, either wholly or in part. Radical change of this magnitude must inevitably inflict social costs and 'dis-welfares' on some sections of the population.

Among the employed work-force, however, there are significant differences. In some sectors of the statutory social services both employers and employees are having to choose between higher wages and fewer jobs or lower wages and more jobs. The workers who are most likely to be affected do not in the main belong to powerful unions and they lack political and industrial muscle. The economy will not be jeopardized if nurses, teachers, social workers, home helps, dinner ladies, and hospital cleaners go on strike. Only their own quality of life will suffer, along with that of their patients, pupils, and clients.

Then there are the victims of unemployment. It is frequently suggested that the statutory social services, especially social security, have reduced the risk of social unrest at a time of high unemployment, but they are only one of the mitigating factors. The Redundancy Payments Act of 1965, which was implemented by a Labour administration, provided a statutory framework for easing workers out of declining industries and attracting them into new areas of economic growth, but there is relatively little job protection in Britain and throughout the 1970s and 1980s employers have made increasing use of lump-sum redundancy payments in the reduction of their work-forces. The average payment under the Act is no more than £1,400 but, as Nicholas Jones points out, many workers receive much more than that, and a large number of settlements are never officially notified or recorded. Official returns probably account for just over half of the payments made. Jones draws attention to an Income Data Services study carried out for the BBC this year which showed that:

> 'Around £2,000 million was paid out in the public sector alone with the single biggest payout in the steel industry – £900 million shared between 113,000 redundant workers at the British Steel Corporation. . . . The average payment in the steel industry was £8,000, with many of the older workers receiving anything from £10,000 to £20,000 or more.'
>
> (Jones 1984: 4–5)

Jones reports that on average payments made in the private sector tend to be lower, although the range extends from as little as £1,000 to over £20,000. Redundancy payments have become a major and largely unacknowledged social service with a rate of growth which has more than kept up with declared redundancies, and they are popular with workers, who are 'still queuing up to take the money' (Jones 1984: 5).

Paradoxically the exception to the general acquiescence of the work-force in the reorganization of British industry is the coal miners, who have for many years enjoyed the most generous industrial workers' redundancy scheme of all. Even here the scheme has been so successful that most of the miners aged fifty and over (who receive the most generous payments) have already left the industry, while 'The terms have been increased substantially for the younger men, with the offer of £1,000 for each year they have been in the industry' (Jones 1984).

The cost of these generous settlements amounts to about '£200 million in the last financial year and another £240 million in the coming twelve months', and the BBC study estimates that the total cost of redundancy payments is in the region of £6,000 million.

It should, however, be noted that redundancy payments in the coal and steel industries received special treatment and assistance through the EEC, and their full cost does not therefore fall on the British taxpayer. The NUM case against pit closures is not a dispute about the level of redundancy payments but a total rejection of the view that welfare can be a satisfactory substitute for work and that one generation of workers has the right to trade away the employment prospects of future generations.

In the short run the alternative to spending taxpayers' money on redundancy payments is to spend it on the subsidization of uneconomic pits. The government, according to Christopher Huhne, is currently 'budgeting cash grants for the NCB worth £4,000 per employee. This represents more than 42 per cent of the predicted national average wage and is an increase, after allowing for inflation, of 200 per cent since 1978–9.' Put more dramatically:

'It would have been cheaper for the taxpayer to pay each Treforgan colliery (the worst loss maker in 1981–2) employee more than double the then male manual average wage NOT to mine coal. Even on the NUM's calculations it would have been a lot less expensive to pay them off.'

(Huhne 1984)

Against this view the NUM contends that there is a difference between the NCB and the government in terms of profit and loss because 'The average cost of an unemployed person is more than £5,000 a year in benefits and lost taxes' (Huhne 1984). Nevertheless other factors must also be taken into account since the recipient of a redundancy payment will not be able to claim supplementary benefit until his capital has fallen below the figure of £3,000. Furthermore workers in less favoured industries may not receive much more than a lump sum of £3,000, an amount which is soon used up in the months following redundancy.

The NUM naturally argues that more investment would make uneconomic pits profitable, but the question of a short-term subsidy to one group of workers raises the issue of equity across the whole section of the work-force that is employed in declining and unproductive industries. It is clear, however, that considerations of equity, defined as fairness, have so far had little influence in deciding which specific casualties of social and economic change are to be helped or to what extent, for how long, and on what terms help will be given.

We are left with a situation in which real wages continue to rise in one section of society for a factor of production – labour – which is in over-supply. Disagreements intensify regarding the relative importance of the various causes of high unemployment, including the extent to which social expenditure has imposed extra 'burdens' on the economy and reduced the mobility of labour. Disagreements also persist about the extent to which the incomes of the employed should be used to subsidize the unemployed. In addition, as it is frequently pointed out, unemployment imposes a double burden on taxpayers because it not only absorbs more tax revenue but it reduces the total amount of taxable income. Unemployment also imposes other less quantifiable costs on society in so far as it is deemed to be associated with depression, delinquency, and social unrest.

The idea that there is an association between high levels of unemployment and social unrest is frequently challenged by advocates of free market monetarist economic policies. Nevertheless it is misleading to talk about a free market as long as there are extensive social services which mitigate the hardships of the unemployed. If these services were reduced to an absolute minimum, the theory might work in purely market terms, but the risks of serious social unrest would then increase dramatically, with unimaginable economic and political costs falling on the whole community. Alternative approaches to the problem, based on neo-Keynesian theory, would mean more investment in public works of one kind or another in the hope that the multiplier effect would boost the economy and reduce unemployment. Nevertheless, without a stringent incomes policy and pay freeze as well as continuing restraints on social expenditure, the most likely outcome of this policy would be runaway inflation. Both approaches depend for their success on the control of trade union power, and this is not likely to be achieved on a voluntary basis.

Continuity and change in welfare policies

Writing in a period of economic growth, Titmuss was hostile to the steady growth of occupational welfare schemes and highly critical of their inequitable features and their relative freedom from public accountability and open scrutiny. In the current economic recession the inequities persist, although the composition of the beneficiaries now includes more manual workers, and there is still no disposition on the part of either public or private sector employers to publicize details of the redundancy payments made under the auspices of occupational welfare.

It is worth noting that Titmuss's whole approach to collective welfare was based on the assumption that there would be sustained economic growth, a process which inevitably involves innovation and hence economic and social change which benefits some workers and deprives others. Socialists tend to appropriate all the collectivist virtues but these virtues are represented in all the major British political parties. There has been a collectivist tradition of thought in the Conservative Party throughout the

present century. The social and political objectives set out in
Harold Macmillan's *The Middle Way* are explicitly collectivist.
Writing in 1938, Macmillan observed that: 'The pace of social
change has been too slow for too long. . . . Bold changes have now
become necessary to provide for the full utilisation of the new
powers that science and invention have conferred', but he added
that: 'The granting of industrial protection should be made
conditional upon industrial reorganisation' (Macmillan 1966:
15).

Although Macmillan rejected both 'collectivism' and 'laissez-
faire individualism', he expressly demanded an extensive and
adequate range of social service provision, including 'a comprehensive system of social insurance by which a minimum supply of
necessities at all times could be guaranteed' (Macmillan 1966:
362). Macmillan's rejection of *laissez-faire* seems more final than
his rejection of collectivism; indeed his rejection of collectivism is
as unconvincing as Margaret Thatcher's patronage of the NHS.
In his 1966 preface to *The Middle Way*, referring to the earlier
period in British history 'when there were 2¾ million unemployed in this country', Macmillan stated that:

> 'As long as I live I can never forget the impoverishment and
> demoralisation which all this brought with it. I am deter-
> mined, as far as it lies within human power, never to allow this
> shadow to fall again upon this country.'
>
> (Macmillan 1966: xxiv)

From 1951 to 1974 all Conservative governments supported
collectivist social policies and, notwithstanding their individualist rhetoric, they protected the universalist framework of
the social services. This element of continuity in Conservative
thinking was shared by successive post-war Labour administrations and by the Liberal Party. As far as social policy is
concerned, the years between 1945 and 1979 will be remembered
as a period of broad consensus about welfare objectives.

It is often argued that the Thatcher administration has
rejected this post-war legacy since it is committed to policies
based on individualist economic doctrines such as reducing the
scale of the public sector in order to encourage the free play of
market forces, and generating a reserve army of the unemployed

in order to bring down the rate of inflation. From this point of view the reserve army of the unemployed is the causal mechanism in a functional theory of poverty in which the existence of a reserve army is intended to hold down the level of wage demands among the employed. All the theory currently lacks in order to fit the facts is a harshly deterrent system of selectivist social services designed to stigmatize all but the deserving poor, or those whose state of dependency can be considered respectable because it is classified as unavoidable. In any event a much stricter definition of respectable dependency will be needed if the government's present economic policies are to succeed. It would, however, require a singularly obtuse government, hell-bent on creating social conflict, to make this bizarre theory come true.

In fact the situation is rather more complex. It is true that the range of respectable or unavoidable dependencies within the statutory social services is being pared down by the present government, and the scope of less eligibility extended. The prime minister has advised the unemployed that one way out of their poverty is to start small businesses. The decision to abolish earnings-related supplements – combined with the taxation of unemployment benefits – reduced the spending power of the short-term unemployed; in addition increases in rent levels and national insurance contributions have adversely affected the living standards of families with low incomes, despite recent improvements in child benefits. So far we have seen only tactical moves against the values and aims of our major social services but the government's recent decision to review the whole structure of the social security system presages strategic measures. The logic of the government's current economic policies – which are unlikely to succeed in default of compatible social policies – calls for a radical reshaping of social security provision in which more recourse to selectivity and deterrence would widen the gap between 'avoidable' and 'unavoidable' states of dependency.

Nevertheless in some instances the government has been relatively generous in its treatment of certain categories of industrial worker in specified declining industries. However, this relative generosity tends to vary according to industrial power and the availability of EEC support rather than need, which may explain why the government has encountered the sharpest resistance where its policies have been most generous.

The real point at issue is whether these economic policies will succeed in reviving British industry and reducing un-employment. If they should fail, workers who have voluntarily or involuntarily exchanged work for welfare will face a grim future when their redundancy payments are exhausted. Even if there is a recovery, the prospects for the middle-aged will remain bleak. The scope for setting up small businesses is not unlimited. In the long term the unemployed will face the prospect of living on attenuated and increasingly stigmatized forms of social security. If the other major social services are cut back the private sector will expand to meet unmet needs, but only for those who can pay for them.

If the country wants to return to the 'Victorian values' esteemed by the present government it will have to accept the necessity for deterrence as well as the need for self-help. In the context of social welfare, that will mean a revival of poor law principles and increasing reliance on charity and private social services. How far the government will be willing or able to pursue these residualist policies will probably depend on the balance between political expediency and the innate conservatism of British institutions and British public opinion.

It is therefore vitally important to distinguish between the short-term and the long-term features of the government's social welfare policies in both the statutory social services and the occupational sector. Three of Titmuss's analytical contributions are useful for an understanding of current events – his formulation of a social division of welfare, his interpretation of social welfare institutions as agents of redistribution over time and his analysis of questions of equity (Titmuss 1974).

In his description of the social division of welfare, Titmuss showed how inequalities were institutionalized, with those who are able to secure the full benefits of occupational and fiscal welfare enjoying significantly better life chances than those who are largely dependent on statutory social services. The outcome of this arrangement is an inequitable distribution of resources over time. It is understandable, given the period in which he was writing, that Titmuss appears to have treated the division of welfare as more or less static; individuals were not expected to move in and out of the sector of occupational privilege over their own working lifetimes. The phenomenon of mass unemployment has now created a more volatile division of welfare. Economic and social change has undermined the framework on which the old division of welfare was based but future legislative change may well give institutional authority to the new division which is currently emerging.

As a temporary expedient redundancy payments have been used to make unwanted workers into more or less transient beneficiaries of occupational welfare so that the radical restructuring of British industry could be carried out with a minimum of suffering and unrest in the short run. Access to these benefits, however, has been decided more by a combination of chance and expediency than by considerations of equity. In the long term the division of welfare will be determined by the outcome of the present review of the social security system.

Many of the present beneficiaries of redundancy payments will never work again. In times of dependency their welfare will be mainly the concern of the statutory social services, and the same will apply to many of the other long-term non-employed – the elderly, the chronically sick, and the disabled. The quality of the statutory social services will depend on whether they are given an institutional or a residual role in the new division of welfare. If an increasing proportion of the able-bodied work- force is obliged to rely mainly on occupational and fiscal welfare schemes, the statutory sector will become a residual service run on selectivist principles for the non-employed, the unemployed, and the marginally employed.

If the economy does not recover, redundancy payments will have helped to create a reserve army of the unemployed as well as a political context within which it will be possible to replace the post-war system of institutional welfare with residual statutory social services based on deterrent forms of selectivity. If the Thatcher administration had wanted to put its individualist theories to the test it could have given priority to the task of dismantling the statutory social services in 1979, thereby adding a new dimension of risk to the lives of older workers threatened with unemployment and school-leavers vainly looking for their first jobs.

Conclusion

In the present economic crisis it is unlikely that any government would try to do more than hold the line on welfare expenditure, but there is an important difference between permitting inflation and a piecemeal drift towards selectivity to erode universalism on the one hand, and actively preserving the universalist structure on the other. As Titmuss once observed, selectivity has a necessary and useful role to play in social policies, but the risk of stigmatization can only be kept in check if selectivity is applied within a broad and recognizable infrastructure of universalist services. Without the universalist infrastructure, selectivist services become indifferent to exceptional needs rather than responsive to them, and exclusive rather than inclusive in coverage – and the worst effects of economic cuts are experienced by the weakest and most vulnerable members of the community. The immediate question is whether the present government will stop short of radical cuts in the services which are used by the most vulnerable members of society, the unemployed, the old, and the physically or mentally disabled.

In the Titmussian tradition institutional welfare values and a universalist structure of social services are seen as complementary and indissoluble features of a welfare society. Nevertheless the experience of the past forty years suggests that for a variety of reasons we have failed to provide within our universalist framework adequate selective support to the poorest members of society. At the present time we face an awkward dilemma. It is easier to defend universalist than selectivist services from dismemberment because a broader cross-section of voters have a vested interest in their continuance. There are, however, major economic and political impediments to the further extension of universalist services and there is much to be said in support of more positive discrimination in favour of the poor. A great deal depends on whether selective services are intended to enhance or to lower the self-esteem of recipients.

Logic suggests that we ought to be making more use of selectivity but common sense suggests that this is a politically inexpedient time to do so.

In 1979 Mrs Thatcher announced that she intended to destroy socialism as an electoral force in Britain and at present she is well on the way to doing so (Jenkins 1983). Paradoxically, the existence of over three million registered unemployed and over a million unregistered unemployed, as well as a growing awareness among the voting public that this figure is not likely to be significantly reduced in the near future, have not been an impediment to this policy – partly because the opposition is so divided and disorganized. Nevertheless radical cuts in statutory welfare could prove electorally unpopular with the relatively affluent and could cause serious disaffection among the poor.

It would be a foolish government which deliberately pursued contentious and socially divisive welfare policies. Political stability and public welfare ultimately rest on a compromise between economic and social policies. Protective welfare institutions are a vital element of modern industrial society, as expressions of public morality and agents of social integration.

This view of welfare is strongly represented in a recent International Labour Office review of social security systems in industrialized countries, whose authors argue that the so-called 'crisis' of the welfare state 'has been caused above all else by lower rates of economic growth and heavy unemployment' and that 'It is grossly unfair to choose social security as the scapegoat and to ignore the growth of all other sectors of public expenditure and of private plans' (International Labour Office 1984: 114). Looking to the future, the authors conclude that:

'In practice, for a variety of reasons, the consciousness of solidarity which should support all our efforts towards social security has tended to get weaker as the role of social security has widened. It is not possible to have social security worthy of the name, without a consciousness of national solidarity and perhaps – tomorrow – international solidarity.'

(International Labour Office 1984: 115)

It seems paradoxical that modern social security systems tend to lose public support as their coverage grows more extensive.

Nevertheless, as the authors of the ILO report point out, in most countries the general public are remarkably ill-informed about the purposes of social security, and little effort is made to clear away this 'fog of public ignorance'. Also, as social security systems become larger and more complex, they also become more impersonal and harder to understand. Public ignorance and indifference are then easily transformed into outright hostility (International Labour Office 1984: 110–11). National systems should therefore give more attention to improving both access and advisory services at both area and local levels.

In *The Idea of Welfare* I suggested that the fact that:

> 'men and women are able to think at all about the collective well-being of such an extensive and complex phenomenon as the nation state . . . might seem to signify a triumph of the human imagination and might give grounds for optimism regarding the capacity of our moral sentiments.'
>
> (Pinker 1979)

In view of its unpredictable nature, however, imagination will not serve as a basis for social policy. Altruism takes several forms, each of which has its peculiar strengths and weaknesses. Familial altruism is both narrow and intense. Public social services represent a broader form of altruism, without encouraging the passionate commitments of familial concern. National systems of universalist social service are artificial constructs, made and maintained by governments, often *against* the immediate interests of familial and other local forms of altruism, but nothing less than unequivocal statutory support for a universalist system of social services will suffice. If that support is seen to be failing, the altruistic disposition of ordinary people is swiftly directed into more conditional and restricted forms of self-help and mutual aid, and social services gradually cease to play a major part in preserving social solidarity and consensus.

It is easy to exaggerate the extent of spontaneous loving care in voluntary social services. Even in families a considered sense of duty is more usual than spontaneity, and the history of social welfare shows that there are some needs which are not adequately met by familial love and obligation. Statutory social services add legal sanctions to ensure that some of these needs are met with equity and efficiency.

In a truly conservative approach to politics, that is, one which is neither individualist nor collectivist in a doctrinaire sense, the major institutions of society are treated as the outcome of custom and piecemeal change. In Britain the outcome is a form of democratic welfare capitalism in which the welfare institutions are based on a provisional system of compromise between familial, local, and national forms of altruism. The contradictions which result from compromise are preferred to radical change and there is a general disposition to defend rather than challenge the *status quo*.

If the Thatcherist challenge succeeds, it will stand the conventional definition of conservatism on its head because its ideology is populist rather than patrician. The radical nature of Thatcherist policies could eventually provoke collectivists into turning conservative in defence of the established order in social welfare. Like poverty, radicalism is a relative concept. As soon as it became clear that the present right-wing government was going to be a radical administration, the conceptual currency of political debate began to take on new values and meanings. The British Labour Party has shifted further to the ideological left; the right wing of the Labour Party has lost power, esteem, and appeal; and the left wing of the Conservative Party, or 'wets', are looked on as yesterday's politicians. In the middle of all this the radical pretensions of the Social Democratic Party begin to look somewhat dubious. The centrist Liberal–Social Democratic Alliance secured an impressive moral victory at the last election, gaining no less than 25.4 per cent of the popular vote, although under the peculiarities of our electoral system this gave them only 23 seats in parliament. (The Conservatives gained 42.4 per cent of the popular vote and 397 seats, with an overall majority of 144, while the Labour Party slumped to 27.6 per cent and 209 seats, with the regional parties taking 4.6 per cent and 21 seats.)

The SDP has been described as 'an idea whose time has come', but it might be more accurate to describe both SDP and Liberal doctrines as ideas which are in danger of being swept away. A point that is frequently made about the two centre parties is that they do not possess a consistent set of political principles and that their policies are not clearly focused. In my opinion their manifestos lack conviction because they purport to offer 'radical' policies. This may be true in minor respects but the centre parties would gain a new authority and popularity if their programmes were presented as the truly conservative set of policies which they have become, in comparison with those of the Labour and Conservative parties. In the current political situation collectivists of the centre might discover that being conservative *faute de mieux* is the next best thing to an honourable calling in defence of the established welfare institutions of our country.

Note

1 This chapter was written in September 1984. Since then major changes in local government have finally reached the statute book and the government's proposals for the reform of social security have been published just as we go to press.

References

Economist (1982) Thatcher's Think Tank Takes Aim at the Welfare State. *Economist* (18 September): 25–6.

Fabian Society (1984) *Social Security: The Real Agenda: The Fabian Society's Response to the Government's Review of Social Security*, no. 498. London: Fabian Society, pp. 3, 7, and 22.

Henke, D. (1984) How to Hurt a Health Service. *Guardian* (18 January): 11.

Huhne, C. (1984) Is Mrs Thatcher in Reality the Miners' Best Friend? *Guardian* (3 May): 19.

Hutton, W. (1983) Recovery? What Recovery? *Listener* (1 September): 5–6.

International Labour Office (ILO) (1984) *Into the Twenty-First Century: The Development of Social Security: A Report to the Director-General of the International Labour Office on the Response of the Social Security System in Industrial Countries to Economic and Social Change*. Geneva: ILO.

Jenkins, P. (1983) The Political Challenge Which the TUC Now Faces from the Government Is the Consequence of Failures of Leadership. *Guardian* (7 September).

Jones, N. (1984) The Blanket Which Covers up Unemployment Figures. *Listener* (12 April).

Macmillan, H. (1966) *The Middle Way* (first published 1938). London and New York: Macmillan/St Martin's Press.

New Statesman (1983) NHS in Crisis. *New Statesman* (25 November): vii.

Pinker, R. (1979) *The Idea of Welfare*. London: Heinemann, pp. 31–9.

Stewart, J. (1984) It's All About Control. *Community Core* 503 (15 March): 14–16.

Titmuss, R. M. (1968) *Commitment to Welfare*. London: Allen & Unwin.
—— (1974) *Social Policy*. London: Allen & Unwin.
Townsend, D. (1984) Patrick Jenkin Ought to Know Better. *Community Core* 503 (15 March): 14–16.
Treasury (1984) *The Next Ten Years: Public Expenditure and Taxation into the 1990s*, Cmnd 9189. London: HMSO.
Walden, B. (1983) The Six Evils Sown by Lloyd George. *Standard* (8 June): 7.

10
Law, order, and welfare*
PHILIP BEAN

Mr David Steel, introducing a debate on law and order in 1981 (Parliamentary Debates, 6th series, vol. 13: 1009), noted that 'law and order could cover a very wide canvas', and he listed the planning of our cities and towns, local authority housing programmes, and so on, as 'law and order' issues. Even so he and others in that debate restricted themselves to more traditional matters such as combating crime and methods of policing. Yet clearly some MPs are able to define law and order more widely than others; and for that matter more widely than many criminologists and those usually concerned with social policy. In this chapter I shall argue that law, order, and social policy are woven together, and that a defence of welfare relates to law and order though not necessarily in the narrow form currently presented. I do not wish to see this argument in simple partisan terms for there is little to choose between Labour and Conservatives on almost all traditional law-and-order matters. Indeed looking

*I am grateful to Vivien Stern and Paul Cavadino from NACRO who provided much information during the preparation of this chapter.

through the post-war period one would be hard pressed, without knowing in advance which government was in power, to say who was responsible for this or that piece of legislation. Rather I wish to show that 'law and order' stems from a view defined by governments in general about the nature of the state, derived from the fact that all governments are concerned with internal and external security, the Conservative government of Mrs Thatcher being no different in that respect from others, although of course it is markedly different in certain selected features. As such the debate is about the protection of the state and the protection given by the state to its citizens. Where protection *of* the state is seen as excessive there will be, and ought to be, a law-and-order debate; so too where protection given *by* the state is seen as inadequate.

Comparisons in the law-and-order debate

But the point made above, that is of the similarity between various governments on law-and-order matters, requires justification. Martin Kettle writing in *Marxism Today* argues that the dominant feature of Conservative law-and-order policy is its basic continuity with the policies of the last Labour government (Kettle 1983). To Kettle that continuity has more to do with civil servants in the Home Office than politicians. (And David Downes in a Fabian Society pamphlet says that neither Conservative nor Labour governments have a better record of crime control as seen against the rate of increase of crime (Downes 1983: 3).) Certainly, the party rhetoric is similar. In a parliamentary debate on law and order, Shirley Summerskill for the Labour Party said, 'My party is pledged to provide more resources for prisons and the probation service and we certainly support the Government fully in any increase in expenditure that they may make on law and order' (Parliamentary Debates, 5th series, vol. 980: 1376). Compare this with Mr Brittan's statement that 'we think it right that priority should be given . . . to law and order' (973: 1484). However, Mr Kilroy-Silk added a more sombre down-to-earth note during a law-and-order debate and distinguished between the rhetoric and reality of both parties.

'We are here today with empty Benches all around us. There are no speakers getting up from the Conservative side and very few from the Labour side. No one cares, no one is interested' (Parliamentary Debates, 5th series, vol. 980: 1363).

Yet in spite of that Mrs Thatcher has been accused of breaking the post-1945 bipartisan consensus on law and order, and by some criminologists of being out of touch with current criminological research. These accusations are misdirected, or if not then misguided, for at the most the bipartisan consensus has been fractured rather than broken and if there ever was a consensus it did not produce measures unequivocally enlightened. And for law and order to be out of touch with criminological research says much about the manner in which some criminologists have benefited from that consensus – financially and otherwise.

Consider measures produced by that consensus. The 1948 Criminal Justice Act, under a Labour government, introduced detention centres, corrective training, and preventative detention as recommended by a Royal Commission set up under a pre-war Conservative government. Detention centres were formally introduced by a Conservative government and the regime was modified during that government's lifetime. Corrective training and preventative detention were removed in 1967 by a Labour government, but replaced by extended sentences. The 1969 Children and Young Persons Act, introduced by a Labour government, produced, and still produces, long periods of institutional restraints, and Conservative and Labour governments alike have increased the numbers and types of facilities for secure accommodation. As matters stand now many young people are detained in maximum secure conditions without ever having been convicted of an offence. In 1979 the massive pay rise granted to the police may have produced indignation by Conservative opponents yet it merely brought forward by two months that agreed by an earlier Labour government. The increase in police numbers was recommended by that same committee (Parliamentary Debates, 6th series, vol. 13: 1017). The Criminal Justice (Scotland) Act 1980 legalized detention for questioning and produced equal indignation, yet the Labour government introduced a similar Bill which fell only when a general election was called. In England

and Wales the Police and Criminal Evidence Act 1984 was based on the conclusions of a Royal Commission set up by James Callaghan. In the field of mental health, successive British governments have been taken to the European Court of Human Rights for legislation introduced largely unopposed by a Conservative government – and nearly always lost. The Immigration Act of 1968, introduced by a Labour government, was no less severe than that passed by the Conservatives in 1962 and 1971.[1] And so it goes on.

Of course there are differences, although it is not always easy to distinguish between real differences and differences of emphasis, rhetoric, or substance. Both parties have been concerned with supplementary benefits fraud as a measure of state protection. The Conservatives, however, increased the methods and means of detection. For example in the six months from May to November 1979 (mostly under a Labour government) unemployment review officers carried out 122,459 interviews on the long-term unemployed, but this was increased to 177,156 from May to November 1979 (Parliamentary Debates, 5th series, vol. 979: 792). Both parties are committed to the retention of detention centres as a means of providing protection by the state, but the Conservatives tried to toughen them up – or at least one or two selected ones. According to the then Home Secretary 'the object [was] to try and deter these young thugs' (1978). This was in spite of warnings that such changes were likely to be fruitless and could be counter-productive; and in spite of a searching parliamentary question when the Home Secretary was asked if he would publish the research findings on which the government based its view that harsher regimes would have a greater deterrent effect than existing ones. No findings existed and subsequent research has borne out earlier warnings; reconviction rates are if anything slightly worse for those under harsher regimes.

This fondness for military discipline has always been a favourite Conservative theme. So too is that of self-reliance. (Occasionally those operating under this slogan became victims of their own rhetoric. 'We need to be a more self-reliant society . . . in which people stand on their own feet,' said the Minister responsible for the disabled (Parliamentary Debates, 5th series, vol. 981: 493).) More serious has been a demand for a certain type of ill-considered retribution, having little or nothing in common with a retributive philosophy. It is salacious and highly selective. The move to introduce capital punishment in 1981 was a case in point. In this respect the bipartisan consensus did break down, for whilst there may be little difference between the actions of governments, marked differences exist among respective followers and backbenchers. When the capital punishment debate was lost those same Conservatives redirected attention to a group of offenders, mainly involved in personal violence, but again a selected group, in order to sustain political impetus.

The result has been the classical 'law and order' debate to which many criminologists have responded and which has become orchestrated into a social movement by certain Conservatives. Mr Teddy Taylor for example repeatedly asked questions in parliament about the percentage rise of certain types of offences such as murder, manslaughter, and violence against the person, yet with a little effort would have been able to find these out for himself. But that would have made less political impact. Others asked questions about 'mugging', presumably being aware that there is no crime of 'mugging' as such. The approach by this group was thorough, leaving the Home Secretary, Mr Leon Brittan, facing a Conservative Party Conference in 1983 eager to taste a long-awaited victory. Responding to 'a call for action' followed by a claim 'to be the only Party willing to stand up to the men of violence, the terrorist, the thug, the child molester', Mr Brittan first outlined measures to keep certain offenders in jail for longer periods. He specified a minimum period which would normally be served by prisoners convicted of certain types of crime. It was a shrewd political move. It satisfied, temporarily at least, populist demands without committing future Home Secretaries to that policy. In essence the proposals adjusted the period spent on parole which the Home Secretary controls anyway. They required no amending legislation and so avoided a full parliamentary debate. And having been seen to create the right impression at the outset, the Home Secretary was presumably free to introduce more

liberal measures later, such as reducing the prison population
(Brittan 1983). But those populist demands are insatiable. They
will doubtless reappear, and Mr Brittan having once been seen
as 'tough on law and order' will find backsliding more difficult.

The measures proposed by Mr Brittan are interesting for they
show, amongst other things, how a selective approach to law and
order has become a social movement in its own right. In this
respect the Conservative governments of 1979 and 1983 are
different, even though the practical effects show that not a great
deal has changed in terms of the legislative content. The style is
different, a level of respectability has been achieved for a certain
type of vindictive demand, and support has been given to a
certain type of unthinking pseudo-retribution. That social movement has achieved its pre-eminence with a selective approach to
crimes which for the most part produced fears created by
sensationalism. For whilst most of these 'law and order' MPs
were eager to establish the point that certain serious crimes (and
particularly those involving firearms) had increased, they were
less eager to do anything other than reproach the convicted
offender. They did not for example consider extending firearms
control. That proposal, initiated by the Police Federation and
supported by the Superintendents' Association and the
Association of Chief Police Officers, was for the registration of all
firearms, which meant shotguns, but was rejected by the Home
Secretary in December 1983. The proposal, entirely correct in
my view, would have required holders of all firearms to require a
certificate from the Chief Constable. Shotguns would then be
regarded as a firearm under the Firearms Act 1968. It was not
however a new proposal. In 1969 the Labour Party Home
Secretary, Mr Callaghan, was more sympathetic, but the Bill to
control shotguns was lost in the general election of that year, and
it was not revised between 1974 and 1979 when Labour was in
Office. So as elsewhere the British gun lobby seems influential,
and if so we should be wary, for in some of its journals there is a
demand to remove all firearms from registration. If this was
successful we could then speak of a complete break with the
bipartisan consensus, and not of a fracture as exists at present.

Law, order, and welfare

Up to this point I have wanted to show that the so-called 'law and order' debate has, in terms of its legislative content, produced little that differed from before. I wish now to turn the discussion towards welfare, and for these purposes define welfare in terms of protection and rights. In doing so we return to the point made earlier, that where protection *of* the state is seen as excessive there will and ought to be a law-and-order debate; so too where protection given *by* the state is inadequate. And to repeat another earlier point: all governments are concerned with internal and external security, the Conservative government of Mrs Thatcher being no different in this respect from others. This view was made very clear by the minister of state for the Home Office, Mr Patrick Mayhew, who said in the debate referred to above that he welcomed opportunities for the House to discuss questions relating to the maintenance of law and order. 'There is no subject to which this Government attaches more importance. It ranks equally with the defence of the realm' (Parliamentary Debates, 6th series, vol. 13: 1015). The link is neatly made: domestic offenders, like terrorists and hostile states overseas, threaten security, internal or otherwise. Parliament legislates, the courts sentence, and the penal system controls. As a political exercise it is no more complicated than that, and well understood by MPs of all shades of political opinion, even if usually stated less forcibly than that by Mr Mayhew. The means and methods by which law and order are maintained may be open to debate, but not the protection of the state or the state's duty to provide security for its citizens.

It is for that reason that law and order – by which I mean the demand for protection and for restrictions to be placed on those who would harm us – is an ongoing debate and not one suddenly manufactured by Mrs Thatcher's government. Certainly Mrs Thatcher, in a speech preceding the 1979 general election, makes it appear as if it were so. 'The demand in this country will be for two things; less tax and more law and order' (*Daily Telegraph*, 29 March, 1979). We can ignore the first of these so-called demands (if only because unfulfilled election promises are not central to my argument) and concentrate on the second. But notice that

Mrs Thatcher asked for more law and order. All societies have rules regulating the use of violence and the sanctity of property, and the state in modern society protects and enforces those rules. (Again we may debate the fairness or relevance of those rules but I shall come to that later.)

It is possible to link law, order, and welfare in a number of different ways. The first can be called the control model. Consider this in the manner in which law and order and the unemployed were bracketed together by Mr David Steel in 1981.

'There is then the current problem, which we cannot balk, of the enforced idleness caused by unemployment. There is an old saying that idle hands make mischief. That is certainly true among younger people who feel deprived of an opportunity to make full use of their daily lives.'

(Parliamentary Debates, 6th series, vol. 13: 1010)

That link between welfare and control is not new. Plato understood it, so did Hegel, so did Bismarck, and Beatrice Webb understood it perfectly, as have all who feared the subversive influence created 'by the idleness of the labouring classes'. The early nineteenth-century reformers were not urged on just by the despair and misery of poverty but by fear of insurrection if poverty was not relieved. And many contemporaries have fashioned policies on that basis. For example James Callaghan, on introducing the Bill which became the Children and Young Persons Act 1969, wanted 'to prevent the deprived children of today becoming the criminals of tomorrow'. It matters not that the link between deprivation and crime is more complex; it has been enough to assert that a link exists, and the fears created by that assertion become sufficient to produce action.

On this simple control model there is a justification for retaining the welfare state; a matter on which I think all governments have agreed. Also on this basis governments have no option but to provide welfare, for welfare helps reduce dissatisfaction although of course does not relieve idleness. Moreover it can be argued that the welfare state promotes law and order by assisting in the process of socialization, such as through the education system or through the social services wherein those who break rules are taught controls (see also Gough 1983: 157). Such matters help promote internal security. But the difficulty with this model is it does not show the levels of government expenditure required to promote control. Would an increase or decrease in unemployment benefits affect crime rates? And if so by how much? Would cuts in the education system threaten internal security? And again, if so by how much?

An alternative model is more interventionist and assumes that law and order can be actively promoted by removing some of the causes of discontent. This was the view of the US National Advisory Commission on Civil Disorder, and indeed was quoted sympathetically by Lord Scarman (1982), that crime and particularly violence are produced by ignorance, discrimination, slums, poverty, disease, and unemployment. Crude methods of control are seen as ineffective, and sometimes counter-productive. In Britain John Alderson, the then Chief Constable of Devon and Cornwall, said:

> 'People who are poor and have a chip on their shoulder against society are inclined to say "I am getting nothing out of life so I am going to be angry." If society then says: "Okay, you can get as angry as you like but I have a well paid fat cat police force and if you get angry I shall just clobber you," then we are making a big mistake.'
> [He concluded:]
> 'One thing is certain – it is no answer to resort to brute force to try to control people.'
>   (quoted in Parliamentary Debates, 6th series, vol. 13: 1013)

As a general rule all governments since 1945 have also accepted this point – in varying degrees, that is. The strength of this model is that those who are most likely to harm us, that is the poor, the deprived, and those who get little out of life, are encouraged to receive and achieve more; but not entirely, for the elderly, who often come under the category of the poor and underprivileged, are rarely serious offenders, while many serious offenders are neither poor nor underprivileged. But again as a general rule the argument is sound. Welfare, in this model, also helps promote law and order.

It is not entirely clear how much emphasis is placed on these two models by current Conservative governments. The first would perhaps be seen as more appropriate to them than the second but both are doubtless seen as defective in certain respects. Yet they provide options and justifications for welfare as required. Typically Labour governments have emphasized the second model, as did Lord Scarman, without stating any particular political preference, for intervention by the state is in line with collectivist thinking. Whether such a collectivist approach works (in the sense that it promotes control and reduces crime) is a moot point, although it may promote other values considered desirable. Moreover and paradoxically, it promotes the welfare and status of those who intervene. Under this model we are all small people unless employed by the state to carry out state policy. Perhaps this is why those who have benefited most from such policies, that is those who intervene, have been the most vocal about their retention. For if there is a sociological truism to be extracted from the Second World War period it is that welfare, if it is to be accepted as policy, must at the same time promote professional interests. Where those interests are threatened, irrespective of the quality of such proposals, the proposer will find it a chastening experience.

These two models are not, and have never been, mutually exclusive – they are, like most areas of policy, to be emphasized by governments as and when governments choose. But under the Conservative governments of 1979 and 1983 new twists are being added to the control argument – or rather very old ones re-vitalized and revamped. One is the desire to make the family the centrepiece of control; a favoured notion of Conservatives keen to resurrect certain cherished Victorian values, and keen also to promote a hierarchical structure of discipline which has always been the hallmark of Conservative political thought. The 1982 Criminal Justice Act made such a start: sections 26–8 provide that courts must, in cases where the most appropriate penalty is a fine, lay it on the parents or guardian of the child or young person unless he or she cannot be found, or the circumstances make it unreasonable. The same provision applies in cases where a juvenile has been found to have committed an offence in care proceedings and compensation is ordered. There are other changes too which emphasize the importance of compensation. All enhance the view that parents must be responsible for the actions of their children and it is parents rather than the state who must control them.

The difficulty is that the family, as constituted at present, is not altogether well equipped to take over that role. The present levels of divorce and separation are testimony to that. Nor is it likely to change for the better in that respect, for economic demands, prompted as they are by an effort to improve economic performance, require a mobile labour force, and more so if it is to be firmly rooted in a free market economy. Moreover, the demand that the family should care for its members (ailing or otherwise) comes at a time when care for the family, which means care by women, cuts across competing demands. It may of course be possible to have the family increase discipline, and the schools likewise, but the family of the 1980s differs greatly from its Victorian counterpart.

Law, order, and protection

Rights and protection, or the right to be protected, are two-edged. They are about those who would harm us, and about those whose duty is to protect us; for the latter must act in a manner which is commensurate with that duty. That is why crimes by the state and by officials of the state are so destructive, for they subvert and mutilate that set of rights which citizens can reasonably expect to be theirs. That much is obvious. What is less obvious is what to do about the changing nature of the modern police force, the major arm of the state's means of protecting itself and its citizens, and the second major twist in the control argument. For there is a growing belief that traditional forms of benign policing are giving way to a form of policing controlled by technologies and aimed primarily at protecting the state rather than the citizen. If this is so, and some commentators insist that it is, then the law-and-order debate is primarily about state control, and questions need to be asked about the manner of that control.

The position of the police in modern society differs greatly from the traditional notion which involved unarmed beat patrols maintaining the 'Queen's Peace' through the maintenance of close personal relationships with local communities. Modern policing increasingly involves more and more technological support and produces a highly mobile force operating at one degree removed from those local communities. Hence the debate between the merits of fire brigade policing, that is putting out social/criminal fires by large-scale control operations, and community policing, that is returning the police to the local community. It is also about how the police are to be controlled, locally and nationally, whether it be by strengthening existing procedures or by introducing new ones (see Downes 1983 and Regan 1983).

As yet we are still some way from the more naked form of state control practised elsewhere, but the frequent access to arms (in 1981 Mr Whitelaw told parliament that 154 members of the Metropolitan Police were fully trained in the use of revolvers (see Parliamentary Debates, 5th series, vol. 975: 724)) and the announcement on 2 April, 1984 that the Metropolitan Police were to be equipped with a certain type of machine gun to protect visiting dignitaries, add a new dimension to the demand for more law and order. It is true that there are no proposals for routine access to this type of arms and that four deputy commissioners are required before they are drawn, but also true that once purchased they will not readily be scrapped. Aside from the menacing nature of machine guns being used by police in a democracy, with all the politically malevolent overtones associated with this, there are simple dangers of safety: each gun can fire 800 rounds per minute and be effective up to one mile, so that those nearby cannot avoid ricochets or faulty marksmanship. As if this were not bad enough, Mrs Thatcher's government then sidestepped responsibility for this decision by pointing out that machine guns were first issued by a Labour government in 1976 (*The Times*, 9 April, 1984). I do not deny that foreign heads of government need protection or that international terrorism has changed the nature of that protection, but more benign measures are and have been available for a long time.

As it clearly is the duty of the police to protect the state, the police cannot remain aloof or be seen as so removed from politics as to be immune from criticism, or, alternatively, claim to act as passive recipients of government policy. Unfortunately the polarization of attitudes towards the police, divided roughly on party political lines, has not produced much that is helpful to the general level of debate. Those who see the police as doing no wrong remain as obdurate as those who see the opposite. In this respect Ian Taylor is correct when he says, as a socialist, that the orthodox and instinctual attitude of the left to the police, that of a generalized opposition, is unlikely to be of general appeal, and he goes on to say: 'A socialist policy is in need of immediate reconstruction for present conditions as well as for some hypothetical socialist future' (Taylor 1981: 155). Unfortunately he does not provide details of that policy.

Irrespective of any ideological or party consideration, high crime rates in modern society push the police further into more sophisticated technological methods of crime prevention. Put simply there will never be enough police to protect everybody. Yet crime prevention linked to modern technology is far removed from the traditional visit of the crime prevention officer advising on the merits of this or that lock or burglar alarm. Preventative technology involves telephone tappings, data banks on suspects (political or otherwise), video recordings, etc. All go towards removing the police from contact with the ordinary citizen, except for the unwelcome contact of surveillance. Remoteness breeds suspicion and fear. The problem, as I see it, is to make the police more the servants of the citizens and less the servants of the state, for only then will the state be reminded constantly of its obligations. Yet the speed and enthusiasm of the police in the manner in which they accepted and used new technologies makes one suspicious of their own commitments; and certainly the citizen's misgivings were not helped by the judgement in the High Court of Croome-Johnson, J. to the jury in the *Finch and Jardine* case in 1983 in his celebrated direction on the use of force in self-defence and in the prevention of crime.[2]

The question about control of a modern police force is one of the most important law-and-order issues of the day. It will not be resolved easily or quickly, and we should be chary of simple solutions. At the same time decisions by central government which appear oblivious to the manner in which the police distance themselves from the community make solutions that much more difficult, the purchase of those machine guns being a case in point. I can sympathize with David Regan's position when he says we have been able to operate in Britain with a benign tradition of policing which ought not to be placed in jeopardy by hasty decisions (Regan 1983). He wants members of police committees to be more active, to assert their existing powers and to make the police more accountable. In this way his proposal preserves the existing structure with the minimum of disruption.

Unfortunately his proposal may increase accountability but does little to promote control – a different matter altogether. Nor would it deal with the problem of existing passive members of police committees who have hitherto allowed Chief Constables too much leniency (Regan 1983: 13). Yet David Regan is right in one sense when he draws attention to defects in the existing structure of accountability and control. In this respect he appears to have support from a former Home Secretary, William Whitelaw, who said in 1980:

> 'I think it has become increasingly desirable that police authorities should see themselves not just as providers of resources but as a means whereby the Chief Constable can give an account of his policing policy . . . and they can express to him the voices of the community on these policies.'
>
> (quoted in Regan 1983: 14)

And he is also right when he says we should be wary of believing that control by a local authority, or indeed by any political party or pressure group, will solve the problems. Other problems may be produced which are worse; one can imagine for example clashes between police and police committees which resolve nothing, except draw ideological boundaries.

Yet it seems to me that without measures of control the police may drift further and further from their contacts with the public and more into professionalized technology where ends dominate and means are brushed aside. A more vigorous police authority with a slightly different membership, that is with fewer magistrates (Levenson 1980), may be a short-term answer. But if that does not work we should consider again the type of proposals put forward by Mr Jack Straw who twice promoted unsuccessful private member's bills to give local police authorities greater controls over policing, including the appointment of middle-ranking police officers (Parliamentary Debates, 5th series, vol. 980: 1153–157).

Control at the local level will not affect the police in relation to the state but will affect protection of the citizens – and hopefully help the police to be viewed with less suspicion and distrust. The problem is not irreversible, though the warning signs are there. According to the British Crime Survey, four out of five victims were satisfied with police contact over their case, but those who were dissatisfied pointed to police inaction, slowness of response, unacceptable attitudes, and poor follow-up. Approximately 40 per cent of adults approach police annually for assistance in matters unrelated to crime; 80 per cent found police helpful but attitudes varied according to age, sex, and profession. Older people, women, and non-manual workers were more satisfied (Hough and Mayhew 1983).

This information, based as it was on a random sample of 11,000 people in England and Wales, inevitably deals in generalities and masks specific instances where there is a lack of appreciation based on the personal experiences of those who are most vulnerable – or if not then an unwillingness to be involved. But the British Crime Survey found considerable fear of crime, varying according to age, and being highest amongst elderly women even though this group was the least likely to be attacked.[3] And that fear of crime will not diminish by reference to the statistical chances of being assaulted etc., though it may be helped by documents emphasizing the political aspects of crime prevention (Age Concern undated). In this respect the law-and-order campaign of the Conservatives in 1979 may have produced votes because people were fearful for their safety (in contrast the Labour Party with its so-called 'generalized opposition' to the police appeared less palatable), but it cannot be said to have produced a greater trust or affection for the police.

In some respects a shrill approval of the police from certain Conservatives adds to their images of themselves as being linked to the state. In contrast the position of certain older and more established professions has become more vulnerable, and the quality of the protection they give to the public is being questioned. It may be that future historians will identify the early 1980s as the beginning of the demise of the professionals' formal prestige. Already under the 1983 Mental Health Act some restrictions are placed on the clinical decisions of the psychiatrists so that certain forms of treatment shall not be given to a patient unless the patient consents, or an independent medical practitioner has certified either that the patient is incapable of giving his consent or that the patient should receive the treatment even though he has not consented to it (see Jones 1983: 20–98). Hard on the heels of this piece of legislation comes a similar attack on the legal profession, beginning with the removal of that profession's monopoly on conveyancing and including the introduction of a formal complaints procedure financed by the Law Society but independent of it. The accountability of the professional is also being reassessed, with mistakes in legal practice becoming more open to redress. And who knows? Perhaps recognition may be given eventually to the views of organizations such as Legal Action Group who have complained consistently of the poor quality of legal services, including legal representation in court, with papers unread, a lack of familiarity with the case, and insufficient knowledge of the law. It adds up, or should do, to a way of unpacking the professional stance, of removing professional mystification and redefining professional work; that is, placing the professional at the level of the craftsman and technician where status has to be earned rather than ascribed in advance.

It may seem an odd quirk of our society that one group, the police, should benefit from the current changes in the law-and-order debate whilst others, the established professionals, should do less well. (The difference is of course relative for whilst the police have in financial terms done considerably better they are still well behind the legal professionals.) But the differences are readily explained; one group protects the state, the other less so. And it is part of my argument that protection of the state has dominated contemporary thinking on law and order. This being so the demand for more community policing will not solve matters for it is the organization of the police force that poses the problem.

If we look at the other side of the protection argument, that is, the protection granted to citizens, matters are different. Here we can talk of underprotection, or at best selective protection. It is true that Conservatives here stressed the importance of being free to walk the streets without fear, and of course this is important. No one denies that, but protection goes further; it is about responding to the claims of groups who have hitherto been neglected or whose status is low. It is about recognizing claims to be revalued in status terms. As such the 'law and order' debate fashioned by some Conservatives is at best shallow and at worst damaging. Consider the position of children. The 1969 Children and Young Persons Act defined delinquent children as being 'in trouble' or in need of 'care'. Defective personal relationships were seen as the cause of, or the major contributing factor to, crime. This Act represents an outdated view of delinquency and a new view of treatment is needed, together with a redefinition of juvenile crime. For too long the child's 'best interest' has been the guiding axiom, but that means doing things *to* children rather than *for* them. The new slogan, if that is the right way to interpret it, is to produce the least detrimental alternative – an altogether more limited, and some would say negative, approach. Yet 'the least detrimental alternative' places restrictions on what can or cannot be done to children, and so recognizes that promoting the child's 'best interest' may not advance rights.

Redefining the crimes of children does not necessarily mean a redefinition of the crimes they commit – though it may; it means a redefinition of the child as victim. The changing view of incest illustrates this point. Hitherto incest was regarded as a product of ignorance and overcrowding, often associated with rural idiocy. Now the child is seen as an exploited victim abused by those whose duty was to protect her; the child is regarded as having a right to expect parents to care for her, and not to exploit her or mutilate her self-image. Sadly it seems that some members of the judiciary appear not to see it that way. A demonstration outside the Old Bailey in 1984 was against intemperate remarks by a judge who said, in a case of assault on a child by a man, 'it could happen to anyone'. The demonstrators regarded such remarks as an encouragement to exploitation and demanded a heavy sentence for the offender – a 'law and order' demand if ever there was one, and a demand for the protection of children.

Similar demands come from women, for too long the recipients of domestic violence. Regrettably women and children find a common bond in this area for there is often overlap where both are similarly maltreated (Martin 1978: 8). Women are not only customarily those who care for children, they also share with them a common heritage of violence and abuse. So too for minorities claiming protection from racialist attacks and insults. The demands from these and similar groups is for a more responsive police force able to provide adequate protection in a pluralistic society. And again this is not a simple party matter. For it is not only voters from the Labour Party who protest against the failure of the police to pursue rapists and assaulters of women more vigorously, or who demand more thorough enforcement of existing censorship laws to outlaw films depicting and glorifying violence against women and children.

If we are to take protection seriously, then promoting family discipline or whatever is an inadequate approach. It ignores the question of rights and takes little or no account of those whose claims have hitherto been ignored. Certainly the attack on professional dominance is in my view to be approved, if only because the professionals have monopolized an area of control without providing commensurate benefits. But the right to be represented in court or elsewhere is of little importance if protection in the social milieu is inadequate. If each person has a claim to protection by virtue of his or her citizenship, then this will not be achieved by any return to 'Victorian values', or by making claims that safety in the streets can be achieved by stricter discipline in the home. Welfare is more than safety, it is a way of respecting all claims however low the status of the claimant. For what is so disagreeable about the Conservative Party's 'law and order' programme of the early 1980s is that it created fear (which produced votes), but then did not allay those fears, except by resort to stricter punishments of selected criminals.

The fear created in the elderly, for example, did not result in an offer to provide free or cheap telephones for those living in high-risk areas; and the fear created in women about their ritual abuse in the home and streets did not result in a demand by the government for those who sell alcohol, one of the most criminogenic substances ever invented, to curb their activities. Nor did there appear to be anything in the Conservative 'law and order' debate which was directed at the wholesale slaughter on our roads, where accidents resulting from dangerous driving cause more deaths than all homicides put together; quite the reverse, for the proposals to change the speed limits on coaches etc. are a direct response to the power of those who represent vocal sectional interests. The model I wish to advance is not one where the state is granted excessive protection while the citizens are protected only in selected areas; it is one where each person counts equally and all have a legitimate claim.

Notes

1 The 1968 Act was rushed through in three days during a panic resulting from the influx of Kenyan Asians. It introduced the concept of 'patriality' as opposed to 'Commonwealth status citizenship'. The justification was that racial harmony could not occur if large numbers of Commonwealth immigrants were allowed in. The Conservatives extended that concept, giving it a more rigorous definition, but did so on the basis of James Callaghan's legislation in 1968. See Husband (1982), especially the chapter 'Immigration Policies in the U.K.' by Tom Rees, ch. 4, pp. 75–96. See also the chapter in this volume by John Ferris.

2 A summary of the judgement is as follows.
Use of force in self-defence and in the prevention of crime, Finch and Jardine (1983) Directions of Croome-Johnson, J. to the jury –

> 'The Prosecution have conceded right from the start in each case that this was the result of a genuine mistake by Finch and Jardine. . . . Once it is accepted, as it is all round for that matter, that Finch and Jardine, and others, did make a genuine mistake, it is the law, and also good sense, and fair for Finch and Jardine that you should settle down and think of these matters as though it really had been Martin in the car. You must put yourselves in the position of Finch and Jardine thinking at the time, and genuinely thinking at the time, that it was Martin in the car. . . .
> It is both good law, and good sense, that a man who is attacked may defend himself. It is both good law, and good sense that he may do, but only do, what is reasonably necessary for that purpose. . . .
> If you think in a moment of sudden or unexpected peril, a person who was being attacked had only done what he thought was honest and necessary, you would, I am sure, consider that that was very strong evidence indeed for you to take into account, that only reasonable defensive action had been taken. . . . At all events the genuineness, and urgency, and genuineness of the belief, and the extent of the urgency in

which it was believed by the person being attacked, is a matter of the greatest weight for you to consider. . . .

Supposing there had been no actual attack, but one was threatened, you do not have to wait to be struck. If the circumstances justify it you may get your blow in first of all to prevent that. The present catchphrase we read about all the time is the 'pre-emptive strike'. It is not a matter that is always encouraged. . . . If it was done, the firing before the attack took place, in an honest, genuine, reasonably mistaken frame of mind, that is something which you are entitled to take into consideration. . . .

He (DC Finch) said all he wanted to do (when he struck Mr Waldorf with his revolver) was not to beat up Waldorf, he simply wanted to knock him out. One cannot help here, I suppose, having in mind, and keeping in mind, the parallel with a boxing match where people try to knock each other out but with no prospect in the process that they would do really serious injury to each other, at least it is not their intention to. We read, now and again, of terrible cases where that happens. That is not the intention of the man striking the blow. He tries to knock the other man out but not to do more than that. If you think that was all that Finch's intention was at the time you may well think there was no intention to do grievous bodily harm.'

The connection between police violence and a boxing match seems fearful.

3 The BCS focused on the extent to which fear of crime was a problem and the ways in which this fear could be reduced. Sixty per cent of elderly women fear crime. In general, women in inner cities express the greatest fear. People in manual occupations who lived on their own were more fearful. Fear of crime affected women's behaviour. Only 5 per cent of men avoided going out after dark in their neighbourhood while 51 per cent of young women, 54 per cent of middle-aged women and 58 per cent of older women stayed indoors. A broad range of people fear burglary. Older women worry about mugging and sexual attacks, while middle-aged women fear thefts from bags and purse snatching. Young women fear sexual assault. The BCS found that those who felt most unsafe were least often victims. For example, elderly persons who lead an active life are still three times less likely to be victims of street crime than persons under sixty years of age.

References

Age Concern (undated) *Action against Crime: Crime Prevention*. London: Age Concern/NatWest Bank.

Brittan, L. (1983) Home Secretary's speech to the Conservative Party Conference, 11 October. Conservative Central Office (mimeo).

Daily Telegraph (29 March, 1979).

Downes, D. (1983) *Law and Order: Theft of an Issue*. London: Fabian Society (Pamphlet No. 490).

Gough, I. (1983) Thatcherism and the Welfare State. In S. Hall and M.

Jacques (eds) *The Politics of Thatcherism*. London: Lawrence and Wishart, pp. 148–68.

Hough, M. and Mayhew, R. (1983) *The British Crime Survey*, Home Office Research Studies No. 76. London: HMSO.

Husband, C. (1982) *Race in Britain*. London: Hutchinson.

Jones, R. M. (1983) *The Mental Health Act 1983*. London: Sweet and Maxwell.

Kettle, M. (1983) The Drift to Law and Order. In S. Hall and M. Jacques (eds) *The Politics of Thatcherism*. London: Lawrence and Wishart, pp. 216–34. (Essays from *Marxism Today*.)

Levenson, H. (1980) *Democracy and the Police*. Labour Campaign for Criminal Justice (mimeo).

Martin, J. P. (1978) *Violence and the Family*. Chichester: John Wiley.

Parliamentary Debates, fifth and sixth series.

Rees, T. (1982) Immigration Policies in the U.K. In C. Husband (ed.) *Race in Britain*. London: Hutchinson, ch. 4, pp. 75–96.

Regan, D. (1983) *Are the Police under Control?* Research Paper No. 1, Social Affairs Unit. London: Esmonde Publishing.

Scarman, Lord (1982) *Report on the Brixton Disorders 10–12 April 1981*. Harmondsworth: Penguin.

Taylor, I. (1981) *Law and Order: Arguments for Socialism*. London: Macmillan.

The Times (9 April, 1984).

11

A defence of social security

JONATHAN BRADSHAW

There is so much that is obviously wrong with the social security system in Britain today that it is a valiant almost silly act to seek to defend it. One has only to point to the spate of proposals for reform that are emerging from all along the range of the ideological spectrum as evidence of widespread dissatisfaction with the *status quo* (Minford 1984; Parker 1984; Dilnot *et al*. 1984). The government itself has set in hand its own reviews which Mr Norman Fowler, Secretary of State for Social Services, claims 'will constitute the most substantial examination of the social security system since the Beveridge report forty years ago' (DHSS Press Release 84/89, 2 April, 1984). Given the timetable of these reviews (they were all completed by the end of 1984), and given the many political, administrative, legislative, and financial constraints, it is unlikely that the reviews will quickly result in very fundamental changes to the existing system. However, given the demands from many quarters for a thorough-going restructuring of social security, it is time for some kind of defence to be mounted.

The central arguments in this chapter are that the social

security system that we have is not as bad as people make out, given the size of the operation and the demographic and economic pressures that exist. Social security expenditure is a hostage to the fortunes of other parts of the social structure. Social security does not have and cannot hope to have clear objectives. It serves many forces and is subject to conflicting and competing aspirations. Given this, social security on a number of criteria does very well and has adapted well in the years since the war to the many demands made on it. It has also emerged reasonably undamaged from the present government's aspirations to cut public expenditure and taxation. The people who sponsor fundamental reforms of social security have yet to be convincing that their proposals are either feasible or a desirable alternative to the system which has emerged through the process of incremental *ad hoc* reform. Britain is not over-burdened by the costs of the social security system; on the contrary, there is room for higher levels of expenditure.

The size of the operation

It is as well to start by being aware of the size of the social security operation. *Table 11.1* summarizes the dimensions of the system. It is a really massive undertaking – far larger than any other part of the welfare state, taking up £39 billion in 1985/86 – nearly 30 per cent of all public expenditure – and spending three times as much as both the health and personal social services and the education budget. It includes twenty-three different principal benefits, and about 90,000 staff are employed to administer these benefits. At any one time a substantial minority of the population are dependent on social security benefits for all or part of their income. In 1982, 75 per cent of household units received some of their net household income in the form of a social security benefit; 30 per cent received more than half their net household income in social security; and 11 per cent were receiving more than 90 per cent of their net income in the form of social security benefits (see *Table 11.2*).

Overall, social security benefits contribute 31 per cent of the net income of the average household, but of course social security

Table 11.1   *The dimensions of social security 1984/85*

benefits	expenditure £ millions	numbers receiving thousands
retirement pension	15,539	9,260
widows' benefit	798	430
unemployment benefit	1,538	970
sickness benefit	246	150
invalidity benefit	1,928	740
death grant	18	—
industrial disablement benefit	377	180
industrial death benefit	57	30
other industrial injury benefit	5	5
maternity allowance	191	140
guardians allowance and child's special allowance	2	5
non-contributory retirement pension	44	35
war pension	544	305
attendance allowance	571	490
invalid care allowance	11	10
non-contributory invalidity pension	201	215
mobility allowance	356	350
supplementary pension	792	1,520
supplementary allowance	5,365	2,790
child benefit	4,291	12,455
one-parent benefit	122	570
family income supplement	131	205
maternity grant	18	—
housing benefit	2,461	6,255
administration	1,500	
total expenditure	37,207	

Source: Tables 2.12 and 2.12.2, Cmnd 9143–II, *The Government's Expenditure Plans 1984/85 to 1986/87.*

benefits are more important to some people than others. Benefits provide more than 70 per cent of the net income of pensioner households, 61 per cent of the net income of households with an unemployed head, and 50 per cent of the net income of single-parent families. Many of the most vulnerable people in our society are dependent on benefits: 2.2 million children live in families whose income is determined by the level of supplementary benefit or family income supplement and the very old are also particularly likely to be dependent for all or part of their income on supplementary benefit. Seven million people are now dependent for their income on supplementary benefit (which means by definition that they have few other resources). The seven million includes 60 per cent of the unemployed, a third of all pensioners, and a half of all single parents.

Table 11.2   *Proportion of net household income made up of social security benefits*

proportion of net income	proportion of households
none	24.6
up to 10 per cent	25.5
11 per cent–20 per cent	9.0
21 per cent–30 per cent	5.6
31 per cent–40 per cent	4.0
41 per cent–50 per cent	3.5
51 per cent–60 per cent	3.9
61 per cent–70 per cent	4.0
71 per cent–80 per cent	4.5
81 per cent–90 per cent	4.2
more than 90 per cent	11.1
all	100.0
total number of households	7428

Source: Family Expenditure Survey 1982.

That social security is a very large enterprise is not by itself an argument in its defence, but the fact that social security expenditure is critical to the living standards of so many people means that it can only be tampered with with trepidation. The size of the budget also means that there is a limit to which it can be treated as a residual or marginal aspect of policy, to be employed as a handmaiden to the management of macro-economic policy or to achieve partisan political objectives. This is best illustrated by the experience of the Thatcher government since 1979.

The resilience of social security

The present Conservative government came to power in 1979 with a clear commitment to cut public expenditure and taxation and generally roll back the welfare state. In education and housing policy, very substantial cuts were made in pursuit of that policy. A budget as large as that for social security could not escape the government's attempts to make savings. It is worth rehearsing the cuts that have been made.

1. The link between the rates of long-term benefits and earnings was abandoned in 1980. Upratings were also deferred for two weeks.
2. Earnings-related supplement to short-term benefits was abolished from January 1982.
3. Short-term benefits were abated by 5 per cent in lieu of taxation. These abatements were not immediately restored when taxation began but eventually the government were persuaded to restore the abatement except for invalidity beneficiaries.
4. There were other smaller cuts included in the Social Security (No. 2) Act 1980, including changes to the 'waiting days', abatement of unemployment benefit for occupational pensioners, and reductions in supplementary benefits for strikers' families.
5. The uprating of benefits in 1982 was underestimated by 2 per cent but was subsequently restored in 1983.
6. Child additions to short-term benefits have been phased out over a period of successive upratings.
7. Statutory sick pay transferred responsibility for the payment of sickness benefit to employers for the first eight weeks. This reform resulted in a reduction in public expenditure of £450 million and cuts in the level of benefit payable to families with children. However the reform was neutral with respect to the public sector borrowing requirement because revenue was cut as a result of reduction in employers' national insurance contributions.
8. There were minor savings in expenditure arising from the change to four-weekly payment of child benefit, cuts in child

benefit to school leavers, and changes in the basis of the 1982 uprating in supplementary benefits.

9. In 1983 cuts in the new housing benefit scheme totalling £230 million were announced. They included increases in the tapers and the non-householder's contribution, thus excluding many of those formerly in receipt of benefit. The government were persuaded to amend their proposals and to delay the introduction of the full package of cuts until November 1984, but savings in a full year will amount to £185 million.

10. In 1984, as part of the uprating package, the 'available scale margin' was increased (saving £86 million), and existing claimants of FIS did not receive an uprating (saving £11 million). These savings were partly offset by improvements to heating additions, leaving net savings of £66.6 million. A further £17 million was saved in 1984, and £8.5 million subsequently, by paying unemployment benefit fortnightly in arrears.

There are no very reliable estimates of the cumulative value of these cuts in social security expenditure. In November 1982 the government estimated that the social security changes they had made since 1979 saved £1,410 million in 1982/83 (Hansard, col. 282, 18 November, 1982). This is a very large sum but it represents only 4.3 per cent of the social security budget in that year. Since 1982 the government have been unwilling to publish an estimate of the savings they have achieved. However calculations by the staff of the House of Commons library, reported in *The Times* (25 June, 1984), estimate that since 1979 *cumulative* total savings up to 1983/84 were £4,300 million and would be £6,700 million by 1984/85. This is still only 4.3 per cent of social security expenditure over the period 1980/81–1984/85. Most of the increase in savings of £2,400 million between 1983/84 and 1984/85 comes not from the more recently announced packages of cuts but the accumulating impact of uprating benefits in line with price movements rather than earnings.

Apart from the major decision taken early in the government's period in office to break the link with earnings, cuts have been moderate and somewhat *ad hoc*. It is difficult to discern in them a clear strategic purpose. It appears that each year the DHSS has been required by the Treasury to make cuts in its expenditure commitments to keep within the government's overall expenditure targets and have reluctantly chosen items for cuts which do as little harm as possible to the key elements of social security. It is possible that the reviews of social security were partly created in an effort to inject some rather longer-term planning into future cuts in social security.

There is no doubt that the cuts in social security expenditure have been one factor responsible for the substantial increase in the numbers of people in Britain dependent on means-tested benefits. They have also borne hard on individual claimants of benefits: the Social Security Advisory Committee expressed particular concern at the increase in the non-dependants deduction in housing benefit and concluded that the cuts had 'gone beyond what is fair and reasonable'. However, despite the impact of the cuts on the nature of the benefit system as well as their effects on the circumstances of individual claimants, the social security budget has continued to grow. It has actually grown in real terms by 26.3 per cent between 1978/79 and 1984/85 – at about the same rate as the growth in defence expenditure (26.8 per cent) and not much slower than the increase in the 'law and order' budget (37.1 per cent). Social security has also grown as a proportion of all public expenditure, from 21 per cent in 1976/77 to 30 per cent (planned) in 1986/87. Expenditure on social security has since 1979 also been con-sistently higher than that planned by the government. In 1979 the government planned that social security expenditure should increase from £15,197 million in 1979/80 to £15,910 million in 1982/83, but in the event it had increased to £18,698 million – five times faster than intended (all figures at 1978/79 prices) (Hansard, col. 384, 11 June, 1984).

Dr Rhodes Boyson declared of the social security budget: 'This vast and growing programme cannot be exempt from restraint. It must be kept within overall economic targets if our economic strategy is to bear fruit' (reported in *The Guardian*, 19 July, 1984). But try as they might the government's objectives have been undermined by natural pressures for growth in the social security budget.

Pressures for growth

The first of these pressures have been demographic changes – particularly increases in the numbers of pensioners and a continuing steady increase in the numbers of single parents. The increase in the numbers of recipients in these two groups has been considerably more than the decline that has occurred in the number of children.

The second and much more important pressure on social security expenditure has come as a result of the massive increase in the level of unemployment that has occurred over the last five years. Expenditure on benefits for the unemployed increased fourfold between 1979/80 and 1984/85 compared with an increase in prices during the same period of only about 60 per cent. Expenditure on benefits for the unemployed increased from 7.6 per cent to 17.6 per cent of the social security budget between 1979 and 1984 (Treasury 1984b). Unemployment also affects other parts of the social security budget apart from benefits for the unemployed. Thus the number of invalidity beneficiaries has increased *pari passu* with unemployment; there has been a substantial increase in the number of families claiming family income supplement (FIS); more people are retiring earlier; fewer people are having benefits reduced because of part-time earnings; and there is increased demand for housing benefit, free school meals, and exemptions for health service charges – all partly the results of the decline in demand for labour.

A third pressure on the social security budget has come as a result of improvements in benefits. Most of these cost pressures occurred in the 1970s but since 1978 a new state earnings-related pension scheme (SERPS) has begun to be phased in. The first full pensions will not be received until 1998 and the total cost implications of SERPS will not be fully felt until it reaches full maturity in 2020. The provision of equal treatment in social security more or less imposed on the government by a European Community directive has also led to the extension of rights to certain benefits which will cost an extra £31 million in 1985/86 (Hansard, col. 699, 26 June, 1984). The government itself has also been responsible for a number of reforms which have led to increased expenditure. Following the ending of the electricity discount scheme in 1980, new additional requirements for fuel were introduced into supplementary benefits. By 1984 they were costing an extra £140 million in real terms (Hansard, col. 26, 18 June, 1984). The ending of the invalidity trap in 1983 cost £9 million (Hansard, col. 259, 18 July, 1984) and the new disablement benefit will cost an extra £20 million. Some benefits have cost more from being uprated further than they need to have been to retain their value in relation to inflation. These include mobility allowance, which has been increased in real value by 10 per cent between 1979 and 1984.

A fourth cost pressure has come from increases in the utilization of some benefits. These increases are for the most part unplanned, unexpected, and not always fully explained. The number of families claiming FIS has increased from 81,000 in December 1979 to 201,000 in December 1983. This increase may be the result of a number of factors including fewer opportunities for overtime, fewer second earners, increases in the number of one-parent families, real increases in the prescribed limits, and also, possibly, improvements in take-up. In addition the take-up of one-parent benefit by those not on supplementary benefit and who stand to gain by claiming has steadily increased to about 78 per cent in 1982 (Millar 1984). The number of claimants of attendance allowance increased sharply by over 100,000 between 1982/83 and 1984/85 and recipients of mobility allowance increased by 85,000 during the same period. Neither of these increases has yet been adequately explained.

So even in the face of a clear ideological commitment to reduce public expenditure, social security expenditure has grown. This reflects the fact that it is demand-led and cannot therefore be cash-limited. Half of social security expenditure is on contributory benefits where specific rights are supposed to be guaranteed by the contributory condition, though this principle may have lost some of its force since the abolition of contributory earnings-related supplement and the abatements and cuts in other insurance benefits. Nevertheless, if a government wants to cut social security benefits it more often than not has to go to parliament to change the law; and because very large numbers of MPs' constituents are dependent on benefits, no attempt to cut benefit succeeds without a very uncomfortable passage. Thus for example the government was eventually persuaded to make good the abatement in short-term insurance benefit, thanks partly to the co-ordinated and vociferous objections of their own backbenchers.

Political concern with social security policy is not merely a matter of backbenchers defending their constituents' interests, nor just a measure of the effectiveness of the able pressure groups operating in this field. It also reflects a considerable body of support among general public opinion. Public opinion, however, is difficult to interpret (Hennessy 1984; Taylor-Gooby 1984). People express different attitudes with different levels of commitment and many of the attitudes expressed are inconsistent. There is a tendency to favour tax cuts *and* increases in services, or a tendency to favour cuts in social security but, when faced with the choice of specific benefits to be cut, oppose cuts in them all. There is also evidence that the general public are particularly ignorant about social security issues, tending to overestimate both the level of benefits and the amount spent on administration. Perhaps this is not surprising given the level of discourse about the matter in the popular media. However, despite the difficulties in interpretation, there is still in Britain a clear majority in favour of maintaining and improving social services. There is also evidence that support for social services has been increasing in recent years. The 1979 British Election Study found that 61 per cent of the population wanted to keep up services as against cutting taxes. The BBC election study in 1983 found that this proportion had increased to 77 per cent. A Gallup poll in May 1979 found that 34 per cent were in favour of tax cuts 'even if it means reductions in government services such as health, education, and welfare', but by August 1980 the proportion had fallen to 20 per cent, and in the Social Attitudes Survey in spring 1983 only 9 per cent supported the statement. A MORI poll asked people to nominate from a list of eleven items their top priority for cuts in public expenditure. In February 1980, 44 per cent nominated cuts in social security, but by February 1983 this had fallen to 23 per cent with 19 per cent wanting increases in social security benefits. The first priority for cuts had become defence. In the MORI survey for the television programme

'Breadline Britain' three-quarters of those interviewed were prepared to pay more tax to enable everyone to afford basic necessities. Attitudes to different benefits tend to vary. Taylor-Gooby (1982) carried out a survey in Medway in 1981 and asked respondents whether spending on benefits for particular groups should be reduced, maintained, or increased, and if increased whether the respondent would be willing to pay more in tax to finance an increase. The results are summarized in *Table 11.3*.

Table 11.3   *Attitudes to social security benefit*

	benefits for sick %	old-age pensions %	single-parent benefits %	benefits for the unemployed %	child benefits %
reduce spending	2	6	5	10	34
maintain spending	42	63	52	62	54
increase spending	56	31	43	28	12
% willing to pay extra tax to support increase	50	26	35	18	8

Source: Taylor-Gooby (1982).

Only a minority wanted to reduce spending on any of the benefits listed and even the level of benefits for the unemployed is widely supported, perhaps reflecting the fact that one household in three has a member who is unemployed. The least-popular benefit appears to be child benefit, but attitudes to this vary. In the Social Attitudes Survey a third of adults aged 18–34 named child benefit as their number one priority for increases and a third of respondents in the 'Breadline Britain' survey thought child benefits were too low.

The objectives of social security policy

Many of those who are critical of our social security system and seek to change it with grandiose (but simple) reforms tend to fail to appreciate the variety and complexity of the objectives served by the system. The objectives of social security benefits are rarely made explicit, either in the legislation that brings them into being or in the application forms or other official material used to market them. Because of their nature and the manner in which policy is made, benefits are likely to emerge from the legislative process with a variety of objectives. Indeed scholars of the process of social policy-making have suggested that the more objectives a policy has, the greater the chance of it reaching the statute book. A kind of legislative Darwinism operates. This is not so much a matter of the 'survival of the fittest' in simple terms as it is to do with the fact that in order to survive, policies have to be very well adapted to the competing interests of political parties, pressure groups, taxpayers, beneficiaries, and others in the policy-making process. While a social security benefit may become adapted to meet the often inconsistent aspirations of those engaged in the policy-making process, the end result may be that the final form of the benefit loses its capacity to meet the original primary objectives of the earlier reformer.

Beveridge sought to create a social security system that abolished want but, in pursuit of that objective, policies had to have regard to a host of other objectives – thus the system needed to avoid undermining work incentives, it needed to uphold marriage and the family, it needed to operate within financial constraints, and in the end, for political reasons, pensions had to be paid more quickly than he intended. One result was that pensions and other insurance benefits were never paid at higher levels than social assistance rates. It often requires a fairly detailed study of the origins of a policy to discern its objectives. Thus for example MacNicol (1980) found that the reasons why family allowances succeeded in reaching the statute book were not so much the extent to which they relieved family poverty or boosted the birth rate (objectives publicly espoused then and since), but rather for reasons of economic control – as an anti-inflation policy, to enforce work incentives, to assist labour mobility, and to cope with the problem of low pay. Child benefits now serve a whole variety of purposes. Townsend, in written evidence to the Review of Benefits for Children and Young Persons, identified seven objectives: reducing poverty, promoting adequate diets for children, improving the disposable income of families with children relative to those without, increasing incentives to take and maintain employment, controlling wage inflation, strengthening the mother's role, and stabilizing low incomes during periods of recession (Townsend 1984).

A detailed analysis of the sorry story of housing benefit has yet to be written, but when it is it is likely to reveal how the original aspirants sought a scheme that would unify and simplify the diverse methods of meeting the housing costs of low-income families; how this was then taken up by the DHSS as a mechanism by which they could meet the government's target of saving manpower and was hurriedly implemented to meet that target by March 1983. In the legislative stage the objectives to unify and simplify gave way to the objective to introduce the scheme at nil exchequer cost and at the same time to avoid significant losers. Thus the scheme never unified the old rent rebate scheme with support for the housing costs of supplementary beneficiaries, and was complicated to avoid losers by the unworkable system of housing benefit supplement. Housing benefit is certainly a particularly sad example of how the primary objectives of reform may be diverted in order to pursue other purposes which are irrelevant to the original or prime purpose of the benefit.

We may wish that things were otherwise and that policies could operate unadulterated by extraneous considerations. We may seek to reform policies so that they become more effective, but in the end we have to recognize that social security serves a variety of social functions and resist judging benefits on the extent to which they achieve a single objective.

The achievements of social security

Of all the great variety of objectives of social security benefits there would probably be most general agreement that the primary objective is to provide freedom from want – or, put in a

Table 11.4 *Real value of selected benefits: equivalent at November 1983 prices (£ per week)*

date	retirement pension (couple)	unemployment benefit (couple)	supplementary benefit* (couple)	child support (3 children)
September 1951	23.10	19.54 (August)	21.83	21.77 (April)
April 1961	31.46	31.46	29.48	19.45
September 1971	40.91	40.91	38.90	17.97 (April)
November 1975	50.27	42.68	40.88	16.15 (April)
November 1979	53.65	43.08	41.55	19.15 (April)
November 1982	55.10	42.41	43.66	18.40
November 1983	54.50	43.75	43.50	19.50

Source: DHSS Abstract of Statistics for Index of Retail Prices, Average Earnings, Social Security Benefits and Contributions, 1984.

* RPI less housing costs.

more modern idiom, to meet basic needs. In dwelling on the failings of the system, critics often fail to acknowledge the extent to which this has actually been achieved by the social security system since the war. In particular we fail to recognize the extent to which benefits have improved in real terms. In *Table 11.4* we show how the value of a selection of benefits has changed in real terms over the last thirty or so years. With the exception of child support the purchasing power of most benefits has doubled over that period.

In comparison with earnings (*Table 11.5*), pensions have improved and other benefits have more or less maintained their level, the major exception to this being child support.

As well as improving on the minimum subsistence levels fixed by Beveridge, the system of social security has also responded to meet new needs that have emerged. Thus for example Beveridge made no arrangements to meet the needs arising from the huge increase in the number of single-parent families. The supplementary benefit system has had to respond to this growth and in addition new benefits – family income supplement (FIS) and

Table 11.5   *Value of selected benefits as a % of male manual earnings*

date	retirement pension (couple)	unemployment benefit (couple)	supplementary benefit* (couple)	child support (3 children)
September 1951	30.3	25.7 (August)	30.3	27.8 (April)
April 1961	30.7	30.7	29.9	19.0
September 1971	31.6	31.6	30.8	14.2 (April)
November 1975	34.3	29.1	28.7	11.0 (April)
November 1979	36.0	28.9	28.7	12.9 (April)
November 1982	38.0	29.2	30.1	12.5
November 1983	36.7	29.4	29.3	13.1

Source: DHSS Abstract of Statistics for Index of Retail Prices, Average Earnings, Social Security Benefits and Contributions, 1984.

* RPI less housing costs.

one-parent benefit – have been introduced. The number of single parents receiving supplementary benefit has more than trebled since 1966. The number of single parents receiving FIS has increased more than five times since the benefit was introduced in 1971. Between them these benefits now form something of an income guarantee whether or not the single parent works and, unlike many single-parent benefits payable in other countries, they do not force the single mother to fend for herself in the labour market until the youngest child reaches the age of sixteen.

The other group for whom new benefits have been developed is the civilian disabled. The post-war social security programme took account of the needs of those disabled in war and those disabled at work but ignored most of the civilian disabled. The inequity of this situation has begun to be recognized and successive governments have enacted a stream of new benefits to help to fill the gap. Invalidity benefit was introduced to replace and enhance long-term sickness benefit. In addition the contributory principle has not been allowed to stand in the way of extending a non-means-tested income replacement benefit to the civilian disabled. Non-contributory invalidity benefit can be received by those who have never worked.

Two new benefits, attendance allowance and mobility allowance, have been created to help meet the extra expenses of disablement. These benefits are tax-free and are disregarded in assessing entitlement to other benefits. They are also paid at quite generous rates. A severely disabled person can now receive £82.85 per week in invalidity benefit, mobility allowance, and higher rate attendance allowance (November 1984 rates). Few other countries have benefits equivalent to attendance and mobility allowance in their social security systems for the disabled, and those that do tend to pay considerably less towards the extra costs of disablement. In addition to these benefits for the civilian disabled the social security system has also begun to recognize the financial needs of those who give up work to care for dependent people through the introduction of the invalid care allowance.

New benefits for single-parent families and for the disabled are two ways the social security system has had to develop since the war to meet changes in society and to cope with new patterns of dependency. But these are not the only challenges that the system has faced. For example when, from the mid-1970s, fuel prices began to rise rapidly in real terms, the social security system had to adapt to meet the new problems of fuel poverty – the inability of low-income households to afford adequate warmth (Bradshaw and Harris 1984). These changes were typically incremental and discordant but we now have, for recipients of supplementary benefit, a system of additional benefits targeted on those with a special need for extra heat, those who are at home all day, those with expensive central heating systems, and those living in hard-to-heat dwellings, and there is even a capacity in the system to respond to severe winter weather. Nearly two-thirds of claimants are entitled to one or other of these additional requirements which cost about £400 million per year.

So far we have pointed to the extent to which benefits have improved in terms of their level and coverage, but the best way to demonstrate the achievements of the social security system is to point to the consequences for the population if all or any part of it did not exist. O'Higgins in chapter 8 discusses the extent to which social security benefits contribute to vertical redistribution – to mitigating inequalities in the distribution of primary or market income. But social security benefits also make a major contribution to a variety of different types of horizontal redistribution.

Since the abolition of child tax allowances, child benefits and FIS together with the children's scale rates in supplementary benefit and the children's needs allowance in housing benefit are the only mechanisms for adjusting the net disposable resources of a family to their needs. Without these benefits the horizontal income distribution would be grossly inequitable. Single people and childless wage earners would receive exactly the same net income as families carrying the financial burden of child-rearing. The distribution of income from employment is already biased against families with children because the labour participation of married women is highest when there are no dependent children in the household. So as well as providing compensation for the extra costs of children, child support in the social security system is also providing some replacement for the income forgone by a second earner in a family in the task of care. In 1982 child benefit represented 10 per cent of the net incomes of two-parent families, 17 per cent of those of one-parent families and 20 per cent of those of all families living at or below 140 per cent of supplementary benefit level (Millar 1984).

Another form of horizontal redistribution is in favour of the disabled. Most of the expenditure on benefits for the disabled goes on invalidity benefits and supplementary benefits which are basic income replacement benefits. For the vast majority of the long-term sick and disabled, these benefits are their recipient's sole means of support. There have been few systematic evaluations of the impact of the benefits that are paid to some of the disabled on top of these basic income maintenance benefits. One study by Baldwin *et al.* (1983) carried out a careful assessment of the income lost and the extra expenses involved in caring for a disabled child. They found that without the attendance and mobility allowances, families with a severely disabled child had incomes which were substantially lower than other families due mainly to the fact that mothers of disabled children were less likely to be in employment, and if they were had lower earnings. Attendance and mobility allowances filled some of the income gap, but only for manual workers with a child under five did they fully compensate for income forgone. So social security benefits play a key role in filling the gap between the incomes of families with children or disabled members and their needs.

Benefits are also the most important mechanism for adjusting income to needs throughout the life-cycle. The following graph (*Figure 11.1*) compares the average gross income of families at

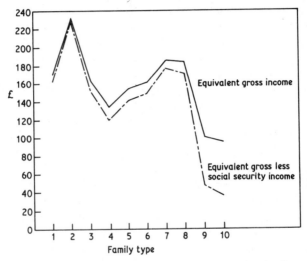

Figure 11.1 Family expenditure survey 1982: income by family type.

each of ten life-cycle stages. The analysis employs a technique devised by Nicholson and O'Higgins (1981) for examining the distribution of income over the life-cycle using cross-sectional data. The households in the Family Expenditure Survey (in this case the 1982 FES (DoE 1983) are allocated to one of ten groups representing a stage of the life-cycle.

The ten groups are as follows:

1. Single adult under 30;
2. Couple, wife under 30;
3. Couple with one child under 5;

4. Couple with two or more children all under 16 and at least one under 5;
5. Couple with children aged 5–16;
6. Couple with children, at least one child over 16;
7. Couple with children all over 16;
8. Couple with no children, head aged 50–65;
9. Pensioner couple;
10. Single pensioner.

The upper line on the graph shows the equivalent income distribution including social security benefits. It can be seen that families with dependent children (groups 3, 4, 5, and 6) and retirement pensioners (groups 9 and 10) have the lowest equivalent income. The lower line on the graph compares the equivalent income excluding social security benefits. While the average income of all ten groups falls it is families with children and particularly pensioners who gain most from social security benefits. Thus social security most benefits those families in the life-cycle stages with the lowest equivalent incomes.

So far we have considered the achievements of social security in maintaining the income of children and the disabled, and throughout the life-cycle (particularly in retirement), but perhaps the most dramatic role social security plays is in supporting the living standards of those unable to gain access to the labour market. In 1982 of those unemployed and seeking work 88 per cent were receiving social security benefits. Of those receiving benefit, over two-thirds were receiving supplementary benefit indicating that they had little or no other resources. Not only are the benefits paid to the unemployed vital to their living standards, but because unemployment affects some areas more than others benefits are of great importance to the living standards of certain regions. This is illustrated most startlingly in Northern Ireland. In January 1983 the male unemployment rate in Northern Ireland was 26.7 per cent, nearly half of the unemployed had been out of work for over a year, and nearly 70 per cent were dependent on supplementary benefit. It has been estimated that if the long-term rates of supplementary benefit were payable to the unemployed, the extra money injected into the Northern Ireland economy as a result would have created 400 extra jobs in 1982 alone (Ditch 1984).

Is social security efficient?

One of the most extensive analyses of the impact of social security on poverty was carried out by Beckerman and Clark (1982) using data from the Family Expenditure Survey. They assessed the achievement of the social security system according to the extent to which it both reduced the numbers in poverty and also reduced the poverty gap – that is the resources needed to be distributed to poor households to lift them out of poverty. They found that in 1975 the number of people living in poverty would have increased seven times without social security benefits. That is, the proportion of the population living in poverty fell from 22.7 per cent to 3.2 per cent as a result of social security expenditure. The proportionate reduction in the poverty gap was even greater – from £5,855 million to only £250 million. They also considered the efficiency of the social security system in relieving poverty. Between 1974–76 only about 40 per cent of social security expenditure was actually directed at reducing the poverty gap. About 42 per cent went to people who were not poor to begin with, and the other 18 per cent went to those who were poor but provided more than enough to raise them above the poverty level. Given that the residual poverty gap is so small they considered whether there is a case for reducing one or other of these leakages. However they concluded that 'it appears that this would be by no means so easy or desirable' (Beckerman and Clark 1982: 5).

Part of this leakage is in means-tested benefits paid to income units within households even though the household in which they live is not poor as a whole. In order to avoid this happening, it would be necessary to reintroduce the household means test which was abandoned in 1942 with considerable relief. Some of the problems of the household means test have recently re-emerged as a result of the government's decision to increase the non-householder's contribution as part of the cuts in housing benefit. This change meant that recipients of housing benefit had their rent increased if there was a person aged eighteen or over in the household, and the non-householder was expected to pay more towards the rent (£8.20 from April 1984). The Social Security Advisory Committee were concerned that non-dependants either could not or would not pay the contribution and that as a result this would 'cause a substantial loss in a largely indiscriminate fashion to families who have very low incomes indeed' (SSAC report, point 11) and would also result in rent arrears. Alternatively, non-dependants might be encouraged to leave home or to leave employment in order to avoid contributing the rent share. Although there is little systematic evidence on the sharing of income within the household, one study based on the analysis of correspondence to the *Daily Star* does indicate that the Social Security Advisory Committee's anxieties about the effects in the increase in the non-dependant deduction may be real ones (Cusack and Roll 1985).

The other main cause of leakage or inefficiency arises from benefits paid without a test of means, including insurance benefits and child benefits. The Institute of Fiscal Studies have focused single-mindedly on this aspect of inefficiency in their proposals for the reform of social security (Dilnot *et al.* 1984). While they acknowledge that 'the objectives of any social security system are many and complex' they assess the efficacy of the system only on the extent to which it relieves poverty – that is, brings incomes up to the supplementary benefit level. Thus using the 1981 Family Expenditure Survey they estimate that only 42.9 per cent of social security expenditure goes towards bringing the pre-benefit poor up to the poverty level. They therefore advocate that reform must be 'achieved by a savage, but selective, retrenchment of the benefit system' (Dilnot *et al.* 1984: 5).

In pursuit of this objective they ride fairly rough-shod over the arguments that might be espoused for the existing system. Thus the notion that insurance benefits entrench rights to benefit more solidly than means tests is 'based on an illusion' (p. 30). The idea that the state should intervene to help people redistribute their income over their lifetime or help them support their children is 'controversial' (p. 43) – after all 'the parents have chosen to have children and have done so for reasons of personal pleasure rather than social obligation' (p. 142). The system only '*may* [my emphasis] need to have regard to other objectives of economic policy, such as the incentive to work or to save' (p. 43).

In any social security system there is a conflict between target efficiency and administrative efficiency. Supplementary benefit costs over 10p to administer for each £1 of benefit paid while retirement pension costs 1½p per £1 paid. Supplementary benefit costs more because it is more efficiently targeted – it is a means-tested benefit which takes detailed account of the resources and requirements of claimants. The IFS propose to overcome this problem of the extra administrative costs of a wholly means-tested scheme by a technical fix. Taxes and benefits would be fixed annually on the basis of a return of income. Anyone who submits a return will be issued with a computerized card.

Under their scheme the tax payable and the benefit credits received have to vary with income, employment status, marital status, the number of children, and housing costs. While end-of-year assessments may be satisfactory for fixing tax payable, this system could not be used to fix benefits. Changes during the benefit year would have to be dealt with by applicants asking for new coding cards as changes occur. Thus the tax/benefit authorities would have to respond to deaths, births, divorces, marriages, children leaving home, increases in housing costs, and a whole variety of other events.

Independently of all these changes in circumstances and employment status there will be variations in income to take into account. It is difficult to see how even with a highly automated system it will be possible to operate the scheme as simply and cheaply as the authors envisage. They argue that the unpopularity of means tests is 'purely instinctive . . . about form rather than substance . . . superficial sloganising'.

> 'What is offensive are specific and potentially humiliating enquiries into the affairs of poor households which discriminate between them and the population as a whole. The intention of the proposals is to effect a considerable reduction in these enquiries by utilising much more extensively information which is, or could be, collected through the tax system.'
>
> (Dilnot *et al*. 1984: 117)

It may not be possible for their scheme to avoid 'specific and potentially humiliating enquiries' given the huge task involved in dealing with changes in income and other circumstances. But the IFS authors have also misunderstood the real nature of the problem of means tests. People do not claim means-tested benefits for a variety of reasons. Certainly humiliating enquiries and their discriminatory nature play a part in deterring applicants but there are a host of other possibly more important reasons for non-take-up, and the problem of the non-take-up of means-tested benefits is not 'superficial sloganising' nor the plight only of 'confused old ladies failing to claim rate rebates' (p. 103), nor is it merely the echo of experiences in the 1930s and before. It is an apparently intractable by-product of delivering benefits according to means (Deacon and Bradshaw 1983).

There is another problem of means tests which proposers of the IFS scheme cannot overcome. This is the poverty trap or high marginal tax rates. In pursuit of the objective of avoiding 5 per cent of single-earner couples with children having a *notional* marginal tax rate of over 100 per cent, they produce a scheme where 28 per cent have an *actual* marginal tax rate of over 80 per cent. The existing tax benefit scheme is far from satisfactory and there are many families with children who face very high marginal tax rates as a result of the effects of benefit losses and tax increases when wage increases occur. However it is very unlikely that a family would lose 100 per cent of any increase in income mainly because FIS, the benefit with the highest loss rate of 50 per cent, continues to be paid regardless of changes in circumstance for a year. They argue that the poverty trap is fundamentally intractable: 'We must either make poor households poorer, or extend high marginal tax rates into more densely populated regions of the income distribution' (Dilnot *et al.* 1984: 94). The poverty trap or poverty plateau problem is actually only intractable if reform is a 'savage' extension of means-tested selectivity.

The IFS proposals are presaged on the assumption that the 'political climate in Britain . . . is now increasingly hostile to additional social security expenditure. The pressure now is not to spend more on social security but to spend less' (p. 2).

It may now be true that the pressure is to spend less on social security, but is it really necessary that the existing system should be overthrown in favour of a wholly means-tested scheme? Do we really not have the resources in Britain to maintain and build on to our existing social security system?

Can we afford better social security benefits?

First there are undoubtedly resources in the tax benefit system that could be better targeted on those in need without resort to means testing and without increasing the public-sector borrowing requirement. For example it is now widely accepted that the married man's tax allowance is very difficult to justify in an era when the majority of married women are independent earners. If it were abolished for those under sixty-five £3,600 million would be released for improvements in benefits – enough to double the level of child benefit (Hansard, col. 80, 9 April, 1984). There are other tax allowances which could also be better directed. Thus the age allowance cost £450 million in 1982–83 and principally benefited pensioners with middle-range incomes (because there is a taper on the allowance for higher income earners). It certainly is of no benefit to the poorest pensioners with incomes below the tax threshold. If this were abolished it would provide the resources to increase the retirement pension by about £1 per week or enable the long-term rates of supplementary benefit to be paid to the unemployed after a year. There are other tax allowances that present rather more complex problems to reform although the benefits derived from them are not targeted very well on those who need help most. Thus for example it is unlikely that any government could abolish the £2,150 million that goes on tax relief on mortgage interest payments because of the opposition from the large number of owner-occupiers and the impact it would have on their housing costs. However, restricting relief to the standard tax rate and setting a lower limit to the size of the mortgage that qualified for tax relief would at least limit the growth of this tax expenditure and strengthen the tax base. The £1,500 million forgone in 1982/83 in tax relief on contributions to private pension schemes could also not be clawed back all at once because of the impact on retirement saving, but this could be limited to the standard rates of tax and its value could be progressively diminished by setting cash ceilings on the existing allowances. So there are resources to be utilized in the reform of some of the tax expenditures.

Townsend has challenged the reviews with more general egalitarian arguments (Townsend 1984). He argues that post-tax incomes in Britain are particularly unequal and that if the richest 20 per cent of the population were taxed more heavily and their disposable income was reduced by one sixth, the disposable income of the poorest 20 per cent could be doubled.

Is social security expenditure excessive in the UK? One of the central economic arguments of the Thatcher (and Reagan) government is that the decline in Britain's economic per-formance can be blamed on the size of government expenditure. In Britain public expenditure as a proportion of GDP has increased from 35.2 per cent in 1964/65 to 46.5 per cent in 1980/81. This is a smaller increase than every other country in the European Community except France. Britain does not have a particularly high level of social expenditure as a proportion of GDP. Indeed in 1981, out of the nine European Community countries, Britain came second to bottom in a league table of social expenditure as a proportion of GDP, spending 23.5 per cent, compared with Holland at the top of the table with 31.4 per cent, Germany with 29.4 per cent, and France with 27.5 per cent. If the comparison is restricted only to social security and social assistance benefits and grants, Britain spends less as a pro-portion of GDP than any other country in the European Community – 13.3 per cent compared with, for example, 28.0 per cent in the Netherlands, 24.4 per cent in France, and 17.9 per cent in Germany (Cameron 1984).

It is not surprising therefore that there is no evidence that our benefits are excessive compared with other countries. Indeed a recently published comparative study found that in general retirement pensions and benefits payable in unemployment were considerably below those payable in the other European countries included in the study. Although the level of sup-plementary benefits tended to be more generous in Britain than the level of assistance benefits payable in the other countries, in those countries only a very small number of people were dependent on such a low level of income (Walker *et al*. 1984).

What about the future?

An analysis by OECD of the growth of social expenditure between 1960 and 1990 concludes that there is no particular cause for alarm in Britain (OECD 1983). In fact the UK is in a relatively favourable position, facing a lower growth in the population generally and in the number of old people. Thus, unlike some other countries, even with pessimistic economic developments, the UK can afford some growth in the levels of provision. Indeed in the period 1981–90 they could grow at a faster rate than in the period 1975–81.

> 'In the UK the future, at least compared to the recent past, looks more promising than elsewhere. Most countries are trying to curb public spending and this objective is being pursued particularly keenly in the UK. Indeed other countries, where the shares of tax revenue, public expenditure and government deficits in GDP are higher than in the UK, appear to be adopting a more relaxed attitude to the future. . . . It is difficult to escape the feeling that in the UK public expenditure restraint has been attached a higher priority than an international perspective would seem to justify.'
>
> (Gillion and Hemming 1984: 20)

Other studies come to similar conclusions. Davies and Piachaud (1984) could find no case either on financial grounds or real resource grounds for a freeze in public expenditure over the next five years.

> 'On the most likely growth assumptions for real GDP, 2–3 per cent per annum, real public expenditure growth of slightly more than this would be permitted on real resource grounds and could be financed without any sizeable increase in the public sector borrowing requirement.'
>
> (Davies and Piachaud 1984: 11)

O'Higgins and Patterson (1984) modelled what would happen to public expenditure up to 1994 on the basis of a range of assumptions broadly consistent with current policies. Public expenditure must increase by between 11 and 19 per cent in real terms by 1993/94, but under most scenarios would decline as a proportion of GDP. Social security expenditure as a proportion of total expenditure would decline from 29.0 per cent in 1983/84 to between 25.5 and 28.8 per cent in 1993/94. They conclude:

'It is unlikely that the government's stated target of zero growth in public expenditure during its current term of office can be met on current policies. It also indicates that this failure should not be a matter of concern, even for this government, since with a reasonable level of economic growth these real increases in public expenditure are consistent with its having a declining share of GDP. This detailed disaggregated analysis therefore suggests that there is no "public expenditure crisis" – or at least that the crisis is not one of economics.'

(O'Higgins and Patterson 1984: 31)

Nevertheless it is the government's intention to ensure that public expenditure remains constant in real terms up to 1988/89 on the grounds that:

'The growth of public spending has over the past twenty years, been the motive force which has driven ever upwards the burden of taxation on individuals and companies alike. The government believes that it is necessary to reverse this process, to decide first what can and should be afforded, then to set expenditure plans for individual programmes consistently with that decision.'

(Treasury 1984a)

The objective of this policy is to be able 'to deliver the cuts in taxation which were promised five years ago but have not yet been delivered' (Gillion and Hemming 1984: 4). Gillion and Hemming also suggest that in pursuit of this objective, social security expenditure is being most closely scrutinized and that the social security reviews will be used to identify 'those areas of social security expenditure where restraint will meet with least resistance' (p. 2).

Given rising numbers of claimants and the ageing of the population, Davies and Piachaud estimate that for the government's objective to be achieved, cuts in social security expenditure in the order of 5 per cent would be required, plus a real decline in the value of benefits relative to incomes of over 10 per cent.

Conclusions

This chapter has gone out of its way to avoid acknowledging the many defects that exist in Britain's social security arrangements. The objective has been to point to the importance of social security and the achievements of the existing arrangements. However, there can be no doubt that change is necessary. The conclusion of this chapter is not the place for setting out detailed prescriptions. Nevertheless it is worth ending with one pre-diction and the advocacy of certain targets. The prediction is that there will be no 'Big Bang' reorganizations of tax and social security policy; change will proceed as it always has – by more or less disjointed incremental reform. There are a number of priorities to be pursued by those reforms. These are no more than the conventional ones identified by most responsible observers of the social security scheme: a substantial improvement in child support targeted particularly on one-earner families; the long-term rate of supplementary benefits to be extended to the un-employed – perhaps initially families with children; the reform of tax expenditures to ensure they serve social objectives; and pro-gressive measures to break down the divisions between income derived from the labour market and income derived from social security – to encourage part-time work, and to assist the un-employed, single parents, the disabled, and those caring for dependants.

References

Baldwin, S., Godfrey, C., and Staden, F. (1983) Childhood Disablement and Family Incomes. *J. of Epid. and Comm. Health* 37 (3): 187–95.

Beckerman, W. and Clark, S. (1982) *Poverty and Social Security in Britain since 1961.* Oxford: Oxford University Press.

Bradshaw, J. and Harris, T. (eds) (1984) *Energy and Social Policy.* London: Routledge & Kegan Paul.

Cameron, D. (1984) Public Expenditure and Economic Performance in International Perspective. ESRC Conference paper, University of Bath.

Cusack, S. and Roll, J. (1985) *Families Rent Apart.* London: Child Poverty Action Group.

Davies, G. and Piachaud, D. (1984) Public Expenditure in the Social Services. ESRC Conference Paper, University of Bath.

Deacon, A. and Bradshaw, J. (1983) *Reserved for the Poor.* Oxford: Martin Robertson.

Department of Employment (DoE) (1983) *Family Expenditure Survey 1982.* London: HMSO.

Department of Health and Social Security (DHSS) (1984) Abstract of Statistics for Index of Retail Prices, Average Earnings, Social Security Benefits and Contributions.

Dilnot, A. W., Kay, J. A., and Morris, C. N. (1984) *The Reform of Social Security.* London: Institute of Fiscal Studies.

Ditch, J. (1984) *Hard Times: Unemployment and Supplementary Benefit in N. Ireland.* London: National Consumer Council.

Gillion, C. and Hemming, R. (1984) Social Expenditure in the UK and Other Major OECD Countries: Trends, Explanations and Projections. ESRC Conference Paper, University of Bath.

Hennessy, P. (1984) Public Opinion about the Social Security System. DHSS Social Research Branch paper.

MacNicol, J. (1980) *The Movement for Family Allowances 1918–1945.* London: Heinemann.

Millar, J. (1984) The Contribution of Child Benefit to Family Income, Working Paper 202. Social Policy Research Unit.

Minford, P. (1984) State Expenditure: A Study in Waste. Supplement to *Economic Affairs* 4 (3) (April–June).

Nicholson, J. L. and O'Higgins, M. (1981) Inequalities of Income over the Life Cycle. London: Policy Studies Institute.

OECD (1983) Economic Outlook 34 (December).

O'Higgins, M. (1984) Inequality, Redistribution and Recession: The British Experience 1976–1982. Unpublished conference paper.

O'Higgins, M. and Patterson, A. (1984) The Prospects for Public Expenditure: or 'Muddling Through' out of Crisis. ESRC Conference Paper, University of Bath.

Parker, H. (1984) *Action on Welfare.* London: Social Affairs Unit.

Social Security Advisory Committee (SSAC) (1984) *Social Security Advisory Committee Report.* Cmnd 7546. London: HMSO.

Taylor-Gooby, P. (1982) Two Cheers for the Welfare State: Public Opinion and Private Welfare. *J. of Public Policy* 2 (4).

—— (1984) The Politics of Welfare: Public Attitudes and Behaviour. ESRC Conference Paper, University of Bath.

Townsend, P. (1984) *Fewer Children, More Poverty: An Incomes Plan.* Bristol: University of Bristol.

Treasury (1984a) The Next Ten Years: Public Expenditure and Taxation into the 1990s, Cmnd 9189. London: HMSO.

—— (1984b) *The Government's Expenditure Plans 1984/85 to 1986/87*, Cmnd 9143–II. London: HMSO.

Walker, R., Lawson, R. and Townsend, P. (1984) *Response to Poverty: Lessons from Europe.* London: Heinemann.

12

In defence of the National Health Service

A. J. WILLCOCKS

For most people in the United Kingdom, the one element of public provision likely to excite interest, to gain acceptance, and to be defended, albeit emotionally, is the National Health Service. In a way which no other part of the so-called welfare state services can match, the NHS remains at the centre of such consensus as our politics of the 1980s can retain. Rational defence is therefore often politically difficult and any criticism almost politically dangerous. Any defence of the NHS must therefore be carefully constructed and inevitably will involve a series of different levels or dimensions.

Such dimensions can, by way of introduction, be briefly stated. The first, and in the eyes of many people the key one, must be the level of principle, that to have to pay for medical care is wrong – indeed some would go further and say that to pay at all (whether voluntarily or not) for medical care is wrong. Such a defence would reject any attempt to transfer any or all of the cost of medical care on to the patient. A second dimension follows from the first, that to have to pay sets a barrier for some to necessary medical care, but this can to a point be tested in operation; were people denied needed medical care because of the cost label and are they now getting all the needed medical care as the cost barrier has gone?

Another level of defence might lie in being able to prove the assertion that our citizens are now healthier than they were previously because of the existence of the NHS. This level also has the possibility of another line of defence in being able to prove that we are healthier, better served, and provided with all we need, in degrees above that of other countries; that in this country in health terms we are better off than those in other countries because of our NHS which in some respects is internationally unique. This comparative approach can also be invoked as a possible defence if it can be proved to be cheaper than the health care systems of other countries. A further and for this chapter a final defence must lie with the assertion (which will have to be proved) that the priorities of market systems of health care are different from those of the NHS, different in a way beneficial to the majority or at least to significant minorities.

A final word of warning by way of introduction: an emotive area of public policy, such as this service, has discouraged the collection of evaluative data. Whatever else the NHS may be good at, evaluation of its achievements is not one. Rarely can so much public money have been spent in the last thirty years or more with so little attempt at serious evaluation. Maybe politicians and public alike think they 'know' it is succeeding.

The defence in principle

For some, for example Michael Foot when writing of Aneurin Bevan, Minister of Health at the time of the creation of the NHS, the service is or was the 'greatest Socialist achievement of the Labour Government' (Foot 1973). For them the 1946 Act offered a service to each according to his need without regard to class, creed, colour, or nationality. By implication therefore this was a service where it would be wrong to put any non-medical hurdle between a need and its being met. Those who hold to this view have to justify the validity of their principle alongside the principles behind the services of other countries, other areas of public provision in this country, and the existence of a thriving and apparently growing private sector in medicine.

At the present time it would seem valid to question how far a generalist argument such as the above can stand its ground alongside increasing emphasis within social service provision of selectivity – service for the poor, the deserving, or some other designated category, rather than service for all. It would probably be true to say that, in most of the developed countries of the world, if a medical service is free or its cost offset by insurance contributions then it will in most cases go only to designated sectors of the community – few if any other countries offer such a service (or such financial help) to all. Why then are we out of line? The answer must in large part lie with this belief in the wrongness of patients paying for their medical services.

Like theology there are inherent limits to rational arguments of principle – at some stage a person has to say 'I believe'. So too, I would argue, with any defence of the NHS on grounds of principle. It cannot be demonstrated at the principle level that the lack of economic barriers to medical care is good or bad. Arguments of life and death have very limited relevance unless other services meeting life-and-death needs are similarly treated as is the NHS.

If it is wrong to insist on access to medical care only after payment of costs, is it wrong to allow paid access for those who wish it (and can afford it)? For some the logic of the 'socialist' argument of 'to each according to his needs' as far as the Act of 1946 was concerned fits ill with the decision to allow the continuation of private treatment for which fees are paid (and often in NHS hospitals). Such a question leads inevitably to the historical point that the creation of health services in 1948 was less a matter of principle and more a matter of political expedience – an expedience to which both major political parties of the time subscribed (Klein 1983; Willcocks 1967). History and especially wartime history demonstrated the need for such a service and the political leaders of the time (of both parties) were swept into an acceptance of the service. Today, therefore, we must ask how valid is the addition of a principle to an example of social policy when its relevance even at the time of the service's creation is at least doubtful.

Another relevant debate must be about how far a principle can be breached but still be relevant. The totally 'free' NHS has ceased to exist, if indeed it ever existed at all. Some of us have to pay something towards our dental services, most of us something towards our prescriptions, and some of us something towards our chiropodial care, to take but a few examples. At each step taken towards a breach in the overriding principle of 'no cost', defenders have seen the death of an ideal whilst 'practical' folk have argued that such measures make possible, through the cash they raise and through the rationing of scarce resources they provide, the maintenance of the basic principle in areas that matter most – hospital care costs. But each concession makes the next more difficult to defend; if we have to pay towards our prescriptions, why not towards the cost of meals in hospitals, the laundering of the clothes we wear in the wards, and so on?

In sum, therefore, the argument of principle is difficult to sustain both because of its doubtful antecedents, the inability to prove it right, and the concessions to that principle throughout the thirty years or more since the NHS began. The point beyond which we will not be pushed can only, in each decade, be the existing *status quo* – it cannot be the totality of a principle which has long since been abandoned. Therefore, although one might wish to join those who defend 'no cost' in principle, it is, I would argue, a very doubtful weapon in the defence of the NHS.

The economic barrier

As a child, I did from time to time wonder why it was that my father went to see his general practitioner when he was ill, whilst my mother, despite illness, often did not go. If the child put an answer to the question it was probably that my mother was more of a martyr than my father, but the political campaigners of the time would have said that the reason lay in the free consultation offered to the male as a contributing member of the National Health Insurance system, a benefit not accorded the non-contributing wife. The barrier of the expected cost kept people away from the medical care they really needed. Therefore the call was to remove this barrier to care so that all would seek the medical care they needed – and this was a major aim of the new service.

Indeed it was confidently believed by many at the time that once the 'backlog' of need (unmet because of pre-existing economic barriers) had been met, then as a nation we would be fitter and the 'real' demand for the service would fall. That this did not happen will be discussed in a later section – here I want to ask if the economic cost was and is a barrier to seeking medical care and if it is the only barrier. It should be added that to remove this barrier to care is not necessarily or inevitably a step towards our kind of health service – there are other ways of achieving this goal, a topic to which I also return.

Is the cost of medical care a barrier to seeking needed care? There are some aspects of medical care costs that need to be borne in mind in considering this question. In the first place the development of the need for medical care can rarely be predicted – it is not like a pair of shoes we know will need to be replaced in a year's time, or like solicitor's fees which we know will fall due when a long-drawn-out legal dispute is settled. If we wish to pay for our children's education we have at least five years' notice of the first bill; if we wish to buy a house we can debate the costs and the validity of our desire to purchase. Medical care is therefore different in significant ways. At the same time the unpredictability of the need for medical care (and the need to pay for it) is matched by the unpredictability of the costs to be incurred. A visit to the general practitioner could result in minimal fees for the consultation, in that plus the cost of medicines, in those plus the cost of a second consultant opinion, in those plus the costs of hospitalization and expensive surgery – the range is almost infinite and as the cost of high-technology medicine increases, so this range widens year by year. The timing of need may bar use at the necessary time, and the range of possible cost may limit the amount of medical service demanded. Alternatively completion of medical care may saddle the patient with a heavy debt to repay after recovery – not a good medicine for full recovery! In this country, the NHS removed that barrier, in large part if not in total removing thereby the anxiety and burdens associated with such uncertainties. The reduction in uncertainty and unpredictability by spreading the cost beyond the individual and over large populations must therefore be of value to each member of that population.

The cost of medical care is often seen as a barrier in itself, but there are other potential barriers in the fact of seeking medical care. The person may well have to contemplate a series of indirect costs. He may lose earnings during a period of sickness, he may lose the 'free' service of a housekeeper wife and need to replace them at cost, he may have to face travelling costs to reach the hospital or clinic, he may need special diets, clothing, adaptation to the house, and so on. Divorced as it is in financial terms from the social security system, the NHS offers no direct contribution from its resources towards these costs, though the patient may have some of these met in whole or in part from other services of the state or voluntary organizations. In as far as these costs may be real and of significance to some people there is clearly a sense in which the cost of sickness may be a barrier to seeking help.

Whatever the detailed situation of each patient is, there is no doubt that the severity or even the existence of direct and indirect costs have been removed and that this in a way, as we shall see later, marks the British system as superior to those of most other nations. That some countries have a long way to go towards health care equity is borne out by a comment by a distinguished American writer on the health services of his own country.

'The path to health care equity may be tortuous, the details unpredictable, and in the current political climate such a goal may seem unattainable. Nevertheless barring a nuclear war or other global catastrophe, by the year 2030, comprehensive health services will surely be available as a fundamental human right to every man, woman and child in the United States.'

(Roemer 1982: 124)

The Act of 1946 in the United Kingdom, in effect, conceded this 'fundamental human right' and no alternative system has done as well.

The failure of the removal of the barrier of cost to reduce the longer-term demand may be explained in many ways. One such explanation is the growing recognition in research and elsewhere that there are other barriers. Some of these are inherent in the individual (a fear of treatment, an unwillingness to miss other important engagements, etc.), in the family (the need to carry out one's familial burdens, or not to add to another's), and in society (the label of weakling or hypochondriac by one's peers) – all these and more may be as potent (or almost as potent) as the economic barrier itself. The reasons why I do not go to the theatre, for example, may be totally unconnected with its cost – the same may apply to my unwillingness to visit a doctor.

Those who saw the economic barrier as the only barrier have sadly been proved wrong.

Are we healthier?

To seek to defend the NHS on such answers as one might find to the question at the head of this section is to face up to serious semantic and organizational issues. In the first place, to provide a convincing definition of health is difficult, if not impossible. Must one go as far as the World Health Organisation when it says that 'health' is a state of complete physical, mental, and social well-being? Or should we go along with McKeown's irritating claim that 'feeling well is something more than not feeling ill' (McKeown 1976)? To justify a claim that the NHS has made us healthier therefore may falter on the difficulties of definition. An alternative might be to talk of the absence of sickness (as will be done below), but it should be remembered that sickness is defined (in practice) by doctors, patients, and society – and their definitions do not always coincide or remain constant. But the preamble of the NHS Act of 1946 talked, *inter alia*, of promoting health and inscribed the word in the legislation and in the title of the organization. For many it could more accurately be called a National Medical Service.

The organizational issue is simply put: can the NHS promote health, make us healthy – or healthier – or must it be limited to curing or ameliorating illness? The killing diseases of a century or more ago were the diseases of the environment, in the sense that people were not to 'blame' for their illnesses, the fault of which lay in bad housing, poor environment, lack of adequate sewerage systems, and so on. The public health legislation of the mid-nineteenth century that sought to control and improve those items has made us as a nation healthier, or at least has stopped us being killed by environmentally caused diseases and helped us to live longer. But the vacuum of death is soon filled – other diseases come along to take their place. Any look at OPCS figures on mortality quickly shows the major killers – circulatory diseases, neoplasms, and respiratory diseases – together accounting for over 85 per cent of all deaths in Britain in the early 1980s. Those diseases are the product of (or caused by) our life-style – smoking, eating the wrong foods, taking too little exercise, and so on. The NHS cannot and should not be blamed for this – it cannot ban smoking or carbohydrates and it cannot compel us to exercise. Any attack on the NHS therefore cannot be directed with rigorous honesty at death rates without accepting what the NHS can and cannot do.

It might have been a reasonable proposition in 1948 that as the beneficial effects of the health service began to take effect, fewer people would be sick and the demand for sickness benefits would therefore decline. This has not happened: figures from the DHSS and its predecessor ministries show the number of days lost for certified sickness in Great Britain as 280.7 million in 1953/54, rising (with some fluctuations) to 358.5 million in 1981/82 – an increase of some 22 per cent when the population at risk rose by a very much smaller figure. Here is no sign of the NHS making us healthier; but can there be any certainty that sickness in 1982 meant the same as in 1954? For some writers like Illich, we (and other developed countries) are medicalizing more and more situations as illnesses, and this, if so, is immeasurable and affects comparisons over time. So again one has to be cautious about using this argument as a defence for the NHS – although one cannot, of course, claim that the situation would not have been much worse but for the NHS.

Many of the mortality rates used by students of epidemiology show pleasing changes since the NHS came into force. Infant mortality rates (usually taken as a sensitive index of health generally in a society) for the United Kingdom in 1948 stood at about 35 per 1000; by 1981 they had dropped to 11.1, a fall of over two-thirds in three and a half decades. In 1980, however, when the infant mortality rate for England and Wales stood at 12 per 1000, World Health Organisation figures show at least five countries with better figures (Canada 10.9, France 10.0, Japan

7.5, Netherlands 8.6, Sweden 6.0) whilst the USA was only marginally worse at 12.5. No great defence for NHS achievement lies in these figures and indeed a recent House of Commons committee has been highly critical of the NHS on this point. As they show, one reason for the relatively poor showing of British figures lies in the very marked differences in infant mortality rate by social class, underlying a persistent pattern of class inequality in health and health care which the NHS has so far not removed. The recent Black Report (Townsend and Davidson 1982) closely describes the failure of the NHS in this respect. What is perhaps true is that other medical systems are even less efficient at solving this problem. It can only be an article of faith (together with some support from patchy information elsewhere) that the NHS structure offers the best opportunity for a closer approach to equity in health and health care. The next section looks further at the position and achievements of the NHS in an international context.

International comparisons

One possible potent defence of the NHS would lie, if it were possible, in the demonstration that we have a more effective, better organized or more efficient service than do other countries. As with so many arguments in this essay, the ground is not too firm – partly because of the difficulty of comparing health care systems which may significantly differ in their forms and content, and partly because of the difficulty of international monetary comparisons. However, it is probably true to claim that the NHS is better in many respects than other countries' services and always near the top of any league of health care service indicators.

There are those who look with some favour on the American system, with its absence of any national health scheme and its dependence almost entirely on a system of voluntary commercial insurance, backed in the case of the elderly by the state insurance scheme, Medicare. For the American system, the priorities and resource allocations are set in the market place, by the insurance system, and to an extent by the consumer. In the NHS those economic decisions are taken by the state and inevitably different priorities and resource allocations may be made. Is the American way the better one? A wealth of comment, both affirmative and negative, could be quoted, but the evidence in the main seems to tend towards a negative answer. For those with insurance cover the cost of medical care is in part met, but for many, perhaps at least 25 million Americans, no insurance cover is possible. This

> 'lack of insurance coverage has three major consequences: it contributes to unnecessary pain, suffering, disability and even death among the insured; it places a financial burden on those uninsured who struggle to pay burden-some medical bills; and it places a financial strain on hospitals, physicians and other health care providers who attempt to provide care to the uninsured'
>
> (Davis and Rowland 1983)

The authors go on to demonstrate how the uninsured make less use of the medical services – to their disadvantage. In a real sense, despite all the limitations of the comparative data, the USA demonstrates the advantages to us of the NHS. On the grounds of equity and compassion we ought not to follow the American route.

But how does the United Kingdom compare with other countries? At a time when the emphasis is increasingly on cost cutting, on efficiency, and on a more managerial approach to the NHS, it is instructive to compare this country's expenditure on health care as a proportion of its gross national product (GNP) with similar proportions elsewhere. Far from what one might be excused for believing, judging by press and similar comments, the NHS is not extravagant by this proportion. Maxwell has compared this proportion over the period 1950 to 1980 with nine other countries, all industrialized like the UK. In 1950 France and Sweden were spending a lower proportion of their GNP on medical care services than the UK (3.4 per cent compared with 3.9 per cent, and in that year the USA was spending 4.5 per cent of GNP). The figures for the years after 1977 are not complete so one must make the similar comparisons in that year. With only 5.2 per cent of its GNP spent on such services the United Kingdom was far below any of the other nine countries, and

France and Sweden were by then spending 7.9 per cent and 9.8 per cent of their GNP respectively. American expenditure had risen by 1977 to 8.8 per cent (Maxwell 1984). Put in other words, whilst the proportion of the GNP has almost trebled in Sweden, more than doubled in France, and almost doubled in the USA, in the United Kingdom it has increased by only about a third. Unless we can demonstrate catastrophic disadvantages to our citizens, the NHS is, by international standards, a very good buy.

To use comparisons of service input or output shows the NHS in a mixed light. It has far fewer nurses per unit of population than most other industrialized countries, is near the bottom of the league for doctors, and has fewer hospital admissions but uses its beds for more patients per year than do most countries. In the words of Maxwell (1984) 'the U.K. is low in the table of inputs and moderate on yardsticks of utilisation. One major reason for relatively low health care expenditure in the U.K. is lower wage rates, rather than lower manning and more efficient utilisation.' The NHS can therefore be defended on the grounds of its apparent efficiency in comparison with other countries, but what of effectiveness? Without any detailed analysis of the many figures necessary for a firm conclusion to such a question, one may quote just one set of figures. Maxwell (1984) shows that in a rank order by percentage of GNP spent on health care in 1975 the UK would rank tenth, whilst for the same year on a standardized mortality rate it would be fourth. Although the evidence may lack a conclusive set of grounds for proving the NHS is better, at least the data show the UK no worse off for its much lower expenditures. In a time when government looks for value for money, such a conclusion must be a powerful argument for maintaining the service as it is.

A postscript to this argument, if there were space, would enable demonstration to be made of some of the reasons for the relative efficiency of the NHS. There is little doubt that national and regional control and limiting of budgets has led to a much greater caution in the use of expensive new treatments, and in the rationalization of their use and location if used. It is interesting to note that the only evidence of the heavy duplication of expensive equipment so common in the hospitals of other countries may come through charities seeking to provide some new piece of machinery for their local hospitals. In as far as hospital authorities accept many of these pieces of machinery they may, in the end, be distorting their own priorities. The setting of priorities, not by some economic marketing system of ability to purchase but by having regard to the needs of the community at large, is theoretically at least one of the great advantages of the NHS over competing systems. In theory cosmetic surgery, for example, can be controlled in favour of geriatric care; unfortunately, though, one of the major areas of failure has been to set priorities in regard to the needs of communities. Side-stepping a long argument, it is perhaps not unimportant to note that the NHS system gives excessive power to the medical profession, a power that ensures the priorities are too often those of the profession rather than of the patients and community as a whole. Whilst one would therefore defend the NHS in general terms there is much about it and its structure that cannot be defended.

There is a counter-argument, sometimes heard, that the patient has a greater opportunity to share in the decisions on his treatment if he pays – he who pays the piper calls the tune. Undoubtedly there is worrying evidence in the UK of doctors who pay scant heed to the wishes of their patients, who seem to regard the patient merely as an object on which he practises his skill. In this sense the NHS, like other parts of the welfare state in this country, gives undue power to the provider professions. As it does that, the gap between the provider and recipient widens (in part because of the skill and expertise that separates them) as does the gap between the provider and the democratic machinery that pays their salaries. I am not convinced that the market system offers a sufficient antidote to this problem, but I, like many others, find the power the welfare state has accorded the providers increasingly worrying. More and more facets of the life of the individual are swallowed up in the umbrella of the helping professions. If only the country could be made more aware of this range of problems, then the welfare machinery, such as the NHS, could well offer the best corrective and set the path to a more self-reliant society.

Priority setting

A brief reference to this defence has already been made, but some underlining is necessary. In a market system, the pattern of medical care (it is argued) will inevitably follow the wishes of those best able to pay – it will concentrate on 'elective' surgery, on fashionable operations, and generally on the ailments of those in work and with money. But with the ageing of all societies, the widespread existence of poverty shows a range of illnesses and conditions unlikely to be met by market systems. There are many who need a separate form of protection for their 'uneconomic' diseases – it is, for example, very unlikely that a geriatrician would make much money in the private sector. For many countries, for example the USA, this need is recognized (however inefficiently) in a fall-back public service or insurance system. These citizens, like the paupers of the past, are consciously denied part of their rights – to participate alongside others. The NHS, in theory, puts their needs alongside those of all others. Again in theory, therefore, the needs of the elderly or the mentally ill, to take but two examples, are protected in as far as the needs of any group are protected – no group gets more because it can pay more, or has an insurance policy. If the NHS had demonstrated the validity of this in practice, then I for one would be prepared to rest my case in defending it on that ground alone.

But as has already been alluded to, this has not happened. There are regional differences proportionately as great now as they were thirty years or more ago. The social class differences in access remain stubbornly unchanged (note in particular the effect of this on infant mortality rates). The immigrant groups probably get less than their needs merit from the service. Ironically this latter group has provided the backbone, or a large part of it, for the provision of medical care over many years, but they, too, have faced their problems of differentiation – few get to consultant status in popular specialities although they do in less popular specialities, and the same applies to the geographical areas in which they can practise. Confronted with issues of this kind, are we to say that the NHS is merely about access or is it about equality of access? Is it about access or about health – the outcome of health care services?

Here is not the place to discuss the issue of equity in health care (for example see Mooney 1982 and 1983), but it must be some-how related to access as regards need for that access. In fact it is not about equality of use (some will need more and ought to be able to obtain more than others) but about some measure of equality in the contribution of the health services to the health of those it serves. In this definition the NHS deserves two cheers at least, and certainly more cheers than the services of most other countries. But three cheers would ignore the major failures of the NHS within this type of definition, and in seeking to defend the health service the question must be, have these failures been enough to remove any valid defence or alternatively, can we see fewer failures elsewhere? Here one would argue that there can be no doubt, despite the failures of the NHS, there is greater equity now than previously in this country and probably more equity than is found in many other countries.

Conclusion

As with most services by government or by the market system, their internal philosophical consistency is usually limited to a point where an absolutist defence is impossible. The NHS is no exception, for in several ways it falls short of its theoretical base, in that some charges are made for some services. The absolutist defence therefore of a free service should logically not be accepted. Instead one has to say that a service free in this and that way but not in other ways is preferable (as being nearer the principle of free care) to services where more is charged or paid for and where some or all of a population are denied access. On such relativist grounds one might with caution defend the NHS.

Are we healthier than we were before 1946? Again the evidence provides only a limited defence for the NHS. Indeed it is almost as easy to defend the proposition that there is now more illness than there was – that the NHS has discouraged self-care and prevention.

The defender is perhaps on firmer grounds (although even

here the evidence is far from totally persuasive) when he claims that comparatively speaking the lot of the citizen in the UK is better than that of citizens in most other countries. The UK spends proportionately less with no serious detriment as a result.

All in all, therefore, the defence of the National Health Service must be a relativist one – there is no absolute position that can logically defend what we currently have. The absolutist perhaps would want change, but in a direction directly opposite to that which inspires this collection of answers.

References

Davis, K. and Rowland, D. (1983) Uninsured and Undeserved – Inequalities in Health Care in the United States. *Milbank Memorial Fund Quarterly* 61 (2).

Foot, M. (1973) *Aneurin Bevan*, vol. 2. London: Davis-Poynter.

Klein, R. (1983) *The Politics of the National Health Service*. Harlow, Middx.: Longmans.

McKeown, T. (1976) *The Role of Medicine*. London: Nuffield Provincial Hospitals Trust.

Maxwell, Robert J. (1984) International Comparisons. In *Health Care U.K.* London: Chartered Institute of Public Finance and Accountancy.

Mooney, G. H. (1982) Equity in Health Care, Discussion Paper No. 11/82. Health Care Economics Research Unit, University of Aberdeen.

—— (1983) The N.H.S. – Caring about Caring? Discussion Paper No. 06/83. Health Care Economics Research Unit, University of Aberdeen.

Roemer, M. I. (1982) *An Introduction to the U.S. Health Care Systems*. New York: Springer.

Townsend, P. and Davidson, N. (1982) *Inequalities in Health (The Black Report)*. Harmondsworth: Penguin.

Willcocks, A. J. (1967) *The Creation of the National Health Service*. London: Routledge & Kegan Paul.

Name index

Subject index